The Puppet Theatre Handbook

THE
PUPPET THEATRE
HANDBOOK

BY

MARJORIE BATCHELDER
Associate Professor of Fine Arts
Ohio State University

WITH DRAWINGS BY

DOUGLAS ANDERSON

1817

HARPER & ROW, PUBLISHERS
New York, Hagerstown, San Francisco, London

To
PAUL McPHARLIN

Table of Contents

~~~~~

[vii]

Contents

Contents

Puppet Plays, Epic Poems, Fables, Fairy Tales, Folk Dances, Folklore, Folk Songs and Ballads, Myths and Legends, Poems and Nonsense Verses, Stories).

Variety Acts; Stage Equipment (Stage Hardware, Lighting Equipment, Dimmers, Scenery, Drapery, Properties, Costume Fabrics, Flameproofed Materials, Scene Paint); Puppet Workshop Equipment (Drawing Materials, Hand Tools, Power Tools, Electrical Supplies, Paint and Dye, Sewing Materials, Scrap Boxes and Files, Supplies for Puppet Construction, Sources for Various Supplies); Recorded Sound Effects and Movies.

NOTES

Illustrations

~~~~~~

[xi]

Illustrations

[xii]

Illustrations

Foreword

~~~~~

Puppets are universal. Look where you will in the pages of history, you will find some tradition of puppet playing. Sometimes there is little more than a vague allusion; at others the puppet theatre becomes an important part of the dramatic scene. Puppetry exhibits a remarkable diversity as one examines it in various parts of the world, yet it has basic qualities which account for its universal appeal.

Small articulated figures have been found in Egyptian tombs. From ancient Greece and Rome similar figures have survived, while classic literature abounds in references to movable images which were often associated with religious ritual. The famous Greek mechanician, Hero of Alexandria, had a complete automatic theatre in which was enacted the *Legend of Nauplius.* While these examples do not prove the existence of puppet shows as we know them today, it is evident that the basic principles of puppet playing were familiar.

Shadow-puppets were known early in Chinese history, and are still a popular form of entertainment. In Java, shadows existed in the tenth century, and the shadow play became the basis of theatrical art. In one form of show, the scenes and characters are painted on long scrolls which the operator unrolls as he recites the story. The stylistic qualities of the shadow-puppets are to be found in these paintings. Likewise, the same details of facial expression and costume are applied to flat wooden puppets shown without a screen. In the fully developed round rod-puppets, the costume is simplified, but other details are traditional. When human actors perform, they not only wear costumes and headdresses closely patterned after the shadow-puppets, but they imitate puppet movement. Much

Foreword

Javanese dancing still retains the side-to-side movement in one plane which is characteristic of shadow play action. Thus in Java we see an unusual example of the unity of puppet and human drama. In Europe, too, during the heyday of the Italian *commedia dell' arte*, there was a free interchange between puppet and human actors. Both used the same scenarios for improvised plays, while characters and costumes were similar. Perhaps the puppets borrowed heavily from the *commedia*, but they have paid their debt by keeping it alive to the present day. Punchinello, Harlequin, Columbine, and many other *commedia* characters still delight us on the puppet stage.

Drama in Japan has been strongly influenced by puppets. During the seventeenth and early eighteenth centuries, the *Kabuki* or popular human drama developed alongside the *Jōruri* or puppet play. To the Kabuki, the puppet theatre contributed the plots which form the basis of Japanese drama, while the music and dance of the *Kabuki* were adapted by the *Jōruri* to enrich its performances.

By the mid-eighteenth century, the Japanese puppet theatre became probably the most lavish in the world. Through the rivalry of two companies, puppet drama reached such heights that it outshone the *Kabuki*. Human actors watched the puppets to learn the niceties of acting. Certain scenic devices, such as the revolving stage, first used in the puppet theatre, found their way into the Kabuki, and thence into other parts of the world. Puppet plays were written by Chikamatsu, Japan's greatest playwright, who found greater freedom in writing for inanimate actors.

The puppets were made two-thirds life size, and were richly costumed. For the principal characters, three operators were used: The first, dressed in the embroidered robes of the samurai, worked the head and right arm; the second, swathed in a hooded black gown, controlled the left hand; the third, also wearing black, moved the feet or the hem of the puppet's dress to simulate walking. Handsomely dressed reciters and samisen players in varying numbers read the lines of the play and provided musical accompaniment.

After this brilliant period, there was a decline. Sometime early in the nineteenth century, a new theatre was founded in Osaka by Bunrakuken; in 1872 the title of Bunraku-za was given to it. Until World War II, when it was destroyed by bombing, this theatre maintained the eighteenth-century tradition of puppet playing, and reached a degree of subtle refinement unexcelled in the history of puppetry.

Much of the world's puppet art has had its origin in folk tradition. In most European countries, the puppet theatre is regarded as a part of folk art, and is duly respected as such. There are many national puppet characters such as Mr. Punch, Petrouschka, and Polichinelle. There are others, such as Hänneschen, Guignol, and Lafleur, who originated as local heroes and usually speak in dialect, wear regional costumes, and reflect the popular ideals of the place from which they come.

The theatres of chivalric romance are good examples of folk puppetry. In northern France, Flanders, southern Italy, and Sicily, the legends of Charlemagne and the stories of the Crusades have been for some two hundred years enacted as crude but vigorous puppet plays. Charlemagne, Roland, the four sons of Aymon, and many other Christian heroes battle incessantly against the wicked infidels in Spain, or at the very doors of Jerusalem. In this proud company of medieval knights, one finds local heroes. Chanchet appears in the Liége versions of the romances, while Lafleur enlivens the Amiens plays. Although they are of peasant extraction, these well-loved characters are quite at home amid the heroic struggles which transpire on the stage. They are necessary, too, for who would clear the battlefield of corpses and perform other menial tasks were it not for Chanchet and his kin?

Although they are based on well-known metrical romances such as *Orlando Furioso*, the puppet plays are read in the local dialect, with a very free interpretation by the showman and his associates. The brilliant descriptions of knights, cities, and battles are not literally interpreted on the stage. An army may be suggested by a knight and half a dozen smaller puppets, the latter held by the operator in one hand. Intricate swordsmanship and brave chargers are described by the showman, and imagined by the audience. In the southern Italian shows the hero brandishes a sword in a crude manner, but in the Liége theatres, the puppets have no arm controls. Horses seem to be regarded as unnecessary complications.

Most of the puppets used in these theatres are large ones (from 2' to 4') operated from above by means of a large iron rod attached to the top of the head, or to the wooden shoulder piece. Strings may be used for controlling hands and feet, or they may swing freely when the puppet is moved. Because of their weight, the movement of these puppets is generally broad and rather limited, although in some local theatres, such as the Ches Cabotans of Amiens, the figures are smaller and more skilfully articulated. The scenery consists of elaborately painted backdrops and wings. The puppets are handsomely costumed in suits of armor, richly decorated with *repoussé* designs, helmets with flowing plumes, and short capes of bright-colored fabrics.

The theatres of chivalric romance are suffering a general decline, being unable to compete with the more modern forms of popular entertainment. One used to be able to visit the Manteo Marionette Theatre in New York City's Mulberry Street almost any night and see the paladins battling—but they are now stored away in a cellar, while the former patrons amuse themselves at the movies.

There are many other expressions of folk culture in the puppet theatre. In German Rhine cities such as Cologne, rod-puppets have been used for decades to present plays based upon old German stories in which fantasy, local happenings, and spectacular effects are ingeniously mingled. Hänneschen, a gay peasant, presides over the Cologne theatre, which was founded in 1802. He is an amusing, irresponsible, bad boy who is often cast as the typical apprentice. In this capacity he has plenty of opportunity for playing all kinds of tricks. He is a pyromaniac at times, causing much trouble with his fires; nor is he above stabbing people's legs with long pins in order to increase the business of his friend Bestava, who is a doctor. Like Mr. Punch, Hänneschen knows the persuasive value of a big club, and is quite satisfied with this means of getting what he wants.

During the nineteenth century in Provence, especially in the cities of Aix and Marseilles, the crib puppet theatres flourished. These popular shows grew out of the custom of singing Christmas carols around the crib in which the story of the Nativity was depicted. Movable figures were later substituted for the stationary ones, and the small theatres were exhibited (for a price) wherever the showman could find a suitable place to set up his show and accommodate his audience. Growing in popularity during the century, these shows became a regular business; one man, Benoit of Aix, managed to keep his in operation some sixty years.

To the religious subjects were added all kinds of spectacular effects, transformations, scenes of hunting and fishing, battles, local songs and dances. These shows were quite crude dramatically and full of anachronisms. Everybody was delighted to observe that the Pope with his cardinals descended from a carriage in front of the stable and proceeded to give his benediction to the Christ child. In one Nativity play there was to be seen the Grand Exposition Palace, with the newly constructed railway near by. No one was surprised when the three kings arrived by rail to pay homage to Jesus, nor were they disturbed by a salvo of cannon shots used to announce the arrival of the child.

The Polish crib plays which are still performed during the Christmas holiday season are another variation of the popular semireligious folk puppet play. As in the Provençal crèches, the story is enlivened by comic interludes in which regional songs and dances are performed by small rod-puppet actors dressed in characteristic costumes.

Popular puppet drama takes a somewhat different turn in the Turkish shadow theatre where Karagoz is the vigorous (and often quite indecent) hero. A ferocious-looking man with a thick black beard and black eyes, Karagoz amuses his audience with his assumed naïveté, his amorous intrigues, and his physical prowess, usually exhibited by the many cuffs on the nape of the neck which he lavishes on his adversaries. Karagoz's friend, Hadjeivat, is a Europeanized Turk who affects a cultured manner and uses many Arabic words in his speech. Conversation between these two

characters comprises most of the play, but other Turks and repre-
sentatives of many tribes and nations appear in lesser roles. Karagoz
mocks all of them, gets into many tight situations, but manages to
escape. The Turkish shadow plays are based upon popular novels,
legends or myths. Persian literature has contributed many plots,
those derived from *A Thousand and One Nights* being always
popular.

In contrast to the puppet theatre of the people where the flavor
of the performances is distinctly popular, there have existed others
of a more sophisticated type, where artists, writers, and musicians
have collaborated to produce shows for special audiences. Such
was the Théâtre des Amis at George Sand's home, "Nohant," in
which she and her son Maurice wrote and produced witty and
satirical hand-puppet plays for their own entertainment and that
of their literary friends.

The Petit-Théâtre, under the inspiration of Henri Signoret and
some forty talented friends, was founded in 1888 for the production of classic plays which were seldom seen in the Paris theatres
of the nineties. Shakespeare, Aristophanes, and Cervantes, as well
as original plays and adaptations, were presented to highly intel-
lectual audiences. The puppets were of the rod type, similar to
those used in the old Provençal crèches.

From 1887 to 1923 there prospered in the cabarets of Montmartre a highly sophisticated type of shadow show. Here the art
of the shadow-puppet, previously a popular but not too elegant
form of entertainment, was developed into a sensitively co-
ordinated ensemble of puppets, music, and drama. It all began one
night at the Chat Noir when Jouy was singing his "Chanson des
Sergots." Henri Rivière tacked up a napkin in the opening of a
small puppet booth and passed across this improvised shadow
screen a group of silhouettes of sergeants he had cut out.

The Chat Noir was a gathering place for artists, writers, and
musicians. There they read their poems, exhibited their paintings,
and tried out their latest musical compositions. In such an atmosphere any novelty was welcome, and Rivière's shadows at once

became popular, for he drew liberally upon the talent at hand.

A hole was cut in one wall to accommodate a larger shadow screen. Backstage there was ample space for musicians and chorus, varied noise effects, lighting equipment, and lines from a gridiron above for changing scenery. A powerful light was placed some 9 feet back of the screen. Three grooved frames were used to get color and depth in the scenery. In the frame closest to the screen were set the scenery pieces, cut from zinc. The next frame accommodated various glass slides upon which clouds, landscapes, waves and so on were represented, while the third frame held slides of single tones of color.

With this elaborate equipment, several kinds of plays were presented. Among the most popular were humorous, satirical pieces for which Rodolphe Salis, the vivid proprietor of the Chat Noir, provided an improvised running commentary. Salis had blond-red hair, a pointed beard, heavy eyebrows shading eyes which were at times blue, gray, green, or yellow. He always wore a gray redingote buttoned up to his neck with two rows of buttons. In his improvisations, Salis was by turns insolent, humorous, or sarcastic; he built up his performances with off-stage noises, choruses and music, while the shadows provided the visual effects. The plots of these shows were slight. One, *The Whist Game*, was a bit of satire on the English. Four whist players are engaged in a game aboard ship. A tempest rages, the ship rolls, the lamp in the cabin sways dangerously, but the game goes on. Corsairs attack —they blow up the powder magazine, the vessel leaps into the air, but the game continues on the floating wreck. Finally, water enters the cabin, the players sink out of sight—no doubt they are still playing!

In other plays of a more lyrical type, the text was recited or sung. One of Rivière's most exquisite pieces was *Marche à l'Étoile*, in which crowds of shepherds, soldiers, women, lepers, and slaves marched toward the star of Bethlehem under a deep blue sky, while the text was sung by its composer, the baritone Georges Fragerolle. In most of his plays, Rivière depended more upon atmospheric scenery, with groups of figures having little or no articulation, passing in procession across the screen, than upon elaborately articulated single figures. His collaborators had plenty of opportunity to use music, words, and color, and it was this richness of material which made the Chat Noir performances memorable. Other cabarets imitated the shows, but none equaled them.

In our own time, the association of puppets with small and specialized audiences is occasionally to be found. After many years of varied experiences, Forman Brown, Harry Burnett, and Richard Brandon opened the Turnabout Theatre in Los Angeles. Equipped with streetcar seats which can be reversed, the auditorium, seating one hundred sixty, has a stage at each end. On one, portrait puppets of famous people from Hollywood and elsewhere do song-and-dance turns, or snappy puppet shows replete with music and lyrics are given. After the intermission, with coffee served in the small green room, the audience, now facing in the opposite direction, is treated to a stage revue with human actors, among whom Elsa Lanchester is usually featured. The novelty of the performance and the intimacy of the theatre make it one of the most popular entertainments of the city.

American puppetry has had a long and exciting history. In his study, "Puppets in American Life, 1524-1914," Paul McPharlin notes that Cortés, setting forth on his military expedition to Mexico, had among his followers a man who worked puppets. However, even at this early date, puppets were already known in America, for the Indian medicine men, like the Egyptian priests of ancient times, used figures manipulated by hidden strings to awe the people during religious ceremonials. Today, in the fire-illuminated kivas of New Mexico, or the ritual huts of the northwest coast, one can see feathers dancing by themselves, or great serpents rising from jars—survivals of who knows what secret magic rites.

By the end of the seventeenth century, a woman named Leonor Godomar was managing a puppet theatre in Peru, but English showmen did not come to the colonies until somewhat later. On December 30, 1742, it is recorded that there played in Philadelphia "an agreeable comedy or tragedy by changeable figures of two feet high, a sight of the sea and ships, and a merry dialogue between Punch and Joan his wife."

During the eighteenth century puppet companies arrived from England, France, and Spain. From July to November, 1749, a puppet company housed in a specially built auditorium played in New York. Toward the end of this century, five permanent theatres were established in Mexico City, and one in Canada. Shadow-figures, hand-puppets, and marionettes (string-puppets) were used at various times.

As the frontiers were pushed westward in the nineteenth century, the puppets went along, sometimes operated by showmen who doubled as acrobats and magicians, or joined forces with a vaudeville company or circus. Large companies arrived from England and made extensive tours. The saga of the Royal Marionettes is an exciting but little-known story in American theatrical history. Such companies offered a bill of plays, songs, dances, tricks, and transformations, which usually ended with an intricate mechanical spectacle.

At the beginning of the present century, puppetry declined as an important form of entertainment. Meanwhile in Europe, and by 1915 in the United States, a new kind of puppet play was being created by artists or cultured people for the entertainment of their own friends. Some of these shows became professional, and proved themselves popular with the public. Among the pioneers in the American puppetry revival were Ellen Van Volkenburg, Tony Sarg, and Remo Bufano. Through the annual tours of Sarg's company, and the publication of technical books on puppet making, the secrets of the old showmen were revealed, and puppetry invaded theatres, schools, and even the commercial world.

In 1937 a national organization, The Puppeteers of America, was founded, counting among its members amateurs, educators, and professionals. Annual puppet festivals were held under its sponsorship until 1942, when they were discontinued during World War II. Resuming the festival in 1946, the national organization continues its job of furthering the growth of the puppet theatre in America. New uses for the puppet have been found in therapy, television, and the movies; new developments in educational work and new opportunities in the professional field lie ahead.

We have suggested that the puppet theatre during its long history has assumed many different forms. This diversity presupposes some basic qualities which give puppets their universal appeal, else they would not equally charm the sophisticated habitués of the Montmartre cabarets and the working people who flocked to the theatres of chivalric romance.

It is significant that the favorite puppet heroes of the popular theatres are basically similar. Whether they are heroic or comic characters, they are symbols of success; whatever gets in their way is, in the end, thrust aside. This victory may be the result of a battle of wits or a more tangible exchange of fisticuffs, but it is always satisfying. The complexities of human life and character are simplified on the puppet stage. Most puppet characters are simple; they do not suffer from the inner contradictions which beset mankind. Orlando is good, noble, and valorous; his Saracen enemies are blackhearted villains upon whom one need waste no sympathy. Mr. Punch has no pangs of conscience, but we tolerate his outrageous behavior because he is able to overcome even the Devil—and no human being can be sure of doing as much!

Many puppet plays point the ultimate triumph of right over wrong; the heroes of Javanese drama have a hard fight of it, but because they are fundamentally good, they always triumph. So do the Christian paladins, even though the Saracens are equally valiant. Lafleur's terrible temper is aroused by wrongdoing, and if he sometimes does considerable damage, it is always bad people who suffer from it. The basic premise of the fairy tale is similar; someone is usually in the power of a wicked person, who in the end is overcome. No matter how harrowing the adventures of the hero (or heroine) everyone knows that finally all will be well.

Puppets are impersonal. Whatever they do becomes more forceful by virtue of being free from any real feeling. We envy them sometimes because they are so completely the part they play. Puppets also gain force because they are mechanically operated. They are never quite real, yet they seem alive. They imitate human beings and animals, but not to the point of merging their identity with them. It is for this reason that even inanimate and completely fabulous beings can be plausible characters on the puppet stage.

In addition, puppets are works of art, being direct expressions of the imagination of their creator, who designs them as he will— comic, tragic, ugly, or beautiful. Because they are not copies of human beings, puppets are free from many of their limitations; in their way they are superhuman. The wise showman realizes this, and chooses for the puppets the kinds of plays in which they can surpass human actors.

Thus one can see that a puppet, whatever its mode of construction, has its own power to divert us. Because puppets are widespread, many ways of constructing them have been invented. This book is primarily a technical manual wherein a great variety of construction methods, including both simple and complex ones, are described and illustrated. But without some idea of how the puppet's unique qualities as an actor can best be used, technical skill is of little value; hence notes are included about puppet acting, playwriting, program organization, and design.

The material in this book was first assembled for a manual to be used by the United States Army in its entertainment and rehabilitation program. Paul McPharlin made the first plan for the manual, and enlisted the assistance of various puppeteers, who gave generously of their knowledge. Douglas Anderson, then a corporal in the Army, was assigned to the Special Services office in New York City to prepare the illustrations, and the author was employed to write the text. When it was finished, the manual turned out to be a comprehensive technical handbook of puppetry, covering the production of puppet shows and the construction of all types of puppets.

This revised edition has been made possible through the courtesy of the Special Services Division of the Army Service Forces, which gave permission for the publication of the material after its use by the Army, and the generosity of the many workers in the puppet theatre who have allowed their contribution to the Army manual to be used herein.

Such a book would have been impossible to write without the benefit of the varied experience of many persons, and the author gratefully acknowledges the valuable assistance of Douglas Anderson, Gayle Michael Anderson, Siska Ayala, Susan Barnes, Peg Blickle, F. L. Brant, Remo Bufano, Lieutenant Colonel R. Robert Cohen, George Cole, Lola Cueto, Merle Swineford Dilley, Perry Dilley, William Duncan, W. A. Dwiggins, Clem Easly, Nina Efimova, the late Bessie A. Ficklen, Harry Fowler, David Gibson, Juan Guerrero, Martha Hargrave, Sue Hastings, John Houghmaster, R. Bruce Inverarity, Edward Johnson, Roberto Lago, Robert V. Longfield, Edward Mabley, Paul McPharlin, Jero Magon, Louise Martin, Vivian Michael, Sergei Obrazsov, Harriet Peasley, Emma Pettey, Romain Proctor, Rufus Rose, Dorcas Ruthenburg, Joseph Shea, Martin Stevens, H. V. Tozer, Ellen Van Volkenburg, Alfred and Lea Wallace, Emma Warfield, Walter Wilkinson, Lemuel Williams, Adolf Woltman, and Ben Yano.

To the following publishers the author wishes to extend thanks for their kindness in granting permission to quote from their publications: The D. Appleton-Century Co.; Harper and Brothers; and Williams and Wilkins. By permission of Paul McPharlin, editor of *Puppetry Imprints*, quotations have been used from Lola Cueto and Roberto Lago, *Mexican Folk Puppets*; W. A. Dwiggins, *Marionette in Motion*; Nina Efimova, *Adventures of a Russian Puppet Theatre*, and *Puppetry, A Yearbook of Puppets and Marionettes*.

In addition to the people who contributed directly to *The Puppet Theatre Handbook*, the author wishes to acknowledge the debt to puppet showmen throughout the ages, for it is they who have made puppetry such a varied and exciting dramatic art. May contemporary and future puppeteers keep it so!

The Puppet Theatre Handbook

CHAPTER I

THE PUPPET THEATRE AND ITS USES

THE UNIQUE QUALITY OF THE PUPPET THEATRE

The puppet theatre offers diversion to people of all ages. While many shows are designed for or given by children, adults in ever-increasing numbers are recognizing the unique quality of puppet entertainment. Sergei Obrazsov in his book *Actor With Puppet*, tells about his experiences with puppets, and how he as an actor gradually learned the special qualities of puppet acting. He made an old man as a study for a character in Offenbach's *La Périchole*. Later, "he conceived the idea of using his *Périchole* puppet for a mock-sentimental song. He made the old man strum a guitar and comb his ungovernable gray hair back with his fingers. He made him sing for a while with great seriousness, then break the mood by a smack of the lips, or an awkward twang of the strings. The audience, almost under the sad spell of the song, would realize that it was all satire, and burst into laughter.

"Obrazsov soon realized that puppets were not imitators of people, but instruments for showing up their foibles. They need not look like real people, he found; they need not even act like people; they had only to move and be symbols of the curious traits of man. As an actor, Obrazsov was particularly interested in reasons why the puppet should exist. How was it justified? What could a puppet do that an actor could not? More and more he came to believe that the puppet has qualities apart from those of the actor. Whenever he put a puppet over his hand and caused it to move, he was able to affect an audience differently than he could in his own proper person. Whether the puppets represent men or beasts, play folk-tale or modern comedy, there is always a flood of life—something so living that one is taken unaware and does not ask, 'Is this realistic, do people act like that?' The puppets are abundantly alive, and whether they mock the ways of man, or invent their own animation, is beside the point. Soldiers, academicians, children, farmers, college students, teachers, engineers, all watch them with the same intense fascination."[1]

THE UNIVERSAL APPEAL OF PUPPETS

It is this universal appeal which makes the puppet show such a versatile form of entertainment. There is a type of puppet and a suitable stage for every occasion and for every audience. The bed-ridden patient in a hospital can be a puppet showman, while the most sophisticated of puppets delight night club audiences from coast to coast. Countless shows are produced annually in American schools by children, while professional showmen tour with fully equipped theatres in which serious adult drama is played. Puppets dance and sing, satirize their human associates, harangue on street corners, ballyhoo commercial products, pop in and out of movies, enact religious drama, and bring the world of fantasy before the eyes of wide-eyed children and tired adults. There is no limit to the power of the puppet to entertain, provided the right program is chosen, and the puppets are adequate for their roles.

PUPPETS IN EDUCATION

Because they are entertaining and fun to make, puppets are excellent for school projects. Many pupils with varied abilities can participate. Emma Pettey describes a puppet show presented in a large Texas school which was composed of children who could not afford to produce a costumed spectacle. "We decided to use a puppet show as a project for the whole school. Andersen's story of *The Emperor's New Robe* was chosen. The seventh grade formed the company cast, worked out and memorized the lines.

The whole school brought scraps of cloth and decorative bits, and the domestic science department costumed the hand-puppets (supplied from the outside). The manual training department provided the stage; the music department worked up the march from *Aïda* as a backstage orchestra to accompany the puppet musicians in the emperor's procession; the art department made scenery and banners, while the physical training department taught the puppets a ballet number by dancing in front of the miniature stage and letting the puppets imitate their movements."[2] In such projects, the children learn and enjoy themselves at the same time. Similar shows are organized in the schools to dramatize life in foreign countries, bring famous episodes of history to life for the pupils, and inculcate good standards of social behavior.

In Mexico, the Ministry of Education has a puppetry program for mass education of the people. Shows are sent to various schools and villages. The puppets dramatize the advantages of reading and writing, of brushing one's teeth and keeping clean. In one show, the little boy who refuses to have his hair cut is terrified when a small lion jumps out of his unkempt and dirty mop; in another, Comino, a favorite puppet, announces that he is no friend to anyone who refuses to accept a free toothbrush, whereupon everybody lines up after the show. The puppet succeeded, whereas previous attempts to interest the children in toothbrushes had failed.

The accomplishment of Javier Villafañe in Argentina, Uruguay and Chile is outstanding. With his puppet theatre, La Andariega, he has performed in hundreds of schools. Following the show, the children are encouraged to record their impressions through drawing or painting. They are shown how to make puppets and establish their own theatre. Puppetry has thus become an important stimulus to creative art and dramatic interpretation.

While it has been widely used in primary and secondary schools, the puppet theatre has been relatively neglected in colleges and universities. This is due to the popular misconception that puppetry is confined to children's entertainment, and a lack of understanding of the special characteristics of the puppet theatre as a form of drama. In a college dramatic curriculum, puppets should be used to present plays which cannot be done as successfully by human actors, or those which might be too elaborate or expensive to pro- duce on the large stage, but which are important for students to see as part of their training in the theatre arts. For studies in staging and costuming, for the appreciation of movement on the stage, in fact, for all those experiments where the small model is inade- quate and the large stage too unwieldy, the puppet theatre is ideal.

It also has its place in the technical training of the actor—for practice in improvisation, for characterization, and for the cor- rection of minor speech defects. For instance, it has been found that persons with unpleasant voices have shown marked improve- ment after having worked with a puppet for which they have used a voice totally different from their habitual one. For people who have good voices, but whose physical characteristics may debar them from anything except limited roles on the large stage, the puppet theatre offers opportunities for the widest possible diversity of roles.

Portable theatres which can be easily set up in a classroom are invaluable for the study of drama. Scenes acted on the stage are much more forceful than they are when merely read from a book. For this type of work, sets of stock puppets (hand- or hand-and- rod-puppets are a good type to use) can be made up for various periods such as Shakespearean, Eighteenth Century, or Classic. Other sets could be designed for presenting plays in foreign lan- guages, while a group of modern characters would be invaluable for improvisations upon current political and social happenings.

When the potentialities of the puppet theatre are understood, it can immeasurably enrich the dramatic program in education, from the first grade through the university.

PUPPETS IN RECREATION

Puppets are ideal for group recreation in churches, camps and social centers because they provide many different activities. A puppet theatre in the home draws the members of the family together; the smallest child as well as the oldest adult can participate.

In Czecho-Slovakia there are numerous community puppet theatres located in the *Sokols*, which serve as gymnasiums and social centers. Here men and women build puppet shows which are presented to the children. Many of these people work as doctors, musicians, lawyers, teachers, clerks, and find in the puppet theatre an outlet for creative work or technical experimentation. The shows are organized to give as many people as possible a chance to participate. Some make puppets, some work on costumes; other groups attend to technical matters such as lighting and staging. Many of these theatres have elaborate scenic equipment— treadmill, cyclorama, revolving or elevator stage, cloud machine and other effects. Complete switchboards and lighting equipment may rival that of the large theatre. Those who read the lines sit below the stage and watch the action directly or in a mrror, while other people manipulate the puppets. It takes several persons just to handle scenery during a show—to set the scenes, to work the treadmill and move pieces on or off, to operate the revolving stage and so on. The American visitor is astonished to find a dozen or more people backstage, each with his particular job to perform.

Adult participation in shows is a form of recreation which might well be encouraged in our country, for it is a rewarding one, both for those who present the plays and those who see them.

PUPPETS IN THERAPY AND REHABILITATION

The puppet theatre is excellent for rehabilitation work with both children and adults. It not only provides lively entertainment, but it is a valuable therapeutic aid which can be used to help many types of patients. Properly approached, nearly everyone likes puppets; their universal appeal is their strongest recommendation. Life in the wards would be considerably enlivened by the occasional appearance of the "Walking Theatre" illustrated on *Plate 31*. One or two men in wheel chairs can organize a traveling show for their own amusement and the entertainment of others

[5]

(*Plates 32-34*). With finger-puppets (*Plate 4*) not even a stage is needed; these figures dance on the bed, run up and down the patient's plaster cast, or stand on his chest and converse with him. The type of puppet used is immaterial so long as it can be made and handled by the patients using it. Elaborate shows can be done if there is time and space, but even the simplest puppets can provide endless entertainment.

In all rehabilitation work, the puppet is fitted to the needs of the patients. What they receive from participating in a show is of far more importance than a professional standard of performance, yet the presence of an audience is an incentive for each person to give his best effort. Any theatrical enterprise has two qualities which are invaluable to people recovering from illness: The participant becomes interested in something outside himself, and whatever he contributes is related to the work of others. Hence individual effort is stimulated, yet it is socialized and extroverted.

Puppetry is helpful for psychoneurotic patients as well as those suffering from organic disorders, muscular tension or broken bones. Adolf Woltman suggests the chief value of puppets for psychoneurotics: "Puppetry is a group activity. It is meaningless without an audience. Therefore several people can be reached at the same time and benefit vicariously in the same way that one enjoys and appreciates a movie or a stage show. The audience may be drawn into the play by talking back to the puppets, making suggestions, shouting warnings, and so on. Such participation leads automatically to a more intimate identification with the characters. The verbalizations of the audience reflect the feelings, drives, and desires of the onlookers and afford good opportunities for the release of hostility and tension. At the same time there should be situations which allow for identification with the ethical good qualities of humans and a strong reaffirmation that love, appreciation, and acceptance are just as much part of human relationships as aggression, hostility, and strife.

"Spontaneity of movement and speech, an essential part of a

[6]

good puppet show, should be made a prime consideration for a therapeutic application. Instead of following a rigid script, a spontaneous show, given on the spur of the moment, will bring forth some of the innermost thoughts. It will help the person who handles the puppet to put into action his feelings and to make them intelligible through speech. Anxieties, fears, and apprehensions that defy description can easily be brought to a conscious level. Furthermore, through repeated expressions of these problems, different solutions can be tried till one is found that is acceptable. At the same time the person who plays out his own desires before an audience will realize that his problems are neither unique nor overwhelming. By letting others share in his difficulties, his problem becomes a group problem. It also leads to the realization that other people, too, have their own struggles. Such an insight is very reassuring in itself.

"A few words of caution are in order. A person who intends to use puppets primarily as a means of psychotherapy should be familiar with deviations of human behavior and should have a fundamental understanding of human problems and difficulties. It is very easy to release anxiety, to provoke hostility, or to stir up fear. It requires skill and clinical knowledge properly to handle such expressions and to channelize them constructively. It is, therefore, most fruitful if the artistic skill of the puppeteer can be teamed with the professional knowledge of a therapist."[3]

Emma Warfield points out that "mental patients can be helped by puppetry: the dull may enjoy watching a production take form; the indifferent may be roused to work in it; the depressed may forget themselves in its detail and color; the introverted may develop initiative and undergo a socializing influence; the artistically inclined chronic paranoid may find an altruistic outlet if given responsibility in directing activity."[4]

Lieutenant Colonel R. Robert Cohen has supervised the use of puppets for the retraining of psychoneurotics at the Aberdeen Proving Ground. A number of visual aids are used in group therapy; the puppet show is regarded as one of the best, because it has concreteness, humor, and movement. Colonel Cohen says: "Puppets are admirably suited to presenting a basic understanding of human emotions to the average soldier, because a puppet as a symbolic character can easily project an abstract idea which a human actor would find difficult and involved. In effect, the puppet is a three-dimensional presentation of an otherwise completely abstract concept. In using puppets with Army men in an understanding of psychoneurosis, puppets make real such emotions as resentment, fear, anger, and sorrow; that is, they present convincingly the fact that these abstractions really exist. Thus, when a soldier has a painful foot he knows it is due to a blister because he can see the blister. In a like manner, when he is told that his bodily reverberations are due to emotion, he can now believe the relationship, because he can see concretely that emotion at work. Furthermore, puppets are valuable because they can change their attitudes quickly. These small characters can change over from extreme euphoria and happiness to marked depression and sadness in considerably less time than it would take a human actor to make the transition. Therefore, the puppet can say things more convincingly within the limits of a short play, and what's more, can say things which no person could say and get away with."[5]

Other suggestions for the use of puppets with mental patients are to be found in the articles listed on page 289.[6]

Puppets may provide many activities for patients with physical disabilities. Handicrafts are valuable because they encourage relaxation from mental activity or care; puppetry involves a great deal of handwork, with the additional incentive of performing for an audience. There are many physical injuries which require exercise to restore movement; making puppets provides necessary activity in many cases. Susan Barnes describes the way in which puppetry is used in the Occupational Therapy Workshop in St. Louis. All the activities involved in a puppet show are analyzed for their therapeutic value. When patients are sent by the doctor for specific treatment, they are carefully studied, and that phase of puppetry best suited to their needs is prescribed. The nature of the case determines the kind of play and type of puppets. For instance, papier-mâché is useful for the extension and flexion of the fingers, while stiff knee joints resulting from fracture can be exercised by cutting out wooden bodies for marionettes on a bicycle jig saw. In this workshop, many types of patients work together on productions according to their needs and abilities.

Some patients lose interest in the things which they normally like to do; for them puppetry may be a new field. It offers opportunity for experimentation, and gives the patient something definite to think about. It may even be something which can be used when the patient returns home. A small stage equipped with lights and a set of puppets may mean a new avocation for a man and his family. Here the value of puppetry would be in the satisfaction derived from planning and making a complete theatre rather than in working with a group of people. The ever-flexible art of puppetry is equally successful as a diversion for many people, or the creative expression of an individual.

PUPPETS IN ADVERTISING

Puppets performing in shop windows never fail to draw a crowd. They may incidentally advertise a product, but it is the fascination of puppet movement which holds the attention. Some years ago crowds all over the country were entertained by the Tatterman diving girl, made of aluminum and dressed in a Jantzen bathing suit, who cavorted in a tank of real water.

In the old French and English fairs puppets were used as advertising devices, and they are equally effective in our modern world expositions. The Kelvinator show produced by the Tatterman Marionettes at the Chicago Century of Progress in 1934 was an excellent example of advertising a product through entertainment. The story of refrigeration was told in a series of dramatic episodes from prehistoric days when man took his meat into the cool recesses of the cave to preserve it, to the modern electric refrigerator. Remo Bufano's huge marionettes enacted the story of pharmacy

[9]

at the New York World's Fair in 1940. Several scenes, including an African witch doctor performing his magic dance, were arranged on a large revolving stage. The scale of the show made it truly spectacular. Another popular show was the A and P Carnival at the Century of Progress Exposition, Chicago, 1933, in which Tony Sarg skillfully combined advertising and entertainment.

Puppets are usually successful in advertising because they create a dramatic situation which, although primarily entertaining, yet advertises the product more or less indirectly. Added to the basic theatrical appeal is the appeal to the eye through movement, color, and form. Mechanical ingenuity and imaginative quality also play an important part in making the puppet show a powerful advertising medium. Most important of all is the compactness of the puppet show; the advertiser can have a complete theatre in a store window.

PUPPETS IN THE MOVIES AND TELEVISION

For advertising, education, and straight entertainment, puppets should have an important place in the movies and television. In a discussion of the commercial possibilities of puppet films, Siska Ayala says, "The future of puppets in the movies is enormous. There is a growing trend to documentary and educational shorts both in cartoon and scale model techniques. Television will broadcast films for entertainment and advertisement, the films because of present technical limitations being better than live action. What puppet forms are best for the camera? At present stop-motion is furthest advanced and best controlled. But there is room for endless experimentation in action range and in combination with live (human or animal) action, running action (shot like regular movies, not stop-motion), and cartoons. There should be trial use of all types of puppets; string, rod, hand, and shadow, and of heroic size as well as small. Charming novelty shorts could be worked out with all these types."[7]

Puppet shows need to be adapted to movie technique. For

[10]

example, fixed features make the close-up unsatisfactory unless the lighting is carefully arranged. If the face is well modeled, it will usually appear alive because the patterns of light and shade change as the puppet moves about the stage. Sometimes realistically modeled puppets are given movable mouths to make them look alive. The result is usually ludicrous rather than real, because the rest of the face is immobile. But if the puppeteer is not aiming at naturalism in his puppets, the "wooden" expression of a puppet may be very amusing, especially in a close-up. So also movable eyes, or ears, or mouth may give enough variety to the face to make it interesting, no matter how close the camera approaches.

The control apparatus of puppets may be a disadvantage if one is attempting a naturalistic effect, but in most cases strings and rods are accepted as part of the show if care is taken to minimize them. Devices such as angle shots, trick photography, and unusual lighting can add to the effect of puppet movies.

Bil Baird, in the movies he prepared for the Office of the Co-ordinator of Inter-American Affairs, has made great advances in the adaptation of puppets to movie technics. Everything—puppets, play, music, script—is designed for the movie medium, and built under Baird's close direction. He supervises the photography, too. Such films combine entertainment and education with a high degree of artistry, and may point the way to a new development of the puppet movie.

Undoubtedly puppet movies have a strong competitor in the animated cartoon, but the former are easier to produce, and give a much more three-dimensional quality. Because there are so many kinds of puppets, it is possible to develop more types of movement than are possible in the cartoon. From the puppet showman's point of view, movies are less satisfactory than actual shows, but they can be shown to much larger audiences, and this has some advantages.

Edward Johnson points out that cost and space are the two major problems confronting the television staff, hence the small size of puppets gives them an advantage over human actors.

Television producers "will be looking for a great variety of programs with visual interest. Puppets can help fill that bill by being just puppets. Care, though, must be taken not to imitate the animated cartoon, for television will make use of many motion picture films for the same purpose that radio now makes use of recordings. Quite a few of these pictures will be animated cartoons, and were we to imitate them we would soon become known only as cheap imitators. No, puppetry must create a style of its own."[8] Andre Vern Longfield mentions that telecasts will be expensive to produce because costumes and scenery can only be used once. Although a single telecast would be seen by more people than would be able to witness a stage play in a year's time, the sponsor's expenses will, nevertheless, be great. "What better opportunity could puppets possibly have to show their true value? One-third the size of their human masters, they will require but a third as much scenery, a third as much costuming, and a third as much room in which to present their productions, and, to the backer's great joy, at a third as much cost. Then, too, by the change of a head and a costume the puppet can become an entirely different person. Lighting is a very important factor in telecasting, and puppets stand patiently for hours, if need be, while lighting experiments are tried on them."[9]

Puppets have already proved their value in television, for they have been used at intervals during the past ten years. What their future will be depends upon the puppeteers themselves and the trends in the development of this science.

PUPPETRY AS A PROFESSION

The foregoing discussion should suggest many possibilities for the expansion of puppetry as a profession. There are too few good touring companies; many more can find business provided they keep up their standards and do not spoil the trade by underselling each other or producing inferior shows. Productions for children have been fairly numerous, but the field of adult puppet entertainment has scarcely been touched. With carefully chosen plays written especially for adult audiences, good professional showmen would be welcomed by clubs for men and women. They should also find a place on the programs sponsored by colleges and universities. As puppetry finds an increasingly important place in the drama departments of universities, opportunities for the puppet showman to carry on his own work and do some teaching should be available.

During the war years, many puppeteers turned to variety, and their acts have been incorporated in the vaudeville circuits playing in movie houses all over the country. In night clubs, too, puppets have enjoyed increasing popularity. United Service Organization entertainers, taking puppetry into all corners of the world, have introduced it to thousands of service men, who are potential audiences for peacetime puppet entertainment. Variety will undoubtedly continue to be a profitable profession, if showmen keep their material fresh and original.

As has been suggested, there are likely to be many openings for puppeteers in the movies and television, especially for commercial shorts. Edward Johnson says: "There is good reason to believe that many studios will maintain several puppeteers on their regular staffs. I have been told by a manager of an important radio station that he has such a plan. Puppeteers holding such jobs would have to have a fairly large number of stock figures made up; figures that could be changed from one role to another quickly. These staff operators would be called upon to make all sorts of model sets, and they would have to be good; so the smart operator will make himself proficient."[10]

We have mentioned some ways in which puppets can provide unique entertainment. Every worker in the puppet theatre must adapt his medium to his own situation. In the following pages we hope that every reader will find something of value. In a general way, we shall show what has been done with puppets. This should provide guidance for the beginner, and a point of departure for the experienced puppeteer.

CHAPTER II

PLANNING THE PUPPET SHOW

HOW TO AROUSE INTEREST IN PUPPETS

One of your foremost problems may be to arouse interest in your projected show. If you are a professional, this is part of the publicity campaign and booking. It is a good idea to have some engagements booked before you spend a long time building the show—or at least to sound out the prospective market to be sure you are on the right track. To introduce puppetry into schools, recreation groups, and hospitals may also require "selling" the idea. Patients in a convalescent hospital may be lethargic as well as bored, and uninterested in making any effort to occupy themselves. A good rousing performance which is lively and amusing, but which does not look too difficult, may be the impetus necessary to start an enthusiastic puppet group. Sometimes alert students will be self-starting; if puppets and equipment are made available for them to experiment with, they will go ahead and start a production. Books have inspired beginning puppeteers and are useful to provide the information necessary to keep a project moving, but cannot take the place of seeing actual puppets. Good photographs, lantern slides, and movies of puppets in action and in process of construction are stimulating. It is also helpful, when introducing puppet construction to groups, to lay out on a table all the necessary materials, with puppets in various stages of completion so that the whole process can be seen. Another excellent way to arouse interest is to sponsor a good professional show and get the collaboration of as wide a variety of people as possible. You will inspire the interest of many persons, and at the same time, you and your associates will have a standard of performance toward which to work. You may not be so good, but you will be aware of that fact, and your triumph in your own show will be tempered with modesty.

Never refer to puppets as dolls, even to children. To suggest to an adult or teen-age group that they should play with dolls, even for dramatic purposes, is the surest possible way to kill any potential interest in puppetry. Besides, puppets are *not* dolls, they are mechanically operated actors; their essential quality is movement. They have a kind of life which the staring doll can never achieve. If your puppet looks like a doll, do something about it—loosen its joints, exaggerate its features, give it more movement. Particularly among men you will find a certain embarrassment about puppets, and it is because they are so often associated with dolls. Men, however, will respect a good piece of craftsmanship; show them a well-carved, finely articulated marionette with nine strings, work it for them, and then let them have a try for themselves. They may not dash off immediately to start making a puppet, but they will understand that it isn't child's play.

In an effort to interest people, some writers about puppet construction have emphasized its simplicity. This is all very well, but the simple kind of puppet often shown as an example of what can be done "with anything you have on hand" would never inspire adult interest in puppets. Adults do not expect something for nothing; they would rather put more work into a show and get the kind of puppets which are sound in craftsmanship and which produce satisfactory dramatic results.

KNOW PUPPET HISTORY
AND CONSTRUCTION METHODS

Many people, having seen a professional string-puppet show or two, decide that it would be fun to make puppets. Usually with little more knowledge than what they have gleaned from watching other people's shows, they start building complicated string-puppets. Before the figures are complete, enthusiasm has waned, and very likely the whole project is abandoned. This is a deplorable state of affairs, especially if children are involved, because they never experience the real joy of puppet production.

Had these enthusiastic people but paused a moment to read a bit of history, they would have realized that the puppet theatre is not just a place where people have fun in their spare moments, but a serious form of dramatic entertainment. It would also have become evident that there are many ways of operating puppets without using strings at all. In addition, a cursory glance through the standard technical manuals of puppet construction would provide enough information to guide the prospective puppeteer in the choice of a suitable puppet type.

Chapter III of this book will give you a variety of construction methods for the different types of figures. However, you should not fail to develop your own ideas because there is still so much to be contributed to the puppet theatre in new technical methods, new plays, new uses for puppets, that you should not necessarily discard an original solution of a problem for an accepted method. On the other hand, learn all you can about what has been done; this will help you to know what not to do, as well as give you hints for your own procedure. Go directly to nature for help in solving articulation problems for human and animal characters, then make your own interpretations in terms of basic construction methods.

It has already been suggested (see p. 1) that the puppet theatre is both similar and dissimilar to the theatre of living actors. The alert puppeteer keeps himself informed about what is going on in the latter, not to imitate, but to learn the fundamentals of theatrical art in order to adapt them to the puppet stage.

CLASSIFICATION OF SHOWS

Assuming that you now have some knowledge of puppet history and a general acquaintance with the mechanics of different types of puppets, you can decide what kind of puppet show you want to give. Shows may be roughly divided into two classifications: Those built for the purpose of making money, and those used as an end in themselves. In the first, the show is designed and built primarily to entertain an audience, to sell a product, or to promote a cause for which the showman is paid. It is, in short, a business, and those who participate in it are doing so for the purpose of earning a living. In the second type of show, participation is of primary importance. Those who build it, manipulate the puppets, speak the lines, and attend to the publicity are doing it for their own entertainment, or because such work is a part of an educational project, or has been prescribed for therapeutic purposes. This does not mean that the show may not be presented to a paying audience, nor that the audience should be ignored in planning it, but it does mean that all those who are concerned with its production must be considered. For example, a puppet show given by convalescent patients in a hospital is planned to give everyone working on it some useful and diverting occupation; at the same time, the ultimate presentation to an audience of their fellows is important because it is the logical goal of any theatrical performance—and also provides entertainment for other patients who need it.

The first step, then, in planning a puppet show it to decide why it is being given, who is to build it, what kind of audience is to see it, and where it is to be presented.

WHAT IS A GOOD PUPPET SHOW

A puppet show, like any other theatrical performance, is a combination of several activities, none of which can be slighted without damaging the quality of the production. Rufus Rose summarizes the ingredients of a good puppet show as follows:

1. A good script, written for puppets.
2. Puppets, scenery and costumes well designed and executed.
3. Carefully planned and effective lighting.
4. Skillful operators with trained voices.

5. Sufficient and efficient stage equipment.

6. Adequate time for rehearsals.

7. A director with a sense of showmanship, who is able to tie all these elements together.[1]

If this seems a rather large order, perhaps impossible to achieve with a small group of neighborhood children, it is, nevertheless important to keep these fundamentals in mind, and realize them as completely as possible.

This chapter is planned to help you get the best possible artistic and mechanical results by efficient organization of all the details which go to make up a show—even a simple one. Simplicity and difficulty are relative terms; it is as difficult for small children to put on a so-called simple show (judged by adult standards) as it is for seasoned puppeteers to stage a three act marionette play with seven scenes and twenty characters. All shows have the same underlying principles, however, and it is with these that we are here concerned.

SELECTION OF A PROGRAM

Select the play and plan the program you are to give. It may be one play, two short plays with a variety number or two, a musical revue, or a vaudeville show. Whatever it is, select play plots and variety numbers which are not hackneyed. If your first impulse is to build a string-puppet piano player, suppress it and think up something else—this act has been done to death. So has the strip tease, the tap dancer, and the opera singer with heaving bosom. Avoid these, unless you are sure you are giving them a fresh interpretation. If you are doing a children's program, the possibilities of *Jack and the Beanstalk* as a puppet play will probably occur to you. So have they occurred to dozens of other puppeteers, and this fairy story is one of the most overworked in the puppet repertory. In other words, try to find out those plays and turns which have been frequently done, then look for fresh material. Don't copy, create.

As you mull over the ideas you have for your show, ask yourself, "Is this play or act something which can be done better with puppets than with any other dramatic medium?" If the answer is "no," discard it and look for something else.

Remo Bufano reminds us that "the important thing about puppets is that they can be constructed to do things that real people could never hope to do and that they can have shapes that real people can only imagine. For example, a marionette can be made with twenty or more arms and legs. He can lift his head off his body and put it back again. He can have a nose longer than his whole body. He can have one great big eye and one tiny one. . . . These are things to remember in picking your play."[2]

Realistic portrait puppets of famous people often amuse an audience, but it is better to satirize them rather than see how closely you can imitate them. Your puppets are at a disadvantage so long as the audience is interested in merely seeing how much they look and behave like human beings. You can produce a much more powerful effect if you can prevent the audience from comparing the puppets with human beings. For example, instead of imitating a famous radio crooner, why not satirize him by exaggerating both his physical characteristics and his manner of singing? You are then producing a humorous commentary upon the whole idea of crooning instead of presenting an inadequate imitation. Some puppeteers maintain that audiences want the old familiar plays and turns. This is perhaps because puppet showmen have failed to provide them with anything else.

The kind of program you present may depend upon the type of puppet you want to use, or you may select the program to suit the talents of a particular group of puppets. If you have some finely built marionettes, find something which will show them to advantage.

For your first show, it is usually best to plan something simple and do it as well as your talent and resources allow. Study Chapter III on puppet construction, and select the type which best suits your purpose, your pocketbook, and the time at your disposal.

The less complex types, such as shadows, hand-puppets, or simple rod-puppets are generally better to begin with than marionettes (string-puppets). However, if you are trying to interest a group of adults who are unfamiliar with puppets, be careful to avoid any suggestion that they are playing at something slight—cutting out shadow-puppets may seem nothing more than making paper dolls, unless they have seen shadow plays. A somewhat more elaborate type of construction, such as the hand-and-rod, might produce far more enthusiasm.

Puppet shows vary in cost from practically nothing to hundreds of dollars. Whatever amount you have to spend should be distributed so that you can provide the puppets with an adequate stage as well as appropriate clothing. Don't spend all your money on handsome draperies, and then have nothing left to buy enough light units to illuminate the stage. You can economize, especially if you are ingenious in the use of available materials, but don't plan a show calling for elaborate costumes and staging unless you can either buy or fabricate the necessary glamour. Try something less pretentious, and next time your resources may be greater. Check on the materials necessary for your show—don't plan to use things which it is practically impossible to get, or which may have to be ordered and will arrive too late for your project. It is well to have everything on hand which you will need, because if work is held up for days while you wait for that piece of jewel cloth to arrive, interest in the show will lag. Careful planning may mean the difference between a production which is fun, and one which is full of headaches for all concerned. In educational and therapeutic work, enjoyment in producing the show is part of its reason for being; more harm than good is done by an ill-planned, hectic project.

DESIGNING AND PLANNING

The entire show should be designed before you begin to build. Each character should be related to the others and to the stage setting; each costume planned in relation to the lighting and to the character portrayed. If you are using puppets one-third or one-fourth life size, the properties and scenery should be designed to the same scale. It is not always necessary to maintain the size relationships of nature—a bird or animal might be larger than normal if it is an important character. You do not have to show a house with the bulk of a real house so long as the puppets can go easily in and out of its door. Puppets usually appear to be as large (or larger than) their human counterparts unless a too-obtrusive violation of scale takes place.

Adequate time to build, rehearse, and advertise the show should be allowed. Too often, especially in amateur productions, construction takes so long that there is not enough time left for rehearsals, and the performance does not do justice to the puppets. It is not easy to do, but a balance between the time used in construction and in rehearsal must be maintained. If time is limited, use simple puppets which can be quickly constructed and then turned over to the puppeteers who are to operate them. Construction always takes longer than you think it will; figure out about how long should be devoted to it, then multiply by two and you may have the approximate time. Do the same thing for rehearsals. As Hastings and Ruthenburg say, "Rehearse. Rehearse some more. Rehearse till you drop."[3] We do not recommend the puppet theatre as a place for killing off people, but only wish to stress the need for enough practice in manipulating puppets to make the show move smoothly. There is nothing more unamusing than a poorly handled puppet wobbling on the stage and stumbling over its own feet as well as its lines.

DISTRIBUTION OF LABOR

Producing a puppet show involves a variety of jobs which can be divided among different people according to their abilities. On the other hand, the versatile individual may handle most of these with a minimum of assistance from others. If you are using the group method, the division of labor might be as follows:

Construction: Making the puppets; building the stage; arranging the lighting; constructing properties, costuming, building and painting the setting.

Playwriting: Either the writing of an original script, or the adapting of a story, play, poem, or other material.

Performance: Directing; manipulating and speaking for the puppets; arranging and supervising the music; ticket taking and ushering.

Business: Booking; making of posters, handbills, programs; writing articles for the press and radio; taking photographs of puppets and puppeteers for newspapers and records; advertising and publicity; ticket selling.

By assigning different people to all these jobs, a large group can be set to work on a show. The larger the group, the more difficult it is to unify all parts of the production. If concentration is more desirable than diffusion, divide the production work into three main types—technical, dramatic and business—which can be supervised by three people having the necessary qualifications. Rarely is one person equally good at craftsmanship, acting and the transaction of business. Most professional companies are made up of a small group of people each of whom is skilled in one of these branches.

Although discussion of the show is to be encouraged among those working on it, some one person must have the final authority to decide what must be done. The more people there are working on the project, and the more elaborate the show, the more important is this guiding hand.

Every show is a new problem in planning and organization; how it is done doesn't matter so much, so long as there *is* planning, and someone is on hand to keep an eye on all that is happening. Let us repeat: *Organization* makes the difference between fun and chaos in any puppet production.

CHAPTER III

PUPPET CONSTRUCTION

BASIC TYPES OF CONSTRUCTION

The many ways of constructing puppets may be grouped into four main classifications: Shadows, hand-puppets, rod-puppets and marionettes (string-puppets). Methods of construction depend upon modes of operation, which determine characteristic movements. It is necessary, therefore, to become familiar with the various types of puppets in order to make the best choice for the kind of play to be given, the audience to be entertained, and the participants in the show.

Shadow-Puppets are flat figures operated by rods or wires against a translucent screen illuminated from behind. The simplest shadow is merely a silhouette cut from cardboard and mounted on a stick. When the figure is articulated it becomes capable of varied and expressive action. For more elaborate figures, colored sheet plastic, or cardboard combined with colored paper, can be used. Since they are quickly made and easily operated, shadows are especially useful for productions given by large groups of people.

Hand-Puppets (known also as fist- or glove-puppets) are worked on the operator's hand; his thumb and little (or third) finger move the puppet's hands, his forefinger the head. These puppets can move rapidly from place to place, pick up and set down all sorts of objects, engage in fights, dance gracefully, or perform slapstick comedy. They are relatively simple to construct and operate.

Hand-and-Rod-Puppets are a development of the hand-puppet. Their construction is similar except that the puppet's arms are longer and are jointed at shoulder and elbow (sometimes wrist) and are controlled by rods. This makes possible more precise and varied

[23]

hand movement, but the difficulty of picking up things is increased. The Michael variation of the type is a fully articulated puppet which can sit, lie down, and do all the usual hand-puppet movements. It is easy to manipulate, has great variety of action, and is more solidly constructed than the average hand-puppet.

Rod-Puppets are supported on a wooden or metal rod. Head and hands are controlled by lighter rods (umbrella ribs are excellent for this). Strings are sometimes used for additional control. These puppets are worked on a floorless stage similar to a hand-puppet booth; the operator may either stand or sit, with the puppet held above his head. Rod-puppets permit an unusually wide range of construction methods—the simplest is a flat cutout figure mounted on a stick, while the most complex is a fully articulated puppet capable of subtle and varied movement. These puppets may be of any size which can be adequately supported.

Marionettes are string-controlled puppets which are worked from overhead. Although there are simple marionettes with uncomplicated stringing, this type is generally more difficult to build and operate than the others described above. Marionettes are excellent dancers; they can perform gravity-defying stunts with ease; they are useful for many trick effects and transformations as well as straight dramatic parts. Because the operator is at some distance from the puppet, the control is less direct than with other types, hence the greater difficulty of operation.

The puppets described in the following pages are representative of the above types. There are simple puppets for the beginner, as well as more elaborate designs for the experienced worker. Many different materials and construction methods are suggested. These have been used by puppeteers in the past, and will serve as a guide for the newcomer in puppetry, as well as inspiration for the ingenious craftsman to invent his own methods.

PUPPET DESIGN

What is a Puppet? Puppets are neither miniatures of human beings nor dolls; they are acting figures controlled by human beings.

Complete imitation of life is not only impossible but undesirable. Puppets have a life of their own which depends upon both their design and operation. Before you begin to build a set of puppets, there are a few important factors to be considered.

Scale. Although some puppets are life size or larger, most of them are much smaller; one-third human scale is average. Some knowledge of human and animal proportions is useful, but the designer should not be limited by them, because unrealistic scale relationships are often powerful or humorous on the puppet stage. Puppets with heads one third the size of their body are sometimes appropriate, but exaggeration without purpose has no meaning. Whether you distort or follow normal proportions will depend upon the type of play you are giving, your own mode of expression and the kind of puppet you are using.

Essential Qualities Stressed. Because of its compact scale, there is no room in the puppet theatre for the unimportant and the unnecessary. Therefore, the most important factor in puppet design is simplicity, with emphasis upon the *essential* quality of what is to be portrayed. For instance, an intricately modeled puppet head in realistic style becomes a mere blur when seen on the stage under theatrical lighting, whereas the exaggerated nose and chin of Mr. Punch are easily visible. You need not necessarily distort, but you must always simplify. Once the essential quality of a character is expressed, further details should be omitted for they only impede. Thus, there may appear perfectly satisfactory characters which have but one or two features. If these are just right, the others are not missed.

Sources for Puppet Design. For ideas about characterization, study the people about you, or look at pictures of historical persons who have the character traits you need for your puppet. Study the basic design qualities of face and figure. To learn how to use these to the best advantage, look carefully at the masks of different civilizations (see p. 264 for references). Mask design runs the gamut from simplified realism, through various degrees of stylization to the grotesque. Whether you want realistic heads or stylized ones, the designers of masks, past and present, will be your best teachers. Compare the stylistic qualities of Greek and Roman masks with those from Bali and Java. See how the American Indian has made masks to represent good or evil spirits, and how the people of the South Seas have used form, color and many varied materials to make their ceremonial masks. Look at theatrical masks for the Japanese nō dramas which illustrate types such as the servant, the old man, the coquettish lady. Notice how Benda achieves his effects.

Remember that the puppet's face *is* a mask; its expression must be integral because the features do not move as do those of the human actor. Some masks and some puppets have one or more movable features, but these do not create an illusion of reality because the face as a whole does not move.

There is a tendency to model puppet faces too hard, with staring eyes and severe mouth. Even at the expense of fine finish, try for expression. More attention to the shape of the eye socket, and less to the painting of the eyeball (which may often be omitted entirely), will help make the eyes seem alive. Experiment with a clay model of the puppet head to see how simply you can make the features in order to gain the expression you want.

Boldness in the modeling or carving, plus simple accents of color, will give character even to figures seen from a distance. When working on heads, they should be constantly studied on the puppet stage under various lights. This will save many errors, by showing where the modeling is weak or the color insipid. Remember that what is important is how the puppet looks back of the footlights.

Puppet character is not confined to the head alone. The kind of body, the cut of the costume, the movement of the hands are just as important, because the puppet must be a consistent whole, or lose its force. It is quite possible to have expressive puppets with no face at all!

What has been said above applies equally to all styles of puppet design—semi-realistic, stylized, or fantastic. It also applies to the designing of puppet animals. These often suffer from too much realism. Here again, reference to masks will help. It is far more important to know and capture the essential character of an animal than to copy its furry or feathered covering. A dog of gingham and a calico cat, as well as a lean and hungry wolf made with visible ribs of sheet aluminum, are plausible on the puppet stage and do not suffer from lack of fur if the movements suggest those of the animal portrayed.

To study either human or animal movement, go to nature. As Rufus Rose suggests: "Man and animals act as they do because of their mechanical construction, which for our purposes involves: their methods of jointing, the distribution of weights in their body parts, and the suspension of these parts by their controllable muscles. In making the marionette, we should accurately copy, in simplified form, this jointing and weighting, and consider the strings in the hands of the operator, as the simplified muscular control of the body parts."[1]

Never be afraid to be unrealistic. The puppet stage is the most appropriate place for those fantastic creations which people the fairy tales and folk legends of all nations. Anything you can imagine, if it is well designed, constructed, and manipulated, can be an effective puppet. Take advantage of the mechanical nature of the puppet, exploit it to its fullest, and don't waste time trying to make an exact imitation of nature.

SHADOW–PUPPETS

Shadow-puppets depend upon their mass for their effectiveness; almost any figure, side or front view, which has a quickly identified, clear-cut outline can be adapted to a shadow puppet, if a smooth jointing system can be worked out. Make line drawings of figures —brush and ink on white paper are good—or try freehand cutting from cardboard for preliminary experiments. Think of the action the figure will need. If it has little to do, it may be just a simple silhouette mounted on a stick (*Plate 1, B*). Perhaps one movement is enough. The fat waiter with the bottle on a tray (*Plate 1, D*) needs only to bow to his customers. Use as few joints as possible and limit them to the action which is required of the puppet. Joints overlap, and are based on the principle of the circle. When you have made a tentative sketch, cut out all the parts from stiff paper and join them together with knotted thread or pins to try out the action.

There are many materials which are effective for shadow-puppets; simple silhouettes cut from black cover paper (a light weight cardboard) are powerful and yet simple to make. Clear stencil paper is semitranslucent and can be painted with oil colors; to make it more translucent, paint it with a mixture of linseed oil (2 parts) and turpentine (1 part). Black cardboard may have openings cut with a stencil knife, over which are pasted pieces of colored Cellophane, gelatin, or colored construction paper treated with the oil-turpentine mixture. Many kinds of fairly heavy colored paper can be handled in the same way. Colored sheet plastics, clear or translucent, make excellent shadows. Several colors can be used by superimposing them and cementing them with the proper solvent. Paper punches of various sizes make nice polka dots; other shapes can be cut out with dies which you may invent or buy. White transparent plastic can be colored with aniline dye, or painted with transparent water color if the surface is rubbed down with fine sandpaper (see p. 285 for kinds of plastic).

There are two general types of shadow construction. In one, derived from the Chinese (*Plate 1, A*), the main control rod is fastened to the front of a collar, with other rods on the hands. The body hangs freely from this center rod, the feet rest on a narrow ledge bolted to the bottom of the screen frame, and the movements are made by manipulating the three rods. The other type, illustrated on *Plate 2, B*, has a small wooden rod fastened to the body, with wires (1) and (2) attached to the movable parts and wound around the center control stick at (3) and (4). The animal on *Plate 1, C* is a combination of methods, with the center rod firmly attached to the body, and the nose rod separate. Notice in this one that a string attached to the tail and tied off to the center rod produces movement by the flick of a finger. The movable eye of

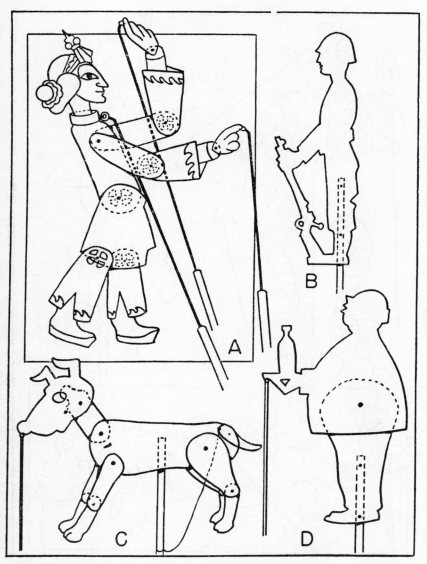

PLATE 1. SHADOW-PUPPETS

A. Chinese type
B, C, D. Simply articulated figures by Vivian Michael

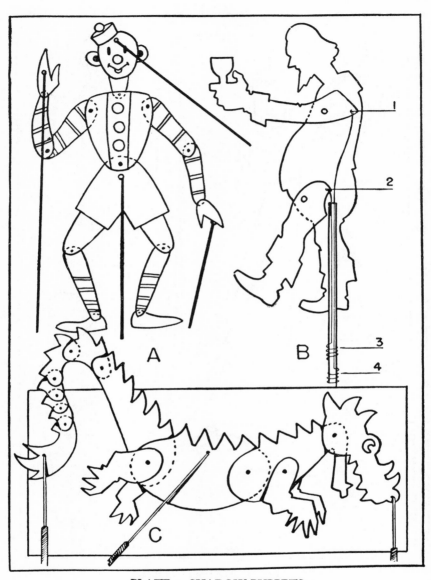

PLATE 2. SHADOW-PUPPETS

A. Front-view dancing clown by M. Batchelder
B, C. Old man and dragon by V. Michael

this animal is also a good trick. A movable jaw is illustrated in the dragon on *Plate 2, C.* The rods for such a creature should be unusually long so that it can fly through the air.

Front-view figures can be constructed in many ways. The dancing clown on *Plate 2, A* is made of sheet Vinylite plastic in bright colors. Upper legs and pelvis piece are made in one, with swinging lower legs. Four rods are used for animation, which can be very lively (see p. 225).

Umbrella ribs are useful for rods, but they are a little thick. If you can hammer out the end of fine but very stiff steel wire and drill a small hole for attaching it to the puppet, you can make your own. ¼" dowels or small square sticks can be used for handles at the other end of the wire, like the pith-stick handles used by the Chinese (*Plate 1, A*).

Number oo wire shanks can be used for jointing, but they are likely to catch on the screen. Fishline closely knotted on either side of the joint is easy to use. A bit of shellac or glue should be put on the knot to keep it from coming untied. Some puppeteers have used heavy Celluloid and riveted the joints—this makes a smooth puppet which moves easily.

From the following list choose the materials you will need to make the kind of shadows you are planning. Tracing paper, black cardboard (cover paper), thin sheet plastic, colored Cellophane, number oo wire shanks, woven fishline, umbrella ribs or wire, colored construction paper, boiled linseed oil and turpentine, transparent paints (oil or water color) and brushes, paste or glue, plastic solvent, scissors, pins, stencil knife, small ticket punch, pencil, and drawing paper.

HUMANETTES

A standard side show novelty, the humanette, has invaded everything from vaudeville to night club floor shows. Simplicity of construction and operation make it a good act where space is limited; besides, it is fun to make, to work, and to watch. The construction of the humanette is illustrated on *Plate 3.*

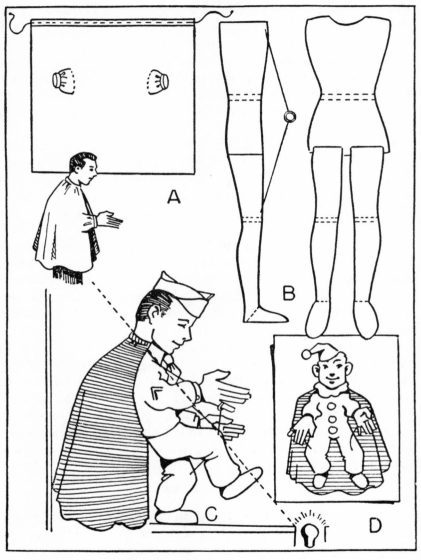

PLATE 3. CONSTRUCTION DIAGRAM OF A HUMANETTE
by Douglas Anderson

Actually, it is no more than a cloth-and-cotton-filled body that fits around the operator's neck so that when he stands behind a table, bed, or specially built box or stage, the illusion is that of a midget body with normal sized head and hands.

A cloak or jacket is constructed as shown in *Figure A*. The drawstring is tied around the operator's neck while his hands fit through the short sleeves. The cloth body of the puppet *B* is about 28" high, with joints at the waist and knees. It is sewn to the cloak. This creates the impression of a puppet *not* worked from behind, and helps hide the operator's body which will be almost invisible if a stage is used and the jacket is of the same color as the backdrop. Care should be taken to keep as little light as possible from falling on the backdrop (*figure C*).

A favorite trick is to fasten a ring to the center of a length of string or fishline and attach the opposite ends to the knees and shoulders respectively. These rings are slipped over a finger on each hand, thus enabling the operator to move the humanette's legs and feet (*figures C* and *D*).

Humanettes can wear children's castoff clothing. The more ridiculous the costume the better. A humanette is not meant for serious drama, but is a slapstick puppet with which one can have a lot of fun. Make it sing, dance, juggle, play an instrument, perform feats of magic, recite verses, and so on. Use your imagination and you will be able to develop a hundred acts for your humanette to perform.

FINGER-PUPPETS

Alfred and Lea Wallace have used finger-puppets for entertaining bedridden service men on the European war front. In crowded wards where even a small stage is difficult to set up, much fun can be had with these little figures which are worked on the operator's index and third fingers. On *Plate 4* are the Wallace designs for Johnnie and Jane Gremlin. A simple paper cutout is shown at *A*. The fingers are thrust through the two round holes to make the puppet's legs, and the paper is bent around the hand at the dotted

[33]

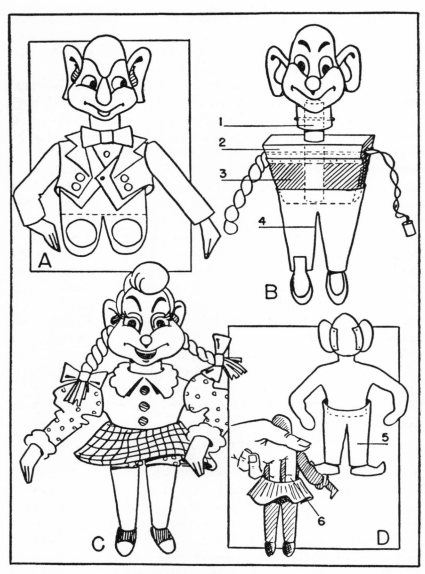

PLATE 4. FINGER-PUPPETS
By Alfred and Lea Wallace

line. An elastic or string can be used to hold the paper in place. At *B* a more durable, three-dimensional construction is illustrated. A wooden shoulder piece (2) has a hole drilled to admit a dowel rod (1) on which the head is pivoted. The neck opening is made large enough to allow some head movement, and there should be some space between the neck and the shoulder piece. Cloth (3) is tacked around the shoulder piece and stuffed in front only. The arms are of wire with a bit of lead on the end to give them a little bounce. They are stuffed with cotton batting and wound with tape. The heads of these figures are made of plastic wood, but any material can be used. *Diagram D,* (5) shows the elastic pants (made from a discarded girdle) which are attached to the torso in front only, so as to permit the fingers to be thrust into them for legs (*D,* 6). Any available material can be used for pants—the advantage of the elastic is that it fits closely to the hand. The feet and shoes are carved from wood and made to fit onto the tips of the operator's fingers. Over this foundation the costume is made. Pink jersey tights can be made for Johnnie—or he can wear half pants cut off at point 4, *diagram B.* Jane Gremlin, all dressed up and ready to perform, is shown in *diagram C.*

The size of finger-puppets is related to the size of the hand which works them—people with long fingers can use taller figures than those with short fingers. The average height is from 6" to 8". By using stuffed or long wooden legs, puppets about 12" high can be successfully worked. They should not be so large that they are awkward to handle, for the charm of these puppets is their delicate, quick movement and their funny postures. They can dance with precise steps, leap, run, kneel, and lie down. Strings from the puppet's hands can be operated by the manipulator's other hand, if such movement is important, but it is often more amusing to work two puppets at a time, one on each hand.

HAND-PUPPETS

A simple, improvised hand-puppet can be made by cutting a hole in a rubber ball, a potato, or a block of soft wood, placing it on the

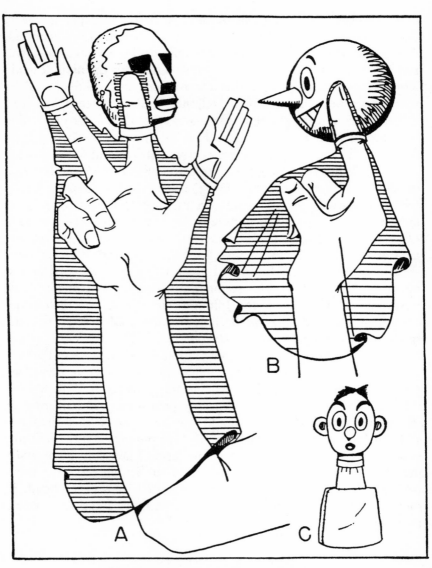

PLATE 5. HAND-PUPPET CONTROL

forefinger, and using a handkerchief or piece of cloth for a costume (*Plate 5, B*). However, hand-puppets ordinarily consist of head, arms, and a sleeve to conceal the operator's arm. The forefinger is inserted into a hole in the head. The hands are attached to short cardboard tubes which fit over the thumb and third finger (or little finger). Because the fingers of the hand are not equally placed, the puppet arm to be worked by the thumb is lower than the one to be controlled by the third finger (*Plate 5, A*). Due allowance should be made for this in designing the undergarment. Usually, a hand-puppet is made to fit either the left or the right hand, on which it is always worked. In *Punch and Judy*, Punch, who is the leading character, is worked on the right hand, with the other characters appearing successively on the left. If the thumb and little finger are used for manipulation, the undergarment may be made like that on *Plate 6, A*. The two extra fingers are kept bent; it helps if there is a small pad attached to the front of the head for them to grip (*Plate 5, C*).

The characteristic short arms of the hand-puppet are sometimes a disadvantage. If necessary, they can be made longer with cardboard tubes or wire. But, as Bessie Ficklen states, "such stiff long arms are difficult to handle. Generally it is best to be content with the ordinary little arms that are worked by the fingers, relying on costume and sleeves to camouflage their shortness. There is a wide choice of sleeves and under-sleeves, cuffs, and bracelets; also a variety of *hands*, of wood, kid, rag, and wire, some with wrists, some without. With a little time and experimenting in combining arms and hands and sleeves, it is always possible to disguise the shortness of the puppet's reach, and even to suggest for him graceful arms and hands."[2]

Shoulders padded with wire and stuffing are often used to give the hand-puppet better form. Chests can also be padded for fatness (*Plate 6, B*) or grotesque effects such as Mr. Punch's humps fore and aft.

The Catalan puppet (so-called from the province of Catalonia in Spain where it originated) has well-formed shoulders and more

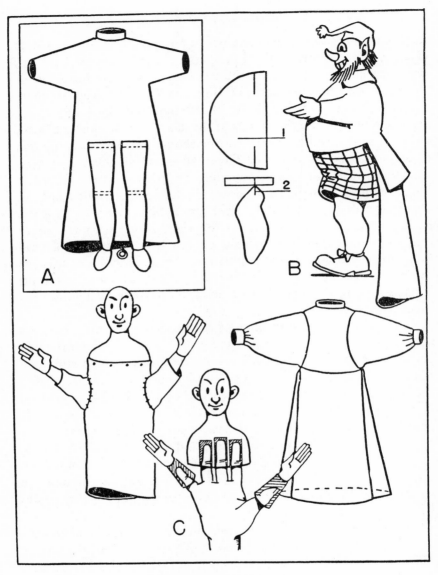

PLATE 6. HAND-PUPPETS
A. Puppet with stuffed cloth legs
B. Wood and stuffing puppet by Peg Blickle
C. Catalan type hand-puppet by H. V. Tozer

naturally placed arms (*Plate 6, C*). H. V. Tozer describes its con-struction: "The head, shoulders, and breast are carved in one piece. The underdress, which constitutes the body, is fastened to the lower portion of the breast and to the arms, which consist of slightly conical tin tubes. Hands are fastened into the narrow ends of the tin tubes and are secured by means of screw eyes; the hands are, therefore, easily removed and others, holding sticks, swords or baskets, may be substituted as required. Dresses may be made very elaborately and accurately owing to the shoulders and the firm foundation afforded by the canvas underdress. Moreover, dresses, may be removed quickly and others substituted for change of scene and character. The sleeves should be longer than strictly required by the length of the arms, and the armholes should extend —it should be specially noted—all the way from the shoulder to the waistline, so that, when the operator's fingers are inserted, the sleeves fall into the folds which give the arms the appearance of extending up to the shouder of the puppet. It will be noticed that the finger tubes, or forearms, protrude from the body and enter the sleeves of the outer dress at the waist level.

"The great advantage of the Catalan puppet over the ordinary type of glove-puppets is that, when dressed, it has the true human shape (down to the hips). Fully dressed and held in its natural position, the Catalan puppet appears to have its arms bent at the elbow, with the upper arms held closely to its sides, and the fore-arms stretched out in front of it. Another advantage is that a very much larger head can (and indeed must) be supported on three fingers than on one, and the larger-scale puppet resulting pro-vides a longer range of visibility and permits, therefore, of larger audiences."[3]

The chief disadvantages of this puppet are its greater weight, and the somewhat more difficult manipulation owing to the neces-sity for using the little finger. No head movement is possible if the puppet is made as illustrated, but if the neck is jointed inside the head (*Plate 13, A*) it will nod when the body is inclined.

In general hand-puppets can do very well without feet. They

are found on some traditional puppets like Mr. Punch—thin, puny affairs which hang lifelessly and serve only to dangle over the front ledge of the booth. Such legs can be sewed to the undergarment (*Plate 6, A*). They can be of stuffed cloth or wood, with a joint at the knee. The dwarf in *diagram B, Plate 6* has carved wooden legs which are jointed at the ankle and hip. A wooden piece ½" thick (1) is used as a foundation for the stuffed body and as a support for the legs, which are attached with a leather strip (2). The wooden shoe is hollowed out, and the leg set into it with a small piece of leather. There should not be too much movement in the ankle joint, or the foot will dangle. These legs are easily controlled; the puppet can dance and use its legs for many different movements.

Efimova has a note on hand-puppet feet: "At one time we yielded to the temptation of making legs for our puppets, but with feet on which they were able to stand. These were merely straight pieces of wood, not themselves manipulated. But it was remarkable to see with what energy and animation they moved across the stage, how they were flung upward vigorously by the sitting or reclining puppet. Sometimes Harlequin kicked his heels against the booth as he sat on its edge, or tapped the footboard of the bed as he hummed a song to lull himself to sleep. So long as the feet are capable of expressive movements, they are useful even if not an essential part of the puppet."[4]

There are various kinds of puppet hands. Some puppeteers prefer a flexible hand of felt or kid, lightly stuffed cloth or any material through which the fingers can feel objects being handled by the puppet. For juggling, expressive stroking of beards, playing of instruments, and such action, soft hands are desirable. Cloth-covered wire hands are sometimes effective; they can be bent into various positions, but have a tendency to look clawlike—which is just right for witches or evil characters. Carved wooden hands are stiffer but also useful in their way—if a puppet has to hold objects, a hole can be drilled and the bouquet, gun, or whatever it is, can be set temporarily by means of a closely fitting dowel. This device is used less frequently with hand-puppets, because they usually carry things with both hands and can suggest most movements even though clumsily.

Heads can be made by any of the methods described on pp. 79-95 but they should not be too heavy.

Hand-puppets should not be made too tall; if the costumes reach below the elbow, it is difficult to show the figures at their full height, because they must be held above the operator's head and worked with the stage floor line at the crown of the operator's head (*Plate 36*). However, some hand-puppet dancers wear costumes which are unusually long and full so they can be swirled around.

A ring sewed to the bottom edge of the undergarment at the back (*Plate 6, A*) is convenient for hanging the puppet in place, so the operator can get it on his hand easily during performance.

Animal puppets can be made in several ways. For those with snapping jaws, such as dragons and crocodiles, use a foundation garment to which hinged jaws are attached (*Plate 7, A*). Very large creatures made this way can be operated from the wings, and the operator's arm may be part of the neck. Used with ordinary size hand-puppets, they are tremendous. Papier-mâché, (with wood for the jaws), is the best material because it is light.

Animal puppets that act like human beings can be made by following the same construction methods used for human figures, but with the substitution of bird or animal heads, feet, or wings (*Plate 7, B*). The cat in *figure C, Plate 7* is made from a cardboard cylinder with front legs, head, and tail of stuffed cloth.

Animals which must show all four legs can be made with a sleeve to hide the operator's arm attached to their bodies as shown on *Plate 8*. The body and neck can be made in one piece (*C*). Cut two identical silhouettes from cloth. Sew the pieces together along the back from (1) to (2). Cut another piece *D* from a double thickness of cloth with (4) laid on the fold. Follow the contour of the animal from (2) to (3). This piece is sewed to the rest of the body to make four legs and give the animal thickness. It is better to make the head separate and run a tube from it to the operator's finger. The animal can be stuffed to fill out the form.

[41]

PLATE 7. HAND-PUPPET ANIMALS

A. Animal with snapping jaws
B. Hand-puppets with animal heads by L. Cueto
C. Cat with cardboard body and stuffed head

Legs can be given solidity, yet have some movement, if a wire is run through them as shown in *diagram C*.

Hand-puppets can ride steeds (*Plate 8, B*). The puppet should have legs, and the mount needs a sleeve to hide the operator's arm—if it is not decked with the long cloth trappings of a medieval knight's horse. The rider and steed can be made in a single unit, or separate from each other as the occasion demands. When Mr. Punch rides his velvet horse, he merely throws one leg over its back and gallops gaily around. He can get on and off or be tossed to the ground, because the operator works Punch on one hand and the horse on the other.

Undulating snakes can be suggested by using stockings fitted tightly over the hand and arm. The fingers should be outstretched and drawn together to a point; the hand thus becomes a snaky head. With glittering eyes such serpents are very effective, particularly if they emerge from witches' cauldrons or snake charmers' baskets. Other types of reptiles can be suggested by using the four fingers of the operator inserted into the toe of the stocking, with the thumb for the lower jaw. Tongue and teeth can be added for monsters. The stocking can be painted and decorated with wings, scales or fins, and a liberal use of spangles and gilding makes the creature impressive. Buttons, beads, sequins and glass marbles are all usable for eyes.

Wire is good to strengthen long ears (like those of rabbits or donkeys), horns, wings and other protuberances. For sawdust or papier-mâché pulp heads, (see pp. 83-85) it is well to bend wire for the outline of the jaws to give them additional strength.

Be imaginative in choosing the covering for your animal. Natural materials such as fur and feathers usually do not look right on the puppet stage; fur is often out of scale to the figures, and feathers tend to look dull and ragged. Animal cloths (if the pattern of stripes or spots is not too large), imitation fur, suède cloth, plush, and chamois, can be tried for the right effect. Feathers can often be suggested with paint on muslin; they can be cut from colored or metallic oilcloth or metal; various combinations of colored

PLATE 8. HAND-PUPPET ANIMALS

A. Four-legged animal with sleeve
B. Hand-puppet horse and rider
C, D. Pattern for stuffed animal
E. Neck tube for hand-puppet

plastic and paint on wooden forms are effective for stylized birds.

Exaggeration of an animal's colors and characteristics often helps to give it the right theatrical touch. Bessie Ficklen says: "A white rabbit covered with a glistening wool fleece is given very pink silk linings to his mouth and ears, and, as an extra charm, enormously exaggerated pink ruby eyes. A strange wild horse is made all of fringe, and a wild cow of raveled rags. A little red fox with a skin of camel's hair fleece has a back of brilliant orange, a throat and breast of silvery white, and, for his paws and the tops of his ears, black velvet. His long tongue, likewise the linings of his mouth and ears are rose color, and his eyes are just the right golden-brown buttons with a gold glitter for high lights."[5] If you have the essential character of the animal, it does not matter greatly what liberties you take with materials and colors.

HAND-AND-ROD-PUPPETS

The hand-and-rod-puppet is a development of the hand-puppet, but the arms are jointed and controlled by rods. *Plate 9* shows two methods of operation. In *A*, the operator's forefinger is inserted into a hole in the head. The undergarment is usually made of some fairly heavy material, such as felt, which is stiff enough to hold its form and support the arms; it is attached firmly to the costume. *Diagram B* shows a wooden or cardboard shoulder piece to which the arms are attached. The head is set on a short rod held between the puppeteer's thumb and forefinger. His wrist is the puppet's waist. If trimness is desired, an elastic in the costume will hold it close to the wrist. The arms and hands can be made of wood, stuffed cloth, or wire and stuffing. Any type of head may be used for this puppet.

The Michael puppet shown on *Plate 10* is designed for maximum action. *Diagram D* shows a wooden shoulder piece (1) and a hip piece (3), joined by a piece of black felt tacked into place. *Diagram C* gives the side view of these pieces. The hip section is flat and slightly hollowed out on the back so that it fits closely to the

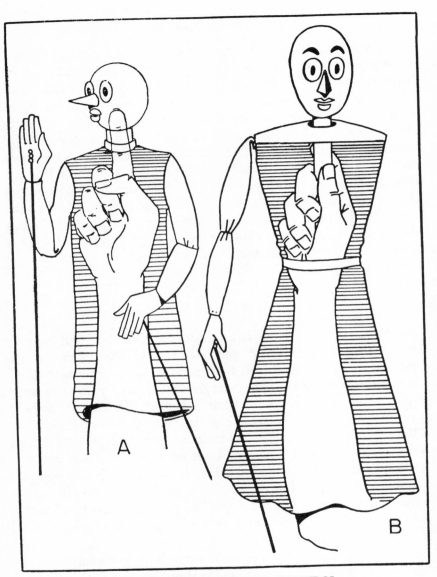

PLATE 9. HAND-AND-ROD CONTROL

A. Operated by finger in head
B. Movable head in wooden shoulder piece

puppeteer's hand. Legs, feet, lower arms, and hands are carved from wood. Ankle, knee, and wrist joints are of leather. The upper arm (2) and leg (4) are of cloth tacked in place as indicated. There should be enough stuffing to round out these forms, but the shoulder and hip joints should be kept flexible. Around the shoulder piece is tacked the sleeve (5) which hides the operator's arm. The skirt or trousers of the costume are tacked around the hip piece. When the costume is in place, the puppet should be laid face down and a tack or two put into the hip piece from the back (inside the sleeve) as illustrated in *figure C (6)*. This is important because it keeps the body from swinging away from the sleeve. Without it the operator has little control of his puppet.

The head on a stick which is ordinarily used for this hand-and-rod-puppet, has only a side-to-side movement. *Diagram A, Plate 10* shows the head pivoted on a wire (1) which passes through the control rod (2). The hole in the head must be large enough to permit it to nod when the string (3) is pulled. The head should be balanced with the heavier part in front; be sure to place the pivot wire far enough back to keep the puppet's chin down except when the string is pulled.

Like hand-puppets, the hand-and-rod type is limited in height. If the legs extend below the operator's elbow, it is difficult to keep the feet at the level of the front ledge. The puppet on *Plate 10* should not exceed 13″ from the soles of the feet to the inside of the shoulder piece for a woman operator; a maximum of 16″ for a man. The best way to judge the correct height for a given group of operators, is to make the figures so that their feet just touch the inside bend of the elbow. If a taller puppet is needed, an extra long head rod can be used (*Plate 10, B*). A disc (1) should be placed just under the shoulder piece to keep the head in the correct position. The rod is held near the bottom. This long rod is not satisfactory for fully articulated figures because the puppeteer's wrist no longer comes at the puppet's waistline, but for characters with long costumes, the device is excellent.

As we have suggested elsewhere (see p. 221), the Michael

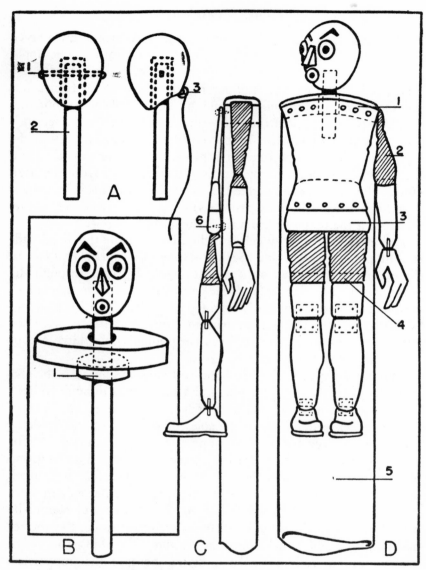

PLATE 10. MICHAEL TYPE HAND-AND-ROD-PUPPET

A. Mechanism for nodding head
B. Design for tall puppet
C, D. Side and Front views of Michael construction

hand-and-rod-puppet is useful for stock characters because the heads and costumes can be readily changed. The figures can be quickly constructed if done on a "mass production" basis. Front and side view patterns for legs and arms should be cut from sheet plastic or cardboard. For the shoulder piece, cut front and top; for the hands and feet, top and side. The hip piece is made from half-inch thick wood. Variations for the male and female form can be made, but keep all the forms as simple and stylized as possible. The puppets can then portray a wide variety of characters with different heads and costumes to give them individuality. Special hands and feet can be used if necessary. In making a group of these puppets, it saves time to carry each process through for all the puppets. For instance, cut out all the parts first, then do all the sanding, next the carving of hands, feet and hip piece. Cut all the felt pieces and have them ready so that the assembling can be done without interruption. Do the same with the leather pieces for the various joints. The first cutting of the parts can be done on the band saw if you have one. Cut the slots for the leather joints first, then the more complicated silhouette such as the side of the legs, and finally the front. By this method, you can have different groups working on the puppets at the same time, which would not be practicable were each puppet completely finished before the next is started.

ROD-PUPPETS

Rod-puppets can be made in many ways. Some are simple, with few joints, others are fully articulated to allow varied movements. These puppets are held above the operator's head by means of a central control stick which may be a metal rod, a dowel, a thin wooden stick, or a heavy wire. Additional rods attached to the hands, head, and sometimes the feet, are used for manipulation. Umbrella ribs are most commonly used, but stiff wire, or plastic rods may be substituted. Various combinations of rods and strings can be worked out for special movements.

[49]

PLATE 11. SIMPLE ROD-PUPPETS

A. Flat unarticulated figure
B. Witch from R. Lago's Mexican puppet theatre
C. Turned wood rod-puppet
D. Wood and wire rod-puppet by R. Lago
E. Mechanism for puppet with long costume

If they are too heavy, rod-puppets are difficult to hold in position on the stage. Three or four pounds is about all one can comfortably manage. All-wood figures tend to be too heavy. If possible use sponge rubber or stuffed cloth for the torso. Hollow out the head as much as possible. Sometimes rod-puppets suffer more from top-heaviness than actual weight. If your figure tends to weave from side to side, make a handle at least 1″ in diameter and set your center rod into it. This is easier to grasp, and helps balance the head. For large figures you will have to devise some kind of support from the floor. You can use a long thick rod resting on the floor and reaching to the stage level, in which the puppet's control rod can be set. This works all right if the operator stands. A pedestal attached to the puppeteer's movable stool, if he sits, is another solution (*Plate 45*). The puppet is held in this support most of the time, but it can be removed from the slot when necessary. Rod-puppets may be of any size, up to the colossal, if they can be supported and manipulated properly.

The simplest type of rod-puppet is a flat figure cut from cardboard and mounted on a stick (*Plate 11, A*). A semiround effect may be obtained by making paper costumes for such figures. One or more movable parts may be used and controlled by rods or stiff wires. A flat rod-and-string-puppet is often effective. The witch illustrated on *Plate 11, B* was cut from Beaverboard with a jig saw. The skirt is a piece of striped cloth tied around the waist. One side of the figure is painted in full color. A single string moves the arms and one leg, in a witchlike hobble. Separate movements of the parts can be made by using individual strings. This principle can be varied for many figures of the jumping jack type which can be cut from thin wood such as that of orange crates, or from cardboard.

For puppets with long costumes where there is no need for a body, the construction shown on *Plate 11, E* is adequate. The head is attached to a long dowel which moves freely in the shoulder piece. A disc holds the head in place. Looped wire padded with cotton batting can be used for the arms, or they can be carved of wood or made of stuffed cloth.

A wire framework is used for the body shown in *diagram D, Plate 11.* The central control rod is a dowel with a spring on one end for the neck. A wire passing through the dowel forms the shoulder line, establishes the width of the torso and pelvis, and forms a pivot for the legs. Other wires are soldered to the main outline to form the thickness of the chest and waist. Additional wires may be added if necessary. This framework can be padded with cotton batting, but if heavy material is used for the costume, this may not be essential.

Simple turned shapes can be used for rod-puppets. The ballet dancer, *Plate 11, C,* has a body turned in one piece, with the head and neck set into it. Arms of dowel rods or turned cylinders are attached loosely to the shoulders. One rod only is used on this puppet because its movement is limited to twirling and swaying. In the motions of a dance, the ballet skirt and the arms fly outward from centrifugal force.

A wood-and-stuffing rod-puppet is shown on *Plate 12.* The center dowel passes through the body and into the neck, which is pinned to it with a nail through a screw eye. The shoulder and hip pieces are thin strips of wood to which the wires forming the body are tacked. The head, hands, lower arms, legs, and feet are wood. Upper legs and arms are cloth. The legs swing on a wire which runs through the center dowel.

Rod-puppets can be made to stand up by placing two discs on the rod as illustrated at *A, Plate 12.* The top one should be placed so that the feet rest flat on the floorboard of the stage when the puppet is placed in position. The discs may be ¼" plywood, metal soldered to the center rod, or spools cut in half and fastened to the rod with brads and glue. *Detail A* shows the slots cut in the front ledge or other convenient parts of the stage to admit the rod. Be sure that the discs are securely fastened, and make the slots large enough for easy entry of the supporting rod. Set the discs far enough apart so that you can place the figure in

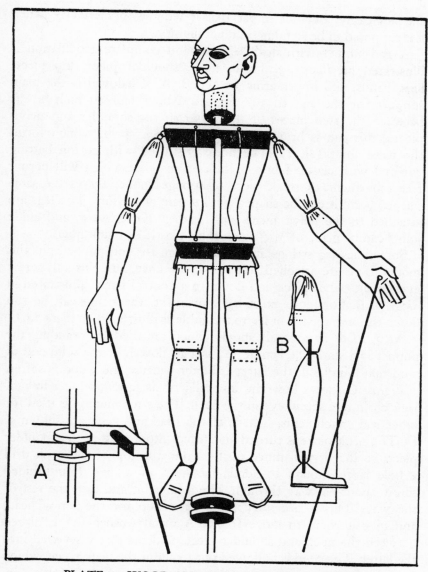

PLATE 12. WOOD AND STUFFING ROD-PUPPET
By Marjorie Batchelder

the slot easily, but not so far that it wobbles precariously when it is supposed to be standing in quiet dignity.

A rod-puppet with flexible waist and complete articulation is illustrated on *Plate 13*. Head, neck, shoulder piece, hip piece, legs, hands, and lower arms are wood. A ⅜″ dowel is the main support for the 24″ to 30″ puppet. About half an inch is left between the two pieces of dowel set in the shoulder and pelvis pieces; this gap is bridged by a screen door spring which forms the waist joint (*A, 1*). The body is stuffed with cotton batting covered with elastic fabric or knitted material which will permit free movement. A thick piece of sponge rubber serves the same purpose, and it can be shaped with a pair of scissors. The legs are attached to the pelvis piece with leather. Knee, wrist, and ankle joints can be made of ¹⁄₁₆″ thick sheet plastic or trunk fiber.

Sometimes leg strings are an advantage for rod-puppets. In this model, they are attached just above the knee, run through screw eyes in the pelvis piece and down to a control bar as illustrated in *diagram B*. For more exact leg movement, the string can be run down through the lower leg to the ankle as illustrated on *Plate 24, C*.

At *3, Plate 13* are half spools which are used for standing the puppet in a slot. The handle (2) is a 1″ dowel, or the solid end of a curtain blind rod; the latter is better because the wood is softer.

Figure C shows how the umbrella rib is fastened by a link of jack chain to a screw eye in the head. The same method is used for other rod attachments. Details of the head and neck are shown at D. The neck piece is turned and fitted into a hole in the shoulder piece, so that it will move easily. From the top of the neck drill a hole large enough to admit the head of a long roundheaded screw about halfway through. Use a finer bit and drill the rest of the way. This is necessary to make a stop for the screw head, and give it room to move freely. A metal washer (4) is placed between the neck and shoulder piece, and the screw set well into the latter. The head is hollowed out to admit the neck piece, which is pivoted on a wire passing through the top of the neck piece. Drill the holes through the head far enough back to throw its

[54]

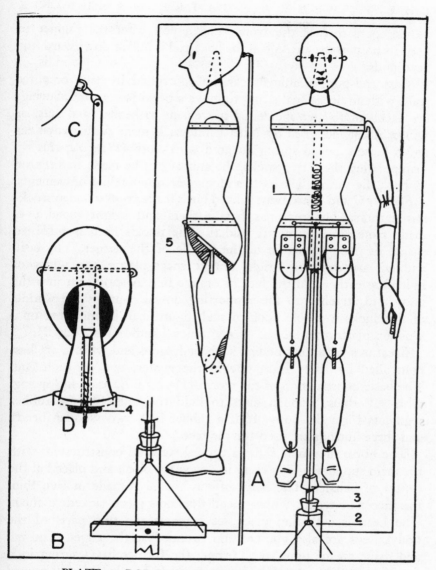

PLATE 13. ROD-PUPPET WITH FLEXIBLE WAIST

By Marjorie Batchelder

heavier part toward the front—unless you want the puppet to keep its nose in the air. When the head rod is pulled downward, the head nods.

Most rod-puppet animals can be controlled by two or three rods, with an occasional string to move a beak, jaw, or tail. Springs are excellent to give incidental movement to heads, ears, tails, or wings. A cat, designed by Nina Efimova, is made with two sticks and a loosely coiled spring covered with cloth (*Plate 14, A*). By manipulating these two sticks, the animal can be made to sit, arch its back, lie down, lick itself and suggest other feline movements.

Figures C and *D* are two stylized birds made from wooden stocking darners. The owl has felt feathers and bright metal eyes made from small furniture gliders. The duck's head is a turned shape, its neck a portion of the handle of the darner. The beak and tail are made of bright orange sheet plastic, the wings of imitation leather and the feet of orange felt. A spring set into the body and attached to the supporting dowel controls the waddle of the duck. A whole flock of such figures can be mounted on a wooden platform attached to a 1" thick handle (*Plate 14, B*).

Creatures with long bodies, such as dragons and worms, are best controlled by three rods; one in the center, one on each end. The basic construction of the worm (*Plate 14, E*) is a long spring, with ¾" thick wooden discs to hold the rods. Sponge rubber segments form the body. Half a rubber ball, two wooden beads, and three buttons are used for the face.

The horse shown at *F* has a typical two-rod construction, with the main supporting dowel set in a wooden block and placed at the center of balance. The body of this animal is made of two thin, flat pieces of wood, with a metal thickness piece tacked to them. The head is a thicker piece set between the two parts of the body. Legs are also cut flat and rounded at the edges. The tail and mane are of upholstery fringe; the former has a spring in it for incidental movement. This horse could be equally well carved entirely from wood, but for easy manipulation it should not be too heavy. Additional joints might be made in the animal's legs

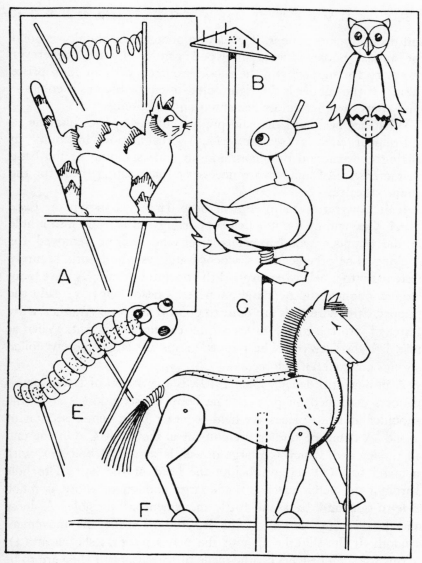

PLATE 14. ROD-PUPPET ANIMALS

A. Cat designed by Nina Efimova
B. Control for group of ducks
C, D. Stylized birds by Vivian Michael
E. Wire and sponge-rubber worm by M. Batchelder
F. Wooden horse

and neck. Sponge rubber, if it can be obtained in chunks, is good for animal bodies. Pieces of wood can be inserted wherever necessary for support and the rubber covered with an appropriate "skin." If the rubber is the right color, it can be used as it comes— with spots of other colors cemented on if desired.

What has been said of hand-puppet animals applies likewise to rod-puppet animals (see pp. 41-45). Imagination, ingenuity in solving construction problems, and an understanding of the basic characteristics of animals are necessary for creating them for the puppet theatre.

Juan Guerrero's Yaqui Indian deer dancer is shown on *Plate 15, A*. One end of the wooden supporting rod is stuck into a hole in the puppet's wooden pelvis piece and can be removed for packing. The other end is sharpened and rests in a cork, securely fastened into a belt worn around the operator's waist. A wire loop, large enough to slip over the puppeteer's head, helps to steady the puppet. Stiff wire rods are used to control the legs. Another wire, fastened into the torso, serves to pull the figure upright. When at rest, it leans forward. The puppet's arms are large, loosely coiled springs covered with cloth.

A peasant girl dancer, *Plate 15, D*, is a variation of Lola Cueto's dancers described on p. 224. The body construction is at *B*; the shoulder and hip pieces are held together by a center section of wood. A detail of the leg attachment is shown at *C*. On the end of the leg rod, which is a large dowel, is set a long bolt (1), with a metal ball (2) set just below the head of the bolt. The hole through the pelvis piece is made large enough to allow as much side-to-side and back-and-forth movement as possible. A loose metal collar (4) is set on the leg rod to make the movement smooth. It fits slightly up into the pelvis piece as shown at (3). Arms for such dancers can be made of springs, or, if they are to be attached permanently to the hips, stuffed cloth is adequate. Some stuffing may be placed around the body pieces, but care must be taken not to interfere with the puppet's movement. The feet

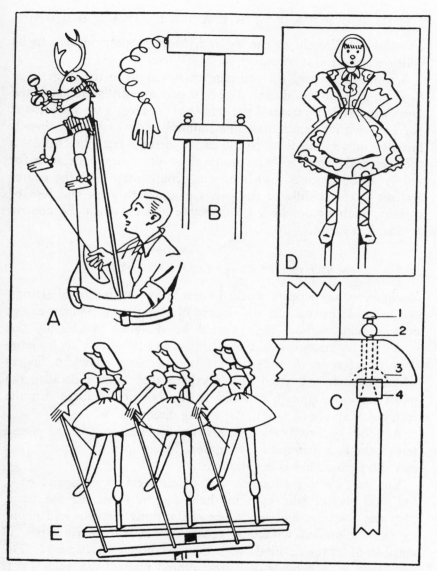

PLATE 15. ROD-PUPPET DANCERS

A. Deer dancer by Juan Guerrero
B, C, D. Mechanism by Lola Cueto for dancer
E. Multiple control for chorus by M. Batchelder

are attached directly to the leg rod. More shapely forms can be built onto this rod if necessary.

A multiple control for rod-puppets is shown in the diagram at *E, Plate 15*. One leg of each dancer is permanently attached to the supporting rod. To control the arms and free leg, a wooden dowel (or bar) with a handle has three umbrella ribs or smaller dowels fastened into it and fixed to the hands. Strings from the hands to the legs make it possible to move these parts simultaneously for simple dance routines. Other chorus groups may have the center rod set in the middle of the pelvis piece, with arms and legs of springs. Such figures have considerable motion when the control is moved in various ways.

MARIONETTES (STRING-PUPPETS)

Marionettes, or puppets worked from above by means of strings, can be made in any size and degree of complexity. Whatever the construction method, they should be designed specifically for operation by strings; avoid such things as hats which are so large they interfere with the manipulation or long clawlike fingers which become entangled in everything they touch. Be sure the joints are loose enough to move freely, but not so loose that the feet, hands and head turn in the wrong direction.

A good quality black silk woven fishline, at least 18-pound test, is the best material for stringing. Black linen or carpet thread can also be used but is less durable.

You can make marionettes out of all sorts of odds and ends, but you should take care in their design; relate all the parts, plan the jointing, and work out the various textures and colors to form a unified whole. A group of fantastic marionettes, all capable of different kinds of action, is shown on *Plate 16*. The centipede at *A* is made of balls. Colored tennis balls, with a soft pleasant texture, form the body, and small rubber balls (or 1″ wooden beads) the legs, nose and antennae. Tiny springs in the feet add to the undulating movement of the creature. A clothespin

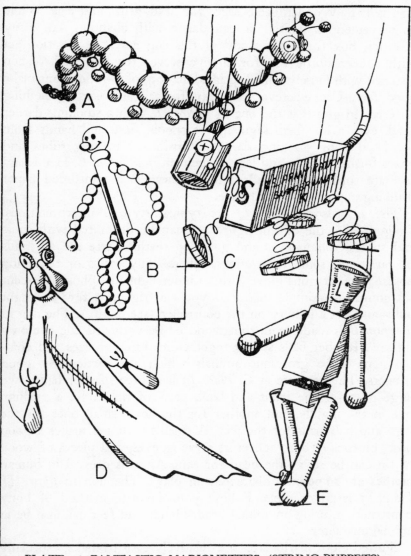

PLATE 16. FANTASTIC MARIONETTES (STRING-PUPPETS)
Designs by Vivian Michael and Paul McPharlin

man is at *B*. Wooden beads serve for head, arms, and legs. While its movement is limited, it can dance with abandon. An army K-ration box forms the body of the dog at *C*. A C-ration tin with a beer bottle top for an eye serves for the head. When fastened with loosely coiled springs, the tops of C-ration cans make good feet. Use whatever is handy for tail and ears. Something different in ghosts is the one in *figure D*, with a stocking darner head, eyes made from segments of spools, nose and hands from the handles of stocking darners. Cardboard mailing tubes and boxes form the body and legs of the man in *diagram E*. Hands and feet are small rubber balls, and the head is a reinforced paper drinking cup or cardboard cone.

The animals on *Plate 17* are typical stylized interpretations. Dragons, like the one in *figure A*, may be decorated with spots and spines, rolling eyes and gnashing teeth. There are all kinds of variations; some have wings, others shiny scales or twitching noses. Some dragons glow with an inner light like phosphorescent sea animals—a simple matter if you can rig up a few flashlight bulbs and put a battery on the controller (see p. 191). The dog in *diagram B* is made from thin wood or Beaverboard cut out on a jig saw. Rubber balls strung together in different sizes and combinations make grotesque animals which are particularly good dancers. The creature at *C, Plate 17* has three sizes of balls; two large ones for the front and back parts of the body, a medium one in the middle, and another for the head; small ones for the legs, and half balls for the feet. A small tin funnel makes a good nose, buttons or auto reflectors serve as eyes, and pieces of wood or tin can be set in the head for ears. Animals dressed in human clothes are sometimes characters in plays. The lion in *figure D, Plate 17* is an example. Follow your favorite method of body construction, using an animal head. Hands and feet can also be in animal character.

Stuffed cloth marionettes are relatively easy to make, especially if you like to sew. It is a good idea to make first a full scale diagram on paper in order to establish the relative size of head, trunk, legs

PLATE 17. ANIMAL MARIONETTES (STRING-PUPPETS)
Designs by Vivian Michael

and arms. You can then cut patterns for these parts.[6] The same basic shapes can be used for all your puppets, but they can be varied for extra fat or thin characters. Cut the patterns from lightweight cardboard, lay them on doubled material (unbleached muslin is good) and trace around them with a soft pencil. Sew on the penciled lines, with a machine if possible, then cut out the parts, leaving about ¼"—and a gap through which to put in the stuffing. Turn the pieces inside out, and stuff firmly with hospital cotton, Kapok, automobile waste or cotton batting. The last is best for general use, although hospital cotton is finer if you have small figures. A double row of stitching at the waist, hip, knee, ankle and elbow should be used for joints. Do not stuff too tightly at the joints or they will be stiff.

A simple stuffed marionette made from a stocking (preferably a cotton one) is illustrated on *Plate 18, C.* Cut off the toe of the stocking as indicated by the shaded area in *diagram* (1), and sew together on the wrong side. Turn the stocking right side out and stuff the head. Wind thread or string around the stocking in two places to form the neck. Refer to your diagram and cut a piece of dowel, heavy cardboard or wood the width of the puppet's shoulders and insert it into the stocking. Screw eyes should be inserted into the shoulder piece (or holes punched if you are using cardboard) so it can be sewed in place. Stuff lightly above the shoulder piece and pad out below as much as is necessary to make the chest. Double stitch for the waist joint. The stocking can be folded over and tacked to make the waist narrower than the shoulders. Stuff the rest of the trunk down to the hip joint and stitch all the way across. Now slit the stocking up the center to form two tubes for the legs and sew up the seams. Run another line of stitching across the top of each leg, and stuff the upper leg. Double stitch for the knee joint. To taper the lower leg to a trim ankle, you can fold the stocking and stuff it firmly, or insert a dowel (¼" or ½" according to the size of the marionette). Stitch again at the ankle, making a flat hinge joint. You can continue stuffing to make a foot, but it is usually better to cut off the stocking as indicated, and make the foot separate.

At *E*, (2) is a pattern for the sole of the foot, which can be cut from cardboard, oilcloth, thin wood or heavy cloth. The upper part of the foot is at (3). Sewed on the heavy lines, it fits onto the sole. Variations of this pattern can be made with a little experimenting. You can also carve the feet from soft wood, or use a sawdust mixture covered with paper (see p. 85).

The marionette's arms are made separately from tubes of stocking material or cloth. The elbow is double stitched, and the upper arm stuffed lightly, then sewed to the shoulder, making a flat hinge joint. If desired, the material can be gathered and sewed to the screw eye in the shoulder piece. Hands can be made in various ways. Two pieces of felt can be cut, stitched around the edges and lightly stuffed. If necessary, fingers can be indicated by stitching. A simple mitten hand can be similarly made from cloth; the pieces should be turned inside out before stuffing. Soft wood such as balsa can be cut into simple hands, or flat ones can be sawed from plywood or thin boards.

Cloth marionettes usually need to be weighted in the feet, hands, and lower part of the trunk (to insure a good sitting posture). Sheet lead, shot, sinkers, solder (without acid core), or dress weights are all usable. Be sure your weights are well padded with cloth so they will not wear through, nor thump when the puppet moves.

Heads for cloth marionettes can be simple ovoids with the features painted, drawn in crayon, or embroidered. It is more effective to cut the head in profile, because it gives an opportunity to make much more plastic features. Lemuel Williams gives the following directions: "Make a pattern on cardboard or tag board and cut it out. Use yellow cloth as a base color for Chinese characters, brown or black for Negroes, and flesh for Whites. A 4″ by 8″ piece will serve. Fold the material double, lay the pattern on it and trace with a soft pencil around the edges. Sew on a sewing machine, leaving the top of the head and bottom of

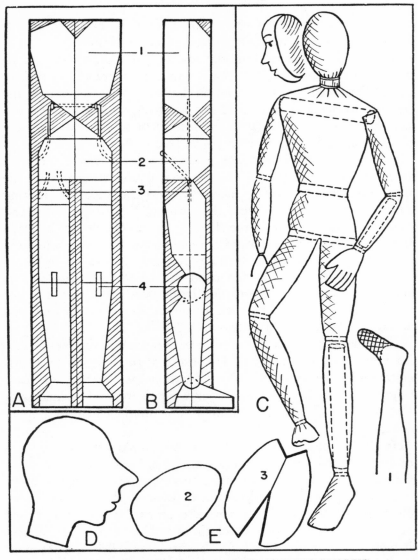

PLATE 18. SIMPLE MARIONETTE (STRING-PUPPET)
CONSTRUCTION

A, B. Wooden 2 x 4 marionette by Lemuel Williams
C. Stuffed stocking marionette
D, E. Details of head and feet

the neck open. Cut out the sewed profile ½" from the seam and turn right side out. Stuff the nose with cotton or Kapok; hold it in place with a finger of your left hand inside the head; now sew with small stitches back and forth from one side of the nose to the other. From the bridge of the nose, sew straight down beside it to the nostrils and straight across under it. Do not pull the stitches too tightly."[7] The rest of the head is stuffed as firmly as possible; you can pull the material into various positions as you work, catching it here and there with a stitch to make the kind of character you want. Eyes, ears, wigs, and other details may be added. Buttons and beads are useful for features. The head can be fastened to the trunk by overcasting—and be sure it is securely sewed.

For the stocking marionette, you can use the profile head instead of stuffing the stocking heel as indicated at *C, Plate 18*, or you can make a papier-mâchè half-mask and sew it to the head (see p. 85 for directions). When painted and covered with the proper wig or headdress, this makes an excellent head.

A simple 18" wooden marionette can be made from an ordinary 2" by 4" white pine or other soft wood. Lemuel Williams' design on *Plate 18, A* shows how the parts can be cut. The torso is (1), pelvis piece (2); these are joined at the center by a cord. Another cord, anchored to the pelvis piece, passes freely through the torso to keep the parts in line, and yet allow some side-to-side movement. The legs can be attached to the body either with a leather hinge (*Plate 13, 5*) or a double cord as shown at 3 *B, Plate 18*. The knee joint shown at (4) is of trunk fiber. A tongue and groove joint of the Dwiggins type (*Plate 20, F*) can be used, or a leather one similar to those used for rod-puppets (see *Plate 12, B*).

Tony Sarg's construction method is illustrated on *Plate 19*. From a block of wood about 2" thick a torso piece is cut (*A, 1*). A hole 1¼" is drilled in the top. With Plastic Wood this block is built up to the desired form, front and back, as shown in the shaded areas (2) and (3). The pelvis piece (4), shown in detail at *E*, consists of three ½" pieces of wood (5, 6, 7), filled in at the

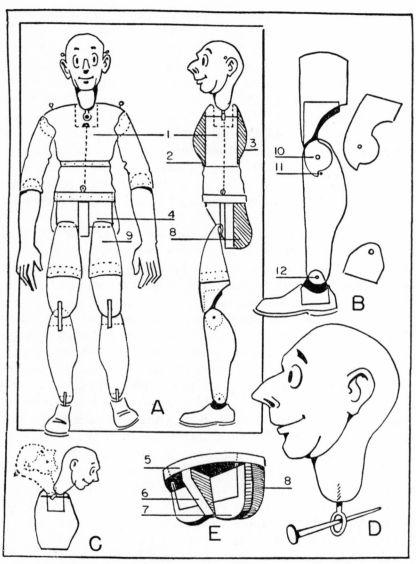

PLATE 19. TONY SARG'S MARIONETTE CONSTRUCTION

back with Plastic Wood (8). These two sections are held together by a strong cord tied to a screw eye in the pelvis piece, run through the torso, and knotted securely. The gap between the two parts is covered with cloth tacked to the wooden parts; light stuffing can be used to fill out the form, but it should not interfere with the free movement of the waist joint. The hands, arms, legs, and feet can be either carved in wood or modeled in clay, cast in plaster and finally cast in Plastic Wood (see pp. 90-92). A cloth top (9) is attached to the upper leg and hung over a wire set in the pelvis piece as indicated. The upper arm is also cloth, lightly stuffed if necessary. *Detail B* shows the knee and ankle joints which are made from trunk fiber. At the knee, the joint is nailed into the upper leg and pinned to the lower leg at (10). A small nail (11) is used as a stop to keep the joint from bending forward. The ankle joint is secured to the foot and the lower leg is pivoted to it at (12). The head attachment is shown at *C*; it is a nail run through a screw eye set in the neck *D*.

The Püterschein system of marionette construction, used by many professional puppeteers, is shown on *Plates 20* and *21*. W. A. Dwiggins, who developed this system, says: "The parts to be moved are simple levers—moved in circular tracks about fixed points or fulcrums. The purpose of our mechanical design is to confine the motions of these levers to given planes, and within certain arcs of travel. The limits for the arcs and the slants of the planes are found out by watching a human being move.

"It is not possible to reproduce in a marionette all the motions of a human figure, nor is it desirable to do so. As in all the arts, a simplified or abstracted presentation is often more vivid than an exact reproduction. The designer watches to see just how a wrist joint moves, for example, and then works out mechanical ways and means for *suggesting* that motion."[8]

The marionette hangs by its head strings. Correct balance of the figure and its natural action depend upon "accurate locating of all points of support, from neck to ground, *in a single plane* perpendicular to the ground" (*Plate 20, B*).

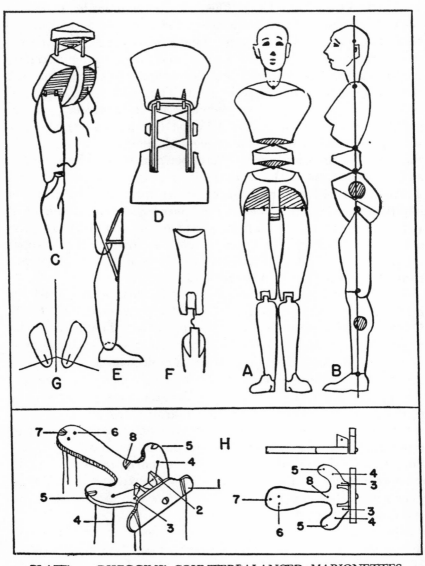

PLATE 20. DWIGGINS' COUNTERBALANCED MARIONETTES
Details of body construction and controller

The head is fastened to the trunk by a screw eye in the stub of the neck and a loop of wire in a shallow cup at the top of the trunk (*Plate 21, B*). The side-to-side movement is controlled by the dimensions of the screw eye and wire loop; up-and-down motions depend upon the depth of the hollow in the trunk—notice that it is higher at the back than at the front, because the head can bend farther in the latter direction. The loop is wound with cord to prevent rattle.

There are three pieces for the trunk: Shoulders, waist, and hips. These three pieces, where they join, are cut in the shape of flat cones meeting at their points (*Plate 20, A, B*). A spine cord running through the points holds the pieces together snugly. The horizontal rotation of the shoulders on hips—the twist of the body—is limited to the proper swing by a loop of cord fastened at both ends in the pelvis piece and running loosely through holes in the waist piece. The cord continues through screw eyes on the under side of the shoulder piece, and is set to the requisite slackness (*Plate 20, D*). This loop of sidestays serves also to keep shoulders and hips in the correct plane when the figure hangs free. The run of sidestay holes and screw eyes is on a cross line a little forward of the spine cord.

Good arm and hand action in a marionette depends upon the proper relation, one to another, of the *axis lines* of the shoulder, elbow, and wrist joints. The upper arm is fastened to the shoulder by two strings (*Plate 21, D*) with some play between arm and body, and the axis of the hinge is at 90° to the shoulder plane. The holes in the shoulder for the two cords are on a line not quite horizontal, the front hole being a little lower, and the center between the two a trifle back of the "plane of balance."

The axis of the elbow hinge is set at 60° to the axis of the shoulder hinge, and the wrist joint is at the same angle to the axis of the elbow (*Plate 21, G. H.*). A single cord holds the two sections of the arm together. The arc of motion of the wrist is shown on *Plate 21, A*; a pin pivot is used to attach hand to arm.

Two cords are used to fasten the thighs to the pelvis piece

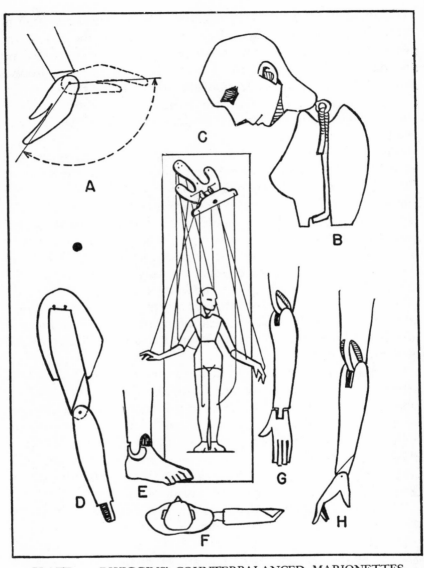

PLATE 21. DWIGGINS' COUNTERBALANCED MARIONETTES
Details of body construction

(*Plate 20, C*); there should be a trifle of motion sideways. One cord holds the lower leg to the thigh (*Plate 20, E, F*). The axes of the knee and thigh hinges are on the balance plane (*Plate 20, B*). The axes of the ankle joints cross the balance plane at their centers, but are set at slight angles off that plane (*Plate 20, G*).

The Püterschein system as here illustrated requires considerably more exact carving and fitting than other methods. But its principles can be applied to simpler mechanisms, for, as Dwiggins says: "The action of the most simple figure will be improved by using the principle of 'all points of support in a single plane.' If an arm is made of cloth tubing stuffed with sawdust, its action will be more natural if the cross-stitching of the joints is contrived to make the parts bend on the designated 'related axes.' "⁹

STRING-PUPPET CONTROLLERS

W. A. Dwiggins points out that designing the controller is half the problem of marionette mechanism. The problem has been solved in many ways and every marionette operator has his favorite method. It does not greatly matter how you devise a controller, so long as it is easy to make and to hold in the hand; is compact while allowing sufficient leverage; provides for as many automatic motions as possible by a mere tilting of the controller; has a minimum of angles, projections, and crevices; and has an easy certain method of fastening and adjusting the strings. Use as few strings as you can on the puppet and keep the controller as simple as possible. There are occasions which demand a complicated control mechanism, but by careful designing you can often provide for a wide variety of movements by simple means.

Although there are many variations of each type, controllers may be divided into two groups—vertical and horizontal. The examples shown on *Plates 20, 21, 22, 23* are basic designs for the control of ordinary puppets. Variations of them can be made for puppets which have to perform special movements. Other methods may be found in *Puppetry 1930* and McPharlin's pamphlet,

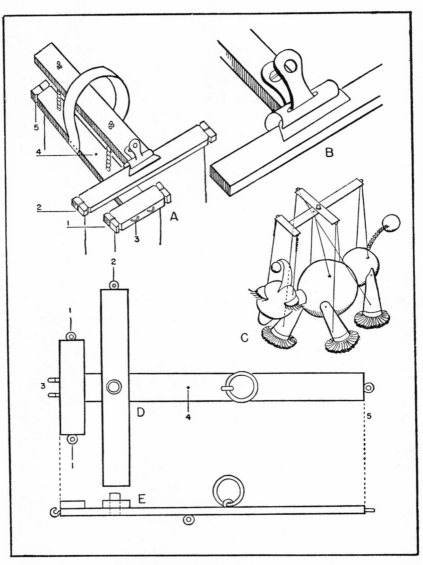

PLATE 22. AIRPLANE MARIONETTE CONTROLLERS

Puppet Construction

Marionette Control. Multiple controllers are often used to operate two or more puppets at the same time, especially for chorus groups. An excellent design by Rufus Rose may be found in *Puppetry 1934.* Dwiggins' paddle type controller is illustrated on *Plate 20, H.* It is made of ⅜" plywood with a screwed-on movable leg bar (1). The raised section at (2) permits the forearm and hand strings to be easily picked up. The hand string is continuous and runs through holes at (3) while the forearm strings (4) are tied off in the same holes. Head strings are at (5), shoulders at (6), back at (7), and forehead at (8). For attaching the strings, a knot is tied in the end, slipped into the curved slot, and wound around until the length is adjusted. This controller is approximately 6" long for an average puppet.

Another paddle controller, designed by Rufus Rose, is shown on *Plate 23, E, F.* It is compact and has no projections. The controller is cut from a piece of ⅜" plywood. Two variations are shown (one half the pattern is given for each). In *diagram E,* a removable leg bar is set on a ¼" dowel at (1), or a 1½" spring paper clip can be screwed in place. Holes can be drilled for tying off the strings, or slots can be sawed. The stringing is as follows: Hands (2), arms (3), head (4), back (5), shoulders (6).

Diagram F shows a wider controller which allows a movable leg bar (8) to be set in slot (7). One half of the bar is shown at (8). It is fastened to the controller by means of a 2½" piece of coat hanger wire secured by staples (10). The ends of the wire should be bent to keep it from slipping out. Washers at (11) allow free movement of the leg bar, which is controlled by the thumb placed at (9). The leg bar is ⅜" thick, 2" wide and 6" long. Controller *F* is 8" by 8"; *E* is 6" wide, 7" long.

The simplest type of horizontal controller is shown on *Plate 23, D.* A single rod (1) has the head strings at (*a*), the hand at (*b*), and the leg at (*c*). A separate bar (2) can be used for the leg strings instead of attaching them to (1).

A typical airplane type controller is shown on *Plate 22.* It consists of three bars ⅜" thick, 1" wide. *Detail D* shows the top

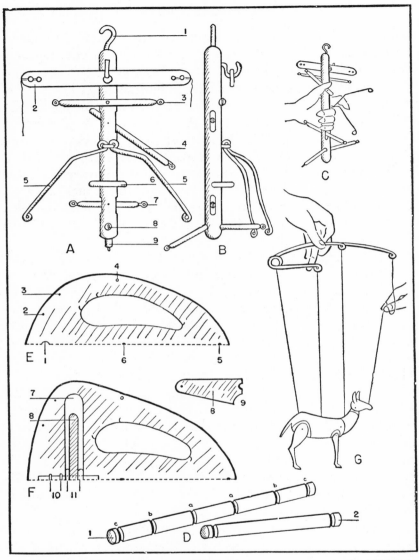

PLATE 23. VERTICAL AND OTHER MARIONETTE CONTROLLERS

A, B, C. Vertical controller by H. V. Tozer
D. Simple controller
E, F. Paddle controllers by Rufus Rose
G. Wire animal controller by Dwiggins

view, with screw eyes for fastening the strings. Head strings are at (1), legs at (2), hands at (3), shoulders at (4), back at (5). At *E* is the side view showing the screw eye to which shoulder strings are tied and the movable leg bar set on a dowel. *Diagram A* shows a double controller with the leg bar clamped to a separate bar by means of a large spring paper clip (*detail B*). This bar is fastened to the lower one with cords. Such a mechanism enables the operator to work a marionette in each hand; by rocking the upper bar, the puppet can be made to walk. Other strings are placed as in *D*, and secured by slots and notches.

Airplane controllers work very well for animals. The length should be determined by the length of the animal. Measure the distance between the point at which the head strings and back strings are attached, and make the controller about that long. Most animals need strings on the shoulders, back (one or two sets depending upon the size and kind of beast), head, and tail. All four feet can be controlled by using a regular leg bar; the back leg strings are crossed, with the right leg attached to the left side of the bar and vice versa (*diagram C*). A fair animal walk is produced by rocking the bar, as for puppets representing human beings.

Good incidental movement can be obtained by suspending the animal head on strong elastic or loosely coiled springs. A flexible wire controller like that shown on *Plate 23*, *G* is often useful to produce animated movement by simple means.

Three views of a vertical controller used by H. V. Tozer are shown on *Plate 23*. It is made from a 1".wooden rod. The construction is explained in *A*; (1) is the hanging hook; (2) is the removable leg bar; (3) the head bar; (4) is a lever for raising properties to the puppet's hand; (5) hand bars; (6) shelf between third and little finger to keep operator's hand in position; (7) rocking shoulder bar which avoids a run-through string; (8) chest bar, and (9) back bar. A side view of the controller is at *B*, and *C* shows the position of the controller in the hand. Notice that good hand movement can be obtained by moving the wires with the

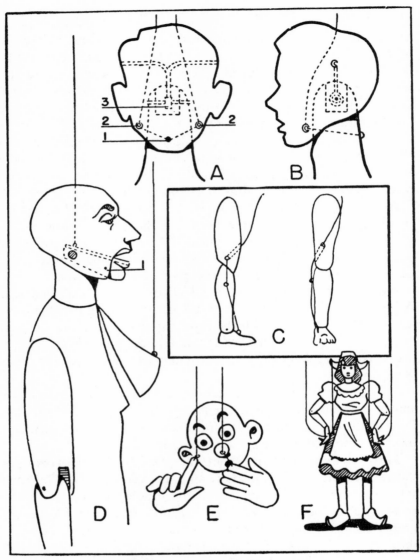

PLATE 24. SPECIAL MARIONETTE STRINGING

A, B. Head stringing by Rufus Rose
C. Leg stringing by Rufus Rose
D. Movable jaw and heaving bosom
E, F. Hand stringing

same hand which holds the controller, thus leaving the other hand free to work the leg bar.

Some movements require special stringing, and this sometimes means modification of the controller. On *Plate 24, A, B,* a mechanism for turning the head is illustrated. A tack (1) is placed at the base of the neck. Strings fastened to it pass through screw eyes (2) or wire loops in the lower jaw inside the head, and out through the top of the head. By pulling one string or the other a sidewise turn is effected. Wires fastened to the head above the ears and slightly behind them, allowing the greater weight of the front to pull the head forward, are brought to a common center and bent vertically down. At their base a loop (3) is made and through it a pin is run from side to side of the neck. A large hole cut in the top of the neck allows the wire to move forward for a nod. The loop must be loose enough on the pin to assure sideward turning of the head.

At *C, Plate 24* is shown a method for leg stringing. The string is tied to the foot, passes through a screw eye on the inside of the lower leg, and through the upper leg. Care must be taken to make the hole in the upper leg large enough to allow unimpeded movement.

Mechanisms for a movable jaw and heaving bosom are shown at *D, Plate 24.* The jaw, pivoted to the head at (1) is weighted to keep the mouth closed. When the string is pulled, the mouth opens.

When string-puppets must bring hands to lips, or place arms akimbo or make similar movements, the strings pass through loops or screw eyes as illustrated at *E* and *F, Plate 24.*

PUPPET HEAD CONSTRUCTION

Puppet heads may be made of many different materials. It all depends upon whether you want to model or carve, what you have on hand, how skillful you are, and how much patience you possess. The following methods of construction are those most commonly used; some are very simple and others will give you full opportunity for sculptural expression. Whatever method you choose, remember that simplicity, carrying power and emphasis (even exaggeration) of essential details should be your guide. The recipes for plastic materials as well as directions for modeling, casting, carving and painting may be used for making other parts of a puppet because the principles are the same.

Potato Heads. With a kitchen or penknife, carve a large potato using broad, simple strokes until you have the desired form. If it is for a hand-puppet, make a hole in it to fit the puppeteer's forefinger. For other types, insert a dowel or other stick for the neck. Paint the head while still wet with tempera or water color; add hair and eyes if the head is to be used immediately, but it is better to put it aside until it has dried somewhat before completing the details. Wrinkles will appear, hence potatoes are best used for grotesque or old heads. Apples can be used in a similar way.

Improvised Heads. Stocking darners, potato mashers, rubber balls, wooden spoons, gourds, and many others things can be used for basic head shapes (*Plate 25*). To these can be added features and hair selected from a scrap box (see p. 285). The best method is to try various shapes and textures; these can be pinned temporarily in place and changed about until the right expression has been found. Persons with no experience in drawing or modeling find they can thus make creditable characterizations. Some modification of the basic form can be made by carving or building it up with Plastic Wood, but these should not be overdone, or the simplicity, which is the greatest value of these heads, will be lost.

Turned Heads. The process of developing these is similar to that used for improvised heads, but it offers a wider range of possibilities (*Plate 26*). The heads are turned on a lathe from soft pine, redwood, or any other moderately soft wood. To save time, cut 3″ by 3″ or 4″ by 4″ wood the length of your lathe, and turn half a dozen or more at a time. Vary the shapes as much as possible to suggest basic head forms. If you want to be a little more careful, the neck may be turned as part of the head; this makes a better

PLATE 25. IMPROVISED PUPPET HEADS
By Vivian Michael

A. Potato masher
B. Rubber ball
C. Stocking darner
D. Paper bag

PLATE 26. TURNED PUPPET HEADS
By Vivian Michael

looking puppet. You may have to finish each head separately on the lathe, after the forms have been sawed apart. Noses and ears can be cut from wood and held in place by airplane cement and brads. Depressions for the eyes, or some flattening of the cheeks, may give better characterization. Your main problem is to give the head sufficient modeling, by the addition of features or by carving, to achieve variety from different angles. Avoid small features. Eliminate as much as possible; you might even leave out a mouth or a nose if the other features are sufficiently dominant. A witch, for instance, with green auto reflector eyes, a huge carved nose, peaked hat, and monkey fur hair, is complete without more details.

Modeled Heads. Mixtures such as papier-mâché, sawdust, and asbestos have been found suitable for direct modeling.

Papier-mâché. Practically every puppeteer has his own formula for making papier-mâché, but the basis of each is old newspaper or other soft paper, which has been soaked overnight in water and reduced to a pulp by running through a food chopper or rubbing on a washboard or between the hands. After the water is squeezed from the pulp, some adhesive is added to bind the mixture together. Commercial wallpaper or flour paste, liquid or casein glue, (casein is hard on the hands), casein paste, are frequently used. The mass is kneaded thoroughly, with a little whiting added to prevent stickiness and to make a smoother mixture.

Flour paste can be made by taking one-half cup of flour and adding just enough water to make a thick paste. Gradually add two cups of boiling water, bring to a boil and cook for several minutes, stirring it until it becomes clear. When cool, add a few drops of oil of cloves to preserve it, or to each pint of paste add two heaping teaspoonfuls of formaldehyde (be careful, it's POISON) and one of powdered alum.

Two cups of paper pulp to one of flour paste is a good proportion. A cooked mixture can be made as follows: Soak two ounces of dry newspaper strips in one quart of water and reduce to a pulp. Melt one-half cup of flake glue and one-half cup of water in a small saucepan. Add this to the paper mixture and boil forty minutes, adding more water if necessary. Gradually add one-half cup dry flour, mixing a little water from the paper and glue mixture to prevent its lumping. Cook twenty minutes more. After it has cooled, squeeze out the excess liquid. Weigh the pulp mixture and add an equal weight of whiting to it. Knead until well mixed and of a good consistency for modeling. Place in a tightly covered can.

Joseph Shea crumples up the newspaper, but does not tear it before soaking. Then he rubs it on a washboard with sufficient water to keep it quite wet. When the pulp is fine, the water is squeezed out and the pulp stored in jars or tins for future use. The paste is not added until time to use the pulp; it will keep indefinitely without the paste. Extra finely pulverized pulp with more paste is used for the outside of the head.

Papier-mâché can be built directly on a dowel rod which has a core of paper wadded to it to hold the wet mixture. Or the cores can be made in advance, of the same pulp, and allowed to dry. A cloth-covered cardboard tube (*Plate 8, E*) can also be used. New pulp can be added to the basic form and the features modeled with the fingers, sculptor's tools or those improvised from orange sticks, toothbrush handles, or dowels sharpened to a point. Papier-mâché can also be pressed into a well-oiled plaster mold and allowed to dry. An old electric light bulb makes a useful base for papier-mâché and a good neck can be built on the head. When the pulp is dry, the bulb is broken and you have a fine, hollow, lightweight head. When thoroughly dry, papier-mâché can be sanded and painted with tempera or oil. A priming coat made of equal parts of whiting and Le Page's glue gives you a smooth surface, which can be made even smoother by an additional coat of zinc white oil paint.

Sawdust Mixture. It is best to use a core for building heads of sawdust mixture. A wad of paper or rags wrapped securely with thread to a 1″ dowel or a small piece of soft wood can be used for marionette or rod-puppet heads. Loops of wire for attaching the head strings of marionettes should be set in the core. For hand-puppets, a hollow cloth-covered cardboard cylinder, with a roll of cloth sewed to the base for fastening the costume, is useful (*Plate 8, E*).

On this core you can build up the basic head form, using coarse sawdust (from a bench saw) mixed to modeling consistency with flour paste or other adhesive. String or thread wound into the mixture as you build the head helps to strengthen it. After drying for twenty-four hours or so, the final modeling can be done with a finer sawdust mixture (the dust from a band saw is good). When the head is dry, sand, fill in the cracks with Old English water putty or sawdust mixture. Some whiting can be added to the mixture to make it smoother, or one or more layers of soft paper strips dipped in paste may be put on to make a smooth surface. Paper towels or napkins are excellent for this. A paintbrush is useful for working the paper onto the head.

Asbestos Mixture. Flaked or powdered asbestos, obtainable at hardware stores, can be mixed with an adhesive in the same way as sawdust or paper pulp. Whiting should be added, and a little formaldehyde. The process of modeling is the same as described above.

The principal difficulty with all these mixtures is the length of time required to dry them thoroughly. If cores are prepared and dried in advance, the drying time is shortened, but even so, several days—perhaps a week—must be allowed. Drying can be hastened by artificial heat, but cracks are more likely to occur, especially with the sawdust mixture. Here the quick drying, easily mixed water putty is useful; it comes in powder form and is mixed with water as needed.

Papier-mâché Over Clay Base. For this method you first model the head from clay (*Plate 27, A*). An oil-base clay such as Plasticine is best, for it holds its form and does not have to be kept wet. Water clay can be used, but the head should be given a thin coat of hot paraffin when completed and before the paper is put on. A simple modeling stand can be made of a ¾" or 1" dowel set in a wooden base. If the stand can be constructed to revolve, so much the better. Shape a mass of clay in the general form (usually some variation of the ovoid) you want to use, and place it on the dowel.

Clay is a more flexible medium than the mixtures described above, and you may be tempted to put in a lot of detail. Don't. Work for a strong modeling which will give a suggestion of life, rather than for intricate fine lines which will have no carrying power. Remember that a puppet's face seems to smile, wink, or look sad as it moves about the stage in and out of different zones of light. Depress the clay with your fingers for the eye sockets; roll a small egg the length of the eye and cut in four pieces length-wise. Set one piece into each socket for the eyelid and smooth into place with a wire loop (a hairpin will do). This will suggest the eye and give a more illusive expression than a completely modeled eye with pupil and iris defined. Build up the nose, and remember the mouth is a built-up area, nor just a line in the face. Lips can easily be made by rolling bits of clay into snake forms, and smooth-ing into the head. Model the ears simply, and suggest the main masses of hair—don't waste time scratching lines to represent hair (see p. 96). Try the head under the stage lights from time to time; have someone hold it and turn it about while you watch from a distance of twenty feet. Does it look characterless? Simplify and strengthen the features. Strong modeling is especially important for papier-mâché over clay because some of the detail is lost.

When the head is completely modeled, cover with layers of newspaper, paper toweling, or other soft paper which has been torn into small pieces and dipped into paste about the consistency of thick cream (*Plate 27, C*). Smooth the paper onto the model, varying the direction of the strips. Six, eight (or more) layers should be applied, depending on the size of the head and the thick-ness of the paper. If desired, two colors of paper can be alternately used for the layers in order to be sure all parts of the head are equally covered. After the last layer is on, massage the head thor-oughly with thick paste until all seams and creases disappear. When the head is dry, the clay can be dug out through the neck hole,

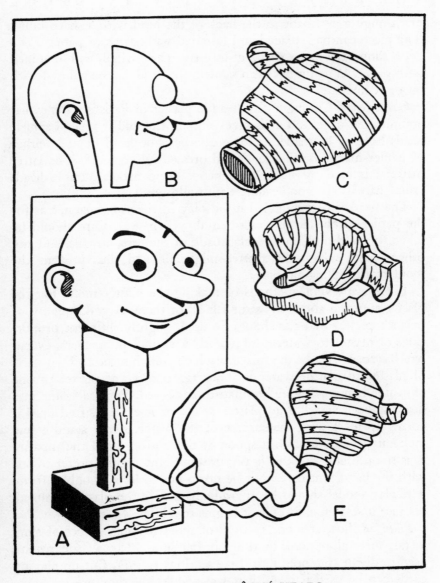

PLATE 27. PAPIER-MÂCHÉ HEADS
By Vivian Michael

or through a cut made in the back of the head with a sharp knife. The piece can be replaced and fastened with strips of paper. *Plate 27, B* shows the paper shell cut into two parts which will be joined with paper. When it has been sanded, the head can be painted with oil or tempera.

Cast Heads. Casting a clay head in plaster of Paris is a somewhat complicated process, but it saves time in the end if several similar heads have to be made, as for a chorus. The head is made either of papier-mâché or Plastic Wood pressed into a mold. The latter material is used by many professionals and makes durable heads which can also be good examples of sculpture.

The head is best modeled in oil clay in the same manner as for the papier-mâché heads described above (p. 85). Care should be taken to avoid undercuts, spaces back of the ears, nostrils, and any other places which the plaster might fill and thus prevent the mold from pulling properly.

There are several methods of making the plaster mold, but the plaster is mixed about the same for all of them. A good quality of potter's plaster of Paris should be used. Slightly different proportions of plaster to water are favored by various puppeteers; everyone has to work out the mixture which suits him best. Two parts of plaster to one of water is about right; three of plaster to one of water is used if a stiffer mixture is desired. Put the water in a deep, smooth vessel. Add plaster as fast as it can be sifted until it comes up level with the surface of the water. Let it stand a few moments, then stir with a spoon at the bottom until the mixture is as smooth and thick as heavy cream. Some people prefer to stir with the hand, but care must be taken not to let air bubbles form. The clay model should be in readiness before the plaster is mixed, because it sets quickly once it begins to stiffen.

Plate 28 illustrates one method of mold making. Pieces of shim metal, sheet aluminum, or thin tin, cut in 1½″ to 2″ squares are used to divide the mold into three sections (*A, B*). Cut-up playing cards can be used if metal is not available, but they are less satisfactory. The dividers are inserted along one side of the neck, up

A

B

PLATE 28. PLASTER MOLD MAKING
By Vivian Michael

over the top of the head at its highest point, and down the other side of the neck. Others are used to divide the front of the face along the line of the nose. Mix enough plaster for the back of the mold, and when it has just begun to set, apply with a spoon, building it up about one inch in thickness. When it has set (it will become warm and fairly hard), remove the dividers which separate back from front, make some holes with a knife to lock the mold, grease the plaster with vaseline, liquid soap (there is a kind especially prepared for the purpose), or hard oil. It is a good idea to grease the dividers which separate the two halves of the face. Cast one half of the face, remove the dividers, make holes in the plaster, and grease the mold before casting the last section. Pry the front sections carefully from the back with a kitchen knife. Any rough places inside the mold can be smoothed and any air bubbles filled with a thin plaster of Paris mixture.

Another method, slightly more difficult but allowing the whole mold to be made at one time, is described by Rufus Rose and has been used successfully by various professional puppeteers. "With a pointed tool, cut a line in the clay model, going up the side of the neck, around the rim of the ear, over the top of the head and in the same manner down the opposite side to the dowel. Anchor a piece of silk button-hole thread [heavy fish line can also be used] to the side of the dowel 2 inches below the neck, run it around the head in the cut, covering it with clay as you go, and anchor the end at the other side of the dowel.

"Next cut a line from the front neck base up over the middle of the chin and mouth, along the nose ridge and across the forehead to the already laid thread which it meets at right angles. Follow the thread to a point halfway between the top of the head and the top of one ear, thence striking out in a generous arc over the back of the head, again meeting the thread at the halfway point between the top of the head and the top of the other ear. At this point, beside the thread, embed in the clay a small button to which is tied another piece of silk thread. Bury this in the cut, tracing it back

[90]

to the front of the dowel and there anchor its end. Be sure all threads are in place and firmly fastened.

"Mix the plaster in a deep vessel, using two-thirds as much water as the volume of plaster. Take the dowel from its base block and using it as a handle dip the model into the plaster. Lift the model up and cover the entire surface with plaster, using a spoon and taking care that it does not gouge the clay. To be sure that the plaster penetrates into crevices, blow it vigorously where these occur.

"Onto a piece of glass about 15 inches square pour a good quantity of plaster. Pile it up about 2 inches high at the center. Place the model, top downward, into this so that it sinks to no less than one inch from the glass. Holding it by the dowel in the left hand, rapidly but carefully build up plaster all over to a thickness of no more than an inch, using an ordinary table knife. Allow no air traps to form. The plaster soon sets enough to support itself as you work.

"When it takes fairly firm pressure to dent the surface, quickly but cautiously pull the threads to cut the mold. The second embedded is the first pulled. Weave it slightly from side to side in pulling so that the mold pieces will dovetail when tied together. It pulls down the front of the face; lift the entire cast free from the glass and carry it to the top of the head. Turn at a right angle toward the ear, then swing around the arc, slanting the cut in a wider radius so that the cap-piece of the mold will come out easily. Stop pulling when you come to the button.

"Now, pull the side thread, following around the rim of one ear, cutting steadily over the top of the head and around the other ear. Now grip the still-anchored end of the thread so that it cannot pull away and complete the cut along the neck.

"Place the dowel back in the base-block and allow the plaster to harden for 20 minutes. Then crack apart the cast by inserting the table knife into a cut and striking it lightly with a hammer. Do not hurry this operation, but work the knife around the cuts at many points. When the cast is free, clean out any clay which may stick to the plaster."[10]

Plastic Wood may be had in one-pound tins, but it is much cheaper to purchase it in larger quantities (see p. 286). Before you start casting the final head, soak the mold for a few minutes in water. Keep your hands dripping wet while working with Plastic Wood to minimize sticking.

Rufus Rose describes his method for making the Plastic Wood head: "Hold one of the front mold pieces in the left hand and lay in a quarter-inch-thick pancake of the pulp just large enough to cover the inside surface. With the thumb, press it into place, so that it oozes into every crevice of the mold. Fill the other front mold piece and fit the two together, holding them tightly in the left hand. Apply a fresh strip of pulp over the division line and knead it into the rest. Support these two mold pieces so that they stay together. Press pulp into the back mold piece. Twist a three-eighths inch loop of one-sixteenth inch wire and anchor the flaring ends in the pulp at the base of the neck. The loop extends outside the pulp, its opening squarely facing front and back. It is used to fasten the head to the body.

"Fit the front and back of the mold together. Working through the opening in the back mold, knit fresh pulp into the division between front and back pieces. Press fresh pulp around the flaring ends of the wire inside the neck. Cast the cap-piece."[11]

Most puppeteers then set the mold in a large vessel of water until the Plastic Wood hardens—about twelve hours. Others use plaster of Paris poured into the mold and swashed around to form a ⅛" coating. When this has set, the mold is removed carefully and the head laid gently on a crumpled cloth bed to dry for forty-eight hours. The inside coat of plaster is then chipped out, and the cap-piece glued in.

It is sometimes easier to fasten the two front sections of the mold together before pressing in the Plastic Wood. This can be done by setting them in Plasticine so they do not have to be supported by the hand. If the divider method described above has been used for making the plaster cast, the three sections can be tied together as Rose explains, but the seams will be worked together from the neck opening instead of the hole in the back of the head. The blunt end of a case knife or a rounded stick can be used to kneed the Plastic Wood, if you can't reach far enough with your fingers. The neck should be made solid with Plastic Wood if the head is for marionettes or rod-puppets; for hand-puppets an opening to fit the forefinger of the puppeteer's hand should be left.

Speed is important in working with Plastic Wood because it dries quickly when exposed to the air. A good quantity of solvent should be kept on hand for moistening places which get too hard to work. When thoroughly dry, the head may be carved or retouched with bits of Plastic Wood mixed with solvent. Old heads may be remodeled by working new features over the old ones. A paintbrush dipped in solvent is useful for smoothing the heads. Any kind of paint can be used to paint Plastic Wood.

Papier-mâché can be used in plaster molds. Fasten the two front sections together and set hollow side up. The mold must be well greased (liquid soap, vaseline or hard oil). Tear paper towels into ¾" strips, dip in clear water and line the mold, pressing paper in firmly and smoothly. Add six to eight layers of newspaper, torn into strips and dipped in paste. The more layers there are the firmer and more durable the head. Keep a smooth working surface at all times and press the paper firmly into the mold. Trim off with scissors any excess paper that comes above the mold. Let the two halves of the head dry in the mold if possible; if it is needed for another head, the pieces can be removed and filled with crumpled paper to prevent warping. When the shell of papier-mâché is dry, remove the first coating of towel, if it is loose, or work in a thick coating of paste if it is partially stuck. Join the two halves with strips of paper dipped in paste. Sand with fine sandpaper. Some puppeteers like to make a smoother surface by giving the head a thin coat of gesso, Reliefo, wood putty, glue and whiting, or shellac and whiting. Tempera or oil color can be used for the final painting.

Carved Heads. Lemuel Williams makes the following suggestions:[12] For carving your puppet heads, you will need suitable wood. Among the soft woods are: Poplar; basswood; balsa; white, sugar, or ponderosa pine. Some hard woods can be used: maple, mahogany, walnut, holly, or rosewood. Whether you use hard or soft wood is a matter of preference, availability, and weight. Hand-puppet heads should be as light as possible; even the lightest of pine wood may be too heavy if the head is large. Some people get good results with balsa wood, which must be carved with a very sharp, thin knife such as a razor blade. Balsa is the lightest available wood. Basswood and poplar are finer grained than pine and carve better, but are less easily found and more costly. Sugar pine (known also as Idaho white pine) is one of the best soft woods for carved puppets, and is easily obtained. Hard woods stand up well, but are harder to carve, less available, and more expensive.

You will require a knife, coping saw, vise, rasps (riffler and cabinet), sharpening stones (coarse, fine, round, and V-shaped), and carving tools. On page 284 are listed various firms from which you may purchase carving tools. You can buy as many as you wish, but a good selection to start with would include: A ½″ or ¾″ flat gouge, a large and a small U, a parting tool (medium V), a small back-bent gouge, a ⅛″ and a ⅜″ flat U-gouge.

Tools should be kept sharp. They should not be ground on high speed grinders, because of the danger of burning, but honed on oiled stones. Avoid using them on wood which has been sanded—this will dull them. Don't lay them down where they may strike their edges on any metal.

Cubes of wood 3″ or 4″ in size are large enough for most heads; use a block an inch or so longer if you want the neck carved with the head. If you can't get the right size blocks, several pieces can be glued together. Be sure the grain in all the pieces runs in the same direction. If you can't tell by looking, run your flat gouge over the surface; in one direction it will dig in, while in the other it will cut cleanly. Be sure the surfaces to be glued together are smooth, then score them by drawing the tooth tips of a saw diagonally across the surface both ways, to form small diamonds. Small dowel pins should be inserted between the pieces for extra strength.

Flake glue should be soaked overnight with just enough water to cover it. The wood should be the same temperature as the glue for best results. Prepared glues like Le Page's are more efficient when fresh, so do not buy them in large quantities. Casein glue should be mixed according to instrctions, allowing a little more time for good measure. This glue goes into a cream state in from twenty to forty-five minutes and becomes waterproof after setting about four days. Weldwood (a waterproof glue) and resin glues are also good for gluing wood.

When you are ready to carve, select a block of the right size. Sketch the profile on one side, and the front view on the side next to it. Saw out the profile with a band saw if you have one, tack the waste back on and saw the front view. The first roughing out may be done with a coping saw if you have no power tools. The block must be held firmly in a vise. Start carving with the nose, the highest point of the face. Some puppeteers like to use a rasp to help in this first blocking out, while others prefer the larger carving tools. Use any method which is easiest and gets the best results. Go slowly and try to keep the forms round. Work on different parts of the head alternately because this will give you a better sculptured form. As in other types of heads, work for simple, unified areas which will show up to advantage under the stage lights.

Painting. Heads may be painted with tempera or oil color. The former is easy to use, but it should have a thin coat of satin finish varnish, shellac, or lacquer over it for protection. The dull finish varnish is best; other materials are likely to be too shiny unless given a coat of wax or rubbed down with pumice powder. Avoid heavy enamels which reflect the light unnaturally, unless you want such effects for a special purpose. In general, the painting should be simple and serve to emphasize the modeling. Paint boldly; tiny lines and subtle gradations of value will not carry from the stage to the spectator at the rear. Wooden heads, if made of fine grained sugar pine and smoothly sanded, may be left unpainted except for details. California redwood, unpainted, is good for characters with swarthy complexions. Cake rouge rubbed into the wood is an easy way to get cheek color because it is easy to blend. The head should be given a thin coat of varnish to protect it. If using oil color, a little French chalk mixed with it will cut down the shine.

The best oil colors to buy are zinc white, rose madder (or alizarin crimson), American vermilion, chrome yellow, ochre, and permanent blue. With red, yellow, blue, green, violet, orange, white, and black tempera you can get most of the tints you will need. A few intermediate colors such as magenta and blue green (turquoise) are also useful.

If you are stylizing the puppets, the painting of flesh tones need not adhere too closely to those of nature—they can be chosen to blend with the costume and setting. If you prefer to be more realistic, variations can be made to suggest different ages and nationalities. Avoid the sickly pink which you get by mixing red and white. All flesh color is basically orange—white, orange with a little blue to dull it, for white people; orange with more blue, makes brown for Negroes (never paint them solid black), and orange with touches of red and white, for Indians and Egyptians. The yellow races are best done with yellow ochre, darkened or lightened with black and white.

Remember that any color can be made grayer by adding a touch of its opposite (see p. 170). Don't be afraid to tone things down if they are too bright when you study the puppet under the stage lights. On the other hand, do not hesitate to make the color stronger if it looks weak under the lights, because it is better to err on the side of vividness.

Wig Making. Hair for puppets may be made in many ways. Efimova warns against using real human hair on puppets, then continues, "The puppet's hair must have sculptural form. This must be sought in an old sheepskin scroll, in the oreole of shining skunk fur, in the flying rhythm of winged creatures, in the lightness of a goat's fluffy hair. The form may be achieved in wood, papier-mâché, anything but real hair. The puppet maker's own ingenuity will dictate to him what material to utilize for each given puppet character."[13] Other possibilities are: crepe hair, dyed Turkish towel (for short Negro hair), frayed rope, sponge rubber, embroidery floss, wool yarn, upholstery fringe (rayon is beautifully silky), steel wool, dish mops, felt, leather, oilcloth, and copper pot cleaners. Most wigs can be glued or tacked directly to the puppet's head, but you can also glue the toe of a stocking to the head for a foundation, and sew on the hair. Sometimes it is convenient to sew the hair to a narrow strip of felt which is fastened to the head.

Under stage lights, many colors can be used to suggest hair tones. Bright yellow, yellow-orange, pink make good blondes; red-orange, vermilion, rust suggest red heads and violet, dark blue, dark green look practically black. The usual range of browns can, of course, be used, but one is not limited to natural colors.

CHAPTER IV

COSTUME DESIGN AND CONSTRUCTION

Puppet costuming is especially important because it not only enhances the scenic picture but helps the audience to identify the various characters. In many folk-puppet theatres, the costume is traditional and is the chief factor in character identification. Costume also helps to point up action or business: Cuffs emphasize good hands; light shoes and bare legs, good dancers; large collars, wigs and headdresses, important and beautifully done heads. The general tone of the play, or the personality of the individual puppet, is suggested through the costume: Long, trailing lines are stately; flaring, puffy ones are gay; queer jags and blotches of color are funny. To the costumer, the puppet's clothes are all-important, but it must be remembered that they constitute but one phase of the total theatrical design and must be in harmony with the scenery, look well under the lighting, and express the character of the puppets they adorn.

Nina Efimova gives this word of advice to the puppet costume maker: "Bring to your work all the earnestness, all the effort you give to the making of the puppet. Don't assume that you are merely sewing doll clothes, but feel that you are constructing something artistic and sculpturesque, only the medium is not paint and plaster, but fur, silk, fine broadcloth, soft peasant linens. And, furthermore, do not for a moment think that you may substitute for these tested materials ordinary calico which you may happen to have, or canvas, or satin. You may say, 'What if I ride on street car Number Three instead of Number Four? The difference is only one.' But the difference is that you may land in the suburbs instead of downtown."[1]

With shadow- and hand-puppets, the costume is an integral part of the construction of the figures. The latter type has no body; the operator's hand inside the costume fills it out and gives it a semblance of form. With other types, however, the costume is made over the puppet body. Due to various methods of body construction, the costume must be made in terms of that particular body.

DRAPING EXERCISES[2]

It is helpful to make experiments with many kinds of fabrics, draped and pinned to puppet bodies, before the costume designs are made. Abstract studies in draping are also useful, not only to see how material behaves, but to suggest ways in which plain areas of a costume can be made more interesting. Cylinders, spheres, cubes, hemispheres and other basic geometric shapes of various sizes can be combined from wooden chopping bowls, cheese boxes, large mailing tubes, beach and tennis balls to make various draping stands which suggest the basic geometrical shapes of human anatomy (*Plate 29*). A sphere on a cigar box is fundamentally a head on shoulders, *A;* a hemisphere (wooden bowl) on a stick is a human pelvis, *D;* two balls atop a large mailing tube become a woman's bust, *B;* two boxes, one on its side the other upright. suggest an arm bent at the elbow, *C.* Several pieces of rayon jersey, about a yard square, are good for experiments. Use one of a plain color, another with a small pattern, and a third with a larger pattern. Try these over the various forms to see how the cloth falls. Hung over the hemisphere, the material will fall as it does in a woman's skirt. Ideas for wimples, collars, veils might be sketched from the cloth arranged over the sphere and box.

Other valuable experiments can be tried by tacking the material to the wall in various ways (*Plate 29, E*). Tack it in the center of one side, and fasten the corners a little lower. Change these relationships every way you can think of, and sketch the results. Tack the top edge of the material along the wall and catch up different

[99]

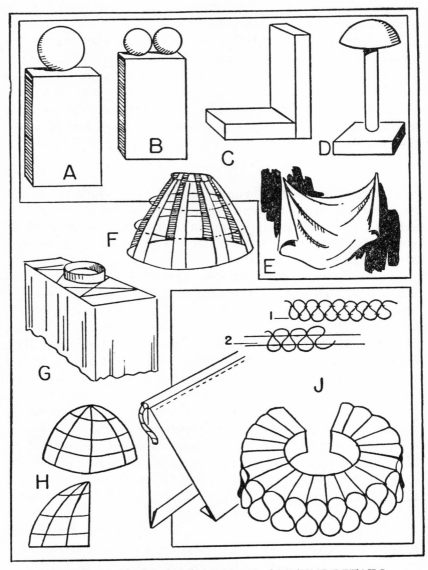

PLATE 29. DRAPING STANDS AND COSTUME DETAILS
By David Gibson

parts of the cloth with other tacks. Try the plain material draped crisscross with the figured in various positions. In all these exercises notice the relationship between the source of the drape and the character of the folds—a tiny pleat, tuck, or fold at the apex will cause the folds to be sharp and deep, while a large tuck will produce deep, rolling folds. Notice the change in the folds with the change in direction of the threads. Bias draping is generally more attractive. Having learned all you can from draping the jersey, try other materials and compare the different ways in which they fall into folds.

In applying this knowledge to puppet costuming remember that the small scale of the figures will effect the manner in which fabrics will drape. Most of them are likely to stand out in large folds instead of falling into soft ones; a complicated bit of draping which may do very well for a human figure becomes bulky and out of scale on a puppet. It would, therefore, be well to supplement the above exercises with others using puppet figures.

A good supply of miscellaneous fabrics of various textures and colors is one of the most valuable assets of the puppet costume designer. It will pay you to make some experiments with colors, textures, and drapery on the stage under varied lighting effects. Using a flash light or spotlight, study the effect of illuminating material from different angles. A good way to learn the effect of light on fabrics is to set up a group including the six basic pigment colors: red, blue, yellow, orange, green, violet—in several values and intensities of each. With a floodlight or spotlight and standard gelatin mediums throw different colored lights successively on the fabrics. You can see at a glance which lights flatter, and which kill the various colors (see pp. 174-76 for further notes on color).

Another good exercise is to set up different colors for the background and arrange others to represent the puppet costumes. Observe that if the latter are in a general way lighter or darker than the background they will show up to advantage; if they are the same value (degree of light or dark) as the background, they will merge with it. Study the relative intensity (brilliance) of the colors, and which ones stand out in a given light. Stand at a distance of twenty feet or more, study the pattern of light and dark which the fabrics make against the background. Half close your eyes and squint. You may find that two colors which seem to have considerable contrast when viewed close up, are actually the same value, and lose much of their contrast from a short distance.

You may not need or have time to do all the experiments suggested here, but the more you do, the more certain will be your results, and the better the quality of your costumes.

DESIGNING THE COSTUMES

With a basic knowledge of how different materials behave, and how various textures and colors look under stage lights, you can design suitable costumes for all your characters. Each costume should be planned to express the character of the person in the play, and at the same time, be related to the other costumes, the setting, and the lighting which is to be used. Within the value range which you choose for the costumes as a group, there should be sufficient contrast to emphasize the leading lady, and also to help the audience distinguish one character from another. There have been puppet shows in which a lady and her servant were dressed so nearly alike that it was almost impossible to tell one from the other. This is a grave error. Be careful about textures, too. Rough, smooth, shiny, dull, glittering surfaces—these are as important in giving variety to your costumes as are color and pattern.

If you have to make a period costume, study not only the costumes, but the architecture, interior design, and decorative details of the period. Try to capture the *essential* lines and shapes which are basic, but never copy any particular costume which you see illustrated. Notice also characteristic materials, how plain and figured goods are combined, and where accessories are placed.

Sketches of the costumes are useful, especially if several people are going to do the construction. The drawings may be finished or rough. Color notes may be painted, or you may use a sketch to suggest the basic lines and masses of the costumes, and attach

Costume Design and Construction

samples of the actual fabrics you are going to use. If you must go fabric hunting, it is convenient to have painted color swatches along to help you get the exact color you want.

SELECTION OF COSTUME MATERIALS

You will save time in shopping if you have a clear idea of the colors and textures of the materials you want. Those painted color swatches mentioned above are invaluable, especially if you have to do some substitution.

The type of puppet you are using will influence the kind of material you will need. For string-puppets, bulky fabric is unsuitable because it interferes with free manipulation. Hand- or rod-puppets may often be dressed in thick materials which hold their shape. Excellent costumes of felt and woolen fabrics have been used with the wire frame rod-puppet illustrated on *Plate 11, D*. The lack of a well-defined body was completely disguised by the costume. Substantial fabrics are best for hand-puppets, especially if they have to play strenuous roles. Rayon jersey is the best material for draped costumes. It can be bought by the yard in many colors and some patterns which are appropriate for puppets. Rayon underwear is also good, and it can be dyed.

LIST OF COSTUME FABRICS

The following list sums up the properties of the most common materials:

1. Soft, easily-draped fabrics, dull finish, varying textures: Flannel, muslin, broadcloth, small-weave monk's cloth, reverse side of sateen, pongee, wool jersey, thin wool suitings, Shantung, duvetyn, all-over laces, cheesecloth, tulle, silk or cotton net, crepe, chiffon, marquisette, crepe de Chine, *mousseline de soie*, Georgette, Indianhead, cretonne.

2. Dull finish fabrics, more or less stiff in nature and not too easy to drape because of their bulky or unyielding textures: Felt, buckram, crinoline, grosgrain satin, taffeta, piqué, corduroy, organdy, tarlatan,

[103]

sharkskin, wool and rayon gabardine, seersucker, linen, burlap, duck, twill, canvas, leather, heavy wool suitings, velvet.

3. Soft, easily draped fabrics, glossy finished: silk or rayon jersey, fine silk brocades, silk or rayon satin, sateen, rayon faille, sequin net, chiffon, "jewel cloth," chiffon velvet.

4. Stiff fabrics not suitable for draped effects in small areas, glossy finished: moiré taffeta, heavy silk or rayon brocade, Skinner or glazed satin, Pliofilm, Cellophane, plush, all-over sequin cloth, glazed leather, oilcloth, patent leather, glazed chintz, metallic cloth.

Every season brings new cellulose fabrics, and plastic cloth is being developed; keep an open eye for new things which may give you unusual effects for your costumes. Knitted fabrics are often more suitable than woven ones for puppet costumes, and they come in a wide variety of weights, colors, and textures. If you have contacts with a mill-end shop, you can pick up useful pieces. Many fabrics which are expensive in department stores may be purchased from theatrical fabric concerns. You should have contacts with these because they carry all kinds of showy trimmings and materials not easily obtainable elsewhere (see p. 282).

All designers for theatrical costumes need a wide range of glittering and spectacular accessories to add glamour where it is needed. Some of these can be procured at theatrical costume companies. Better still are the things one can pick up through various importing companies. You are fortunate if you can get a preferred spot on an importer's mailing list. To locate shops or dealers, look through the advertisements in various theatrical trade magazines and list those firms which offer free catalogues on request or free costume consultation by mail. Catalogues are usually expensive and are not sent to everyone, but any firm is glad to send samples for your inspection. When you have made some purchases and seem to be even a small potential buyer, you can get catalogues. Educational institutions can usually get them without much difficulty.

Among the usual glittery things are: Jewel cloths, sequin materials, metallic brocades, spangle or sequin bandings, elaborate laces, jewels, beads, mirrors, cords, lace trimmings and rhinestone bandings. Accessories which can be collected and kept in the "glamour box" might include: Chinese tassels, flowers, elaborate fringes, chain mail, feathers, ten-cent store jewelry, bits of embroidery, trimmings, braids—in fact, almost anything that catches your eye because of its sparkle or richness.

If you cannot find the exact color and material you want, dye it, and if need be, decorate it with all-over applications of cheap beads, binding tape, *soutache* braid, ribbon, contrasting appliqués, rickrack braid, single spangles, small artificial flowers, embroidery, splattered color, air-brushing, stenciling, block printing, pen and ink, or brushed water color. White, cream, or gray material is good to dye; the last will give you subdued tones.

Often you can save money by imitating with paint some expensive material you have seen. If gold paint on burlap gives the same effect as a ten dollar fabric, you should feel a glow of satisfaction at your cleverness and economy. You could, for instance, buy mesh evening bags for chain mail, but a copper or silver colored pot cleaner, unraveled and placed over rust or white satin may give as good an effect. Metal cloth and trimming usually tarnish with age, so don't lay in too large a stock. You can sometimes revitalize them by brushing the surface with gold or aluminum paint.

COSTUME CONSTRUCTION

Before constructing the costumes, arrange the fabrics you have selected on the stage, establish the general background color you plan to use for the scenery, and try out the lights for each scene. A little time spent before you paint the scenery or make the costumes may save you a lot of changes when all is complete.

Most puppet costuming is a combination of draping, gluing, pattern cutting, and sewing. Some designers do most of the costuming right on the puppet—cutting, fitting and fastening as they go. For some types of puppet, such as the hand-and-rod, pattern-cut costumes which are made complete and removable are more practicable. Whatever method you use, be sure the costume does not impede the puppet's movements, because no puppet which cannot be freely moved is a good puppet, no matter how handsome its dress. Close fitting can be done if managed properly, but in general ample room must be allowed, especially for the shoulder, elbow, and knee joints. The puppets should always move as easily after they are costumed as before.

To cut patterns, take a sheet of heavy tissue paper, pin it on the puppet and cut to shape with small scissors. Use as few pieces as are needed to make the garment fit well, allow for free movement, and look well made. Plan the pattern so the costume will not be skimpy. Ten-cent store patterns of basic garments such as skirts, coats, dresses, and so on, are helpful in giving you general patterns, but puppet anatomy does not always follow that of human beings, and modifications may have to be made. For period costumes, patterns are usually shown in books on stage costuming (see p. 265).

If you are inexperienced in sewing, reference to a good manual on the subject is useful, but you can simplify a great deal. To cut out your costume, pin the pattern to the material and cut with a ¼″ allowance for seams. Pinking shears can be used advantageously except on velvet or cheap rayon materials. Baste the pieces together and fit them on the puppet. Tucks can be used to take up slack and make a good fit, unless your pattern is badly cut. Machine sewing is best—it holds up under stress and strain. Avoid French seams and bulky hems; knitted fabrics should be left unhemmed. For well-pressed pants, run a line of fine stitching 1/16″ from the edge of the crease. For removable costumes, hooks and eyes or snap fasteners are more practicable than buttons and button holes.

Fur should be sewed by hand, because a machine fastens down too many hairs and is likely to tear the skin. Bias tape or thin ribbon should be stitched on both edges to keep it from doubling over. Buttons on marionettes are certain string catchers; they can be painted on, or small pieces of leather or felt can be punched out with a paper punch and sewed on with a single cross-stitch. Individual sequins can be fastened the same way, or secured with a drop of glue. Real buttons can be used if the space between the button and the cloth is filled up by winding the back of the button after it is sewed on with thread dipped in glue. As suggested before, puppet costuming often demands simplifications and short cuts. Work for good line and general effect; make the costume sufficiently sturdy to stand up under whatever use it will receive, but don't waste time imitating careful dressmaking methods unless it is necessary.

ACCESSORIES

In planning accessories for puppet costumes, good taste must always be exercised in striking a balance between theatrical effectiveness and harmony of all parts of the show. You can't load the serving maid who has a minor part with all sorts of glitter, and maintain any sort of unity. Neither can you overdo the size and richness of the king's crown; it may become ludicrous instead of royal.

For jewelry, bathtub chains and ten-cent store products are usually adequate. Often you will have to design the jewels from glass beads, pearls, chains, and other bits of finery, in order to get the right size and shape. Rhinestone banding is excellent for diamond bracelets, chokers, shoulder straps, and neckline accentuation, especially if used on plain cloth.

Artificial or special types of fur are best for puppets, because the usual coat or dress fur is too bulky. Marabou trim, ostrich boa trim, caracul cloth, silk or rayon plush, animal cloth printed to resemble leopard, tiger, frog, or zebra hide are all good fur substitutes. In making a fur coat, no special attempt should be made to duplicate any type of fur in detail. A length of black cony trim can give the effect of a sealskin collar. Thin marabou hand-sewed closely together on a matching color cloth foundation gives the effect of fox. If a thin piece of rabbit fur with short hair can be obtained, analine dyes or brown ink can make a good imitation mink. Fur and plush should be cut on the back with a razor blade so as not to shear it while cutting.

Hats can be handled in several ways. Some types can be cast or carved with the head: small women's hats, halos, tiaras, turbans, derbys, fezzes, skullcaps, miters, berettas, and the crowns for silk hats, toppers, and straw hats. Any large Oriental or exotic head decoration, especially those which require feathers, should be attached to a block cast or carved on the head as a foundation. This is better than using a wire frame which must be tacked to the head. Straw hats can be made with fine raffia and reed, just like a basket. Felt hats can be blocked, or you can sometimes buy them the right size. Rubber balls are useful for such things as the basis of knightly helmets or academic mortarboards; visors and other details can easily be added. Hats which are to be removed and replaced by the puppet must be simple so as not to get stuck in the strings (if you are using marionettes). If too large, hats may make your puppet look grotesque, especially if it has a somewhat large head anyway.

Net gloves and stockings can be made either of fine elastic mesh or heavy cotton net. A simpler method is to paint the leg black and then to spatter or fleck it with flesh-colored paint. Patterned tights, like those of Harlequin or a medieval jester, can be painted on wooden legs; they look very trim.

Shoes can be carved or cast. Boots are made by gluing leather or oilcloth tops over wooden bases. Notice the different shapes—the western cowboy's high-heeled, spurred boots are quite unlike those worn by hunters and trappers. A leather sole tacked to a wood or cast shoe gives a realistic projecting welt.

Belts should not be so conspicuous as to cut your puppet in the middle, thereby emphasizing his large head or other unhuman proportions. If used to set off costume or body lines, they can give to a puppet a tailored look, especially if they match the costume.

Capes should drape well and be quite full, but must not interfere with manipulation. They can be cut as a full circle of material, or from a straight piece gathered into a stand-up collar. They can be lined with slightly contrasting material for dramatic effect. Collars stand up better if lined with crinoline or buckram. Avoid trimming around the bottom of a long cape, and leave it un-hemmed if the material is knitted.

The bustle may be just a bow, or a quarter sphere of wire (*Plate 29, H*). Historical pictures should be consulted for the size of the bustle and method of draping it. Wind sharp edges of the wire frame with adhesive tape.

Some characters need a lace collar, stiffly starched, or a ruff. To make the latter, decide how wide it should be—perhaps 1″ for a 22″ puppet. Cut a strip of organdy about 4″ long and twice the width the ruff is to be, plus ½″ for the hem. Fold in the middle and stitch in a piece of string (*Plate 29, J*). The thickness of the ruff (from about ⅝″ to 1″) should be in proportion to its width. The size varies according to the period of history, the country, and the sex of the wearer, so consult your costume books. Gather into loops as illustrated in *diagram* (1), with the corded edge to the front. Two threads run along the back edge of the ruff are used to gather it to neck size; it is then sewed to a band (2).

Gloves, collars, cuffs, and bosoms for dress shirts can be carved or cast as part of the puppet body. This saves sewing, and the accessories can be easily repainted, thus insuring their freshness.

A farthingale (*Plate 29, G*) is made of moderately stiff wire padded so as not to show sharp edges. The style varies in different periods, so check up before you design yours. Intricate front and back draping can be done, because the frame is treated like a draping platform or box.

The hoop skirt has a series of concentric wire rings fastened together with cloth tape (*Plate 29, F*). There should be enough rings to hold out the material and make a smooth cone shape. Frothy net, tulle, lace or all-over ruffles are best; be careful not to have the material too closely draped on the frame.

Trains musn't get in the way, nor should they attract attention in the wrong places. Don't let them catch on stage props, and don't make them so long the puppet becomes hopelessly entangled. A pleasing length is the "one-third train"—one third of the front length of the skirt extending beyond the heels.

Veils can be effective accessories because they are so feminine. Fine China silk (best bought in white and then dyed) when tinted a pale pink, blue or violet, fluttering about a fairy heroine's head conveys an idea of magic and fairyland. Veils used on historical costumes should be based upon costume pictures of the period.

CHAPTER V

PUPPET STAGES

TYPES OF STAGES

Methods of constructing puppet stages are almost as varied as the making of puppets, and are as likely to reflect the individuality of their designer. Some are crude improvisations, others are as complete as stages for living actors, even though built on a smaller scale. You can make your stage for use with only one type of puppet, or it can be designed for all types. It can have a proscenium, or it can be an open stage which can be seen from at least three sides. The designs included here have been chosen as typical of the principal kinds of stages. Everyone has to make his own plans to suit his theatre, the type of puppets he wants to use, and the kinds of shows he wants to produce.

In general, there are two main classifications: string-puppet stages and those used for the various kinds of puppets worked from below. If you plan to do string-puppets exclusively, there is not much point in making your stage adaptable for hand-puppets and shadows. If your theatre is to be an experimental one, or used by different groups of people with varied interests, a flexible stage which can be used for all puppet types is desirable. Permanent stages and portable ones require different types of construction; decide which is better for you.

EXTERIOR DESIGN OF THE PUPPET STAGE

No matter how small, your show is a dramatic performance, and your stage should suggest the gay and fanciful world of the theatre. This does not mean that dignity and good taste should not prevail, but it does mean that the sight of your stage should create a feeling of expectation in the audience. In your enthusiasm to make the stage attractive, be careful not to overdo its decoration, especially if you are going to use it in daylight. Large figures or patterns painted on the stage, or draperies with too strong colors and designs, will destroy the scale of your puppets and make them appear small. The important thing about the puppet theatre is what happens on the stage. If your exterior decoration can provide additional interest between scenes, well and good, but don't force the puppets to compete with it. Varying textures, changes of color and value between the masking of the stage and the front curtain, small repeat patterns, bits of fringe, and an occasional tassel can be used to give variety and richness without detracting from the puppets. The smaller the stage the more careful you have to be to keep the puppets dominant.

The framework of the stage may be covered with cloth, painted canvas, Beaverboard, thin wood veneer or similar materials. If it is portable, the most compact method is to use draperies which can be removed from the framework. Whatever you use for masking should be opaque. It is disconcerting to see the shadows of the puppeteers on the curtain, or have the stage lights shine through. Suitable materials for masking drapery are rep, velvet, velour, velveteen. You can also use various materials to be found in the drapery departments of dry goods stores, although these usually have to be lined with lightweight black or dark colored material in order to make them lightproof. Striped awning canvas is gay for some types of stages such as hand-puppet booths. Inexpensive draperies can be made of burlap, painted to brighten it up a little.

The proscenium should be kept simple. Elaborate valences with tassels or other decorations which break the line of the stage opening should usually be avoided, although a particular play may need a modified proscenium arch. On string-puppet stages a simple valence is often useful, especially if it can be adjusted in height to mask the operators on the back bridge. In theatres with a high stage the valence can be lowered a little and vice versa.

THE FRONT CURTAIN

Because it is the center of interest, the stage curtain should be different and more eye-catching than the rest of the stage decorations. Several methods of constructing curtains are illustrated on *Plates 30, 31*. *Diagram A, Plate 30* shows a typical pull curtain, which opens in the center and pulls out of sight at the sides of the proscenium. A metal rod or lightweight traveler can be used to carry the curtain, which can either have rings sewed permanently to the cloth or hooks which slip into rings on the rod or traveler. To rig such a curtain, hang the two parts on the rod and close, making sure they meet in the center. Fasten them together temporarily. Take a length of rope long enough to reach from the bottom of your curtain on the right to screw eye (4) and back again. Fasten one end of the rope at (1), run through screw eye (2) and tie off at the second ring (3) of the left curtain, so it will overlap. Continue the cord through screw eye (4), bring it back to (5) on the right curtain and tie. Between points (3) and (5), the rope should be taut. Carry the rope through screw eye (6). The two loose ends can be knotted together or passed through a wooden bead or ball heavy enough to keep the ropes taut when the curtain is open.

In *diagram B, Plate 30* is shown a drop curtain. The material is tacked to a batten which is clamped or bolted to the stage. Each of four cords passes through a separate screw eye placed in the batten directly above the rings. Then the cords pass by twos through screw eyes (1) and (2). The wooden batten in the hem may be removed for packing, or the curtain may be rolled on it and tied to the supporting batten at the top.

Although it is less frequently used and less satisfactory, the draped curtain in *diagram C* is sometimes effective. It is made in

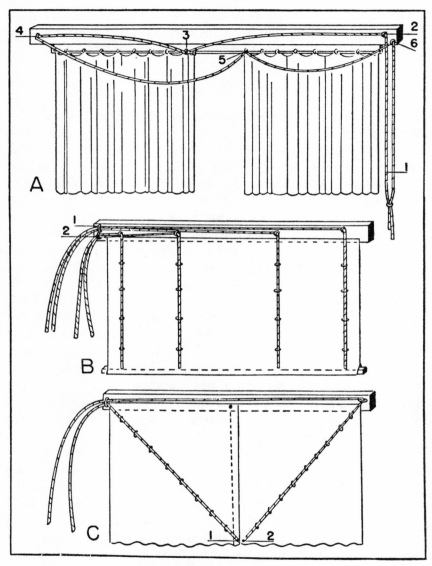

PLATE 30. STAGE CURTAINS

A. Draw
B. Drop
C. Draped

two parts which are tacked to a supporting batten with a 3″ over-lap in the center. Rings are sewed diagonally across each curtain and the cord is run as indicated. There should be weights at (1) and (2).

A roll curtain is illustrated on *Plate 31, A*. The material is tacked flat to a batten. The roller at the bottom can be made of a round wooden rod, or two lengths of 1½″ or 2″ half round. The latter is better because the material can be tacked straight to the flat side of one wooden piece, and the other piece nailed or screwed to it. A spool somewhat larger in diameter than the rod should be fastened on each end, or a disc screwed to either end of the rod to prevent the cord from coming off. To adjust the cord, roll the curtain up and tie it in place. Nail one cord securely to the right spool, wind it around five or six times, run it through screw eyes (1) and (2) and leave it dangling with plenty of footage to spare. With another cord, do the same with the left spool, being careful to nail it in the same position as the other, and wind it the same number of times and in the same direction. This cord runs through screw eye (3). Now take the two cords, hold them with equal tension, untie the curtain, and slowly let it descend. Be sure the curtain rolls onto the rod right side out; if it doesn't, you will have to reverse your original winding of the spools. Run the curtain up and down a few times to be sure it winds straight onto the rod. Tie the loose ends of the cord together through a ring which slips over a hook on the stage to hold the curtain open.

This roll curtain is particularly good for combination stages in which various sizes of proscenium are used because it can establish an opening of any desired height. Its principal disadvantage is its length; it is difficult to fold up the supporting batten and roller, which must be long enough to span the width of the proscenium opening.

If there is enough headroom above your proscenium, you can use a flat curtain which is pulled up out of sight. With this kind of curtain, a special batten to carry the overhead lights would have to be used, because the entire space directly above the

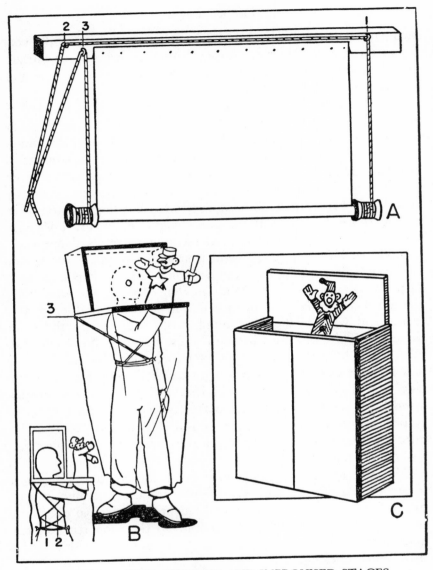

PLATE 31. ROLL CURTAIN AND IMPROVISED STAGES

A. Roll curtain. Adapted from *Be A Puppet Showman* by Remo
   Bufano, copyright 1933, by The Century Company
B. "Walking theatre"
C. Hand-puppet booth of screens

proscenium would have to be clear. With this drop you could establish various heights of proscenium opening. The curtain, made of canvas or other material, could be removed from a hinged wooden, or jointed pipe batten for packing.

The choice of material for the front curtain will depend upon the mechanism you use, the size of the proscenium opening, and the general effect you wish to create. A pull curtain such as the one on *Plate 30, A* can be made of any material which will hang properly in folds. If your masking draperies are plain, a figured material in bright colors might be used. Added richness could be gained with a handsome piece of metallic cloth, or designs appliquéd or embroidered. Various synthetic fabrics such as plastic-impregnated cloths give interesting texture.

A drop curtain which pulls up (*Plate 30, B*) should be made of a soft material which will crush as little as possible. Draped curtains would also have to be of soft material so that they will fall readily into place and drape gracefully when pulled up.

Painted canvas works very well for a roll curtain like that shown on *Plate 31, A*. To make it lightproof, the canvas should be given a coat of dark color on the back before the front is painted. Here you can be fancy-free in your design. You may represent your favorite puppet characters, your company insignia, a whimsical landscape or what you will. Be careful not to get the paint so thick it cracks off when the curtain is rolled up. Instead of canvas, any moderately heavy material can be used so long as it doesn't have to be lined, as this would interfere with rolling, and make the curtain too bulky.

If you are touring, select fabrics which will stand wear and tear—particularly folding and packing in a trunk.

Be sure to use durable cord for your curtain. A light or medium weight one can be rigged with the woven cord commonly used for Venetian blinds. Green sea-island cotton or mason's line are also good. For heavy curtains, you may need to use something heavier, such as woven sash cord. Avoid any kind of rope which will stretch, because the adjustments will not remain accurate.

IMPROVISED STAGES

Puppets have been worked on table tops, dangled over the backs of large armchairs, shown on illuminated screens hung between doorways, and manipulated on small stages set up on hospital beds. The ingenious puppet showman is never at a loss when it comes to exhibiting his actors.

The "Walking" Theatre. On *Plate 31, B* there is illustrated a light, corrugated cardboard box resting on the puppeteer's shoulders. On this stage puppets can act as the showman moves from place to place. Four cords hold the box in place. The pair attached to the front (1) crosses over the operator's back and ties in front; those on the rear of the stage (2) cross over the chest and tie in back. If necessary, padding can be used on the box bottom to make it fit more closely to the shoulders. The puppeteer's head fits through a hole in the bottom of the box, and peepholes are cut in one side so that he can see where he is going, and also watch the puppets. A light wooden framework (3) is fixed to the box to hold the thin draperies which conceal the puppeteer. Hand-puppets are the best type to use with this kind of stage.

Stage Made from Folding Screens. Diagram C, Plate 31 shows a hand-puppet booth made of two ordinary folding screens, with a backdrop which may be a piece of drapery supported on two sticks, a sheet of Beaverboard or corrugated cardboard. Such a stage could be set in front of a wall or drawn window draperies.

Stages Improvised from Hospital Equipment. With the growing popularity of puppets in physical and mental rehabilitation, the puppeteer's ingenuity has been turned toward adapting hospital equipment to puppet stages. The designs on *Plates 32, 33, 34* were developed by Ben Yano, and put into use at Camp Luna, New Mexico.

The Traction Bed and Rolling Litter Stage. Improvised from equipment available in any hospital, this type of stage is useful in ward entertainment where string-puppets are used (*Plate 32*). It consists of two main parts, a rolling litter *A*, and a traction

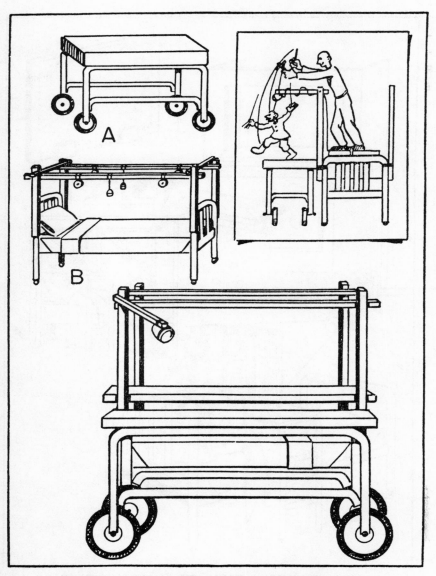

PLATE 32. MARIONETTE (STRING-PUPPET) STAGE
Improvised from hospital equipment by Ben Yano

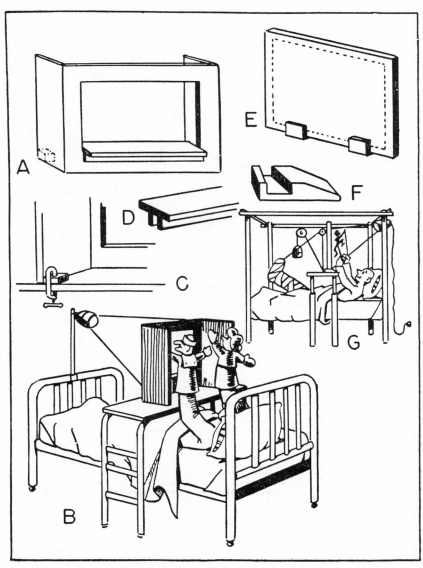

PLATE 33. SHADOW-SCREEN AND HAND-PUPPET STAGE
Improvised from hospital equipment by Ben Yano

bed *B*. The litter is placed by the bed to form the floor of the stage, while the bridge, or portion upon which the puppeteer stands, is made by fastening two sturdy planks to the foot-and head-boards with C-clamps. The bar above the bed can be used to support a backdrop. The bars at the foot or head of the bed may be un-clamped and swung forward to support a spotlight or reading lamp. Care must be taken to apply the brakes on both bed and litter during the performance. After the show, you can unclamp the equipment and wheel it into another ward.

Hand-Puppet and Shadow Stage for the Traction Patient. The traction patient need not be limited to being a member of the audience during puppet presentations in wards. By employing a simple stage (*Plate 33, A*) which is set upon an over-the-bed table *B*, he can participate in simple shows. This stage is constructed from plywood or heavy cardboard strengthened by laths and secured to the table by C-clamps *C*. To the proscenium, a small shelf or platform *D* can be fastened to hold puppet props. The suggested proscenium opening is 24″ by 40″.

A shadow screen *E* is made by covering a wooden frame with cloth or translucent paper. Two wooden braces *F* cut on a miter, slip onto the lower edge of the screen. By clamping these to the table with C-clamps the screen can be held in place. To illuminate the screen, hang a bed lamp or similar light behind and above the operator (*diagram G*).

Wheel-Chair Puppet Stage. The wheel-chair stage (*Plate 34*) permits the patient to become a traveling puppeteer, wheeling his show from ward to ward. It consists of two main pieces, a shelf-like section which clamps to the arms of the chair, and a combination shadow screen and backdrop *B*, which is clamped to the back of the chair. Upon the latter, drops of painted cloth *C* can be tacked, and turned over after each scene.

During the performance of shadow plays the operator stands behind the chair, while the patient in the chair acts as reader or master of ceremonies *D*. Two-man wheel-chair teams can be formed by clamping section *A* to the back of the first chair as

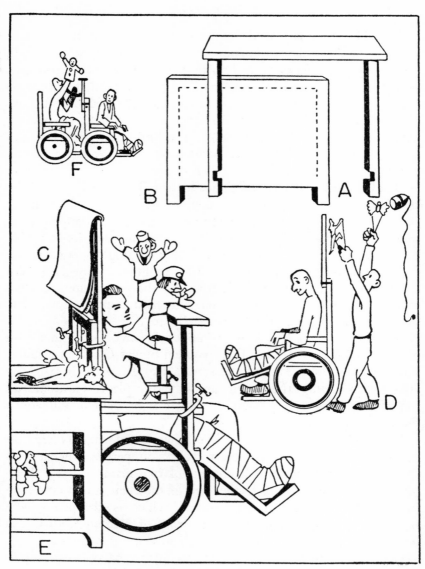

PLATE 34. WHEEL-CHAIR PUPPET STAGE
Designed by Ben Yano

shown at *F*. The personal cabinet *E* can be used to hold extra puppets or to store those not in use.

SHADOW SCREENS AND STAGES

The Shadow Screen Frame. The frame, especially if it is a large one, should be made of clear lumber which will not warp. Canvas stretchers are good, and can be purchased in a variety of sizes. Large screen frames can be made portable with half lap joints at the corners bolted together. Small frames can be made solid.

The frame may be covered with any material which is translucent enough to show up the shadow-figures, yet thick enough to diffuse the light which illuminates them, and substantial enough to be stretched tightly. Unbleached muslin; white bed sheets; white window shades; white paper oiled, dried and shellacked; tracing paper; tracing cloth; rayon taffeta and oiled silk are usable materials. Some are more durable than others. For instance, paper is all right for one or two performances but would not do for touring.

You may tack your screen permanently to the frame, but it is sometimes convenient to remove it for packing. *Detail B, Plate 35* shows a webbing (1) which has eyelets set at 3-inch intervals (2). A cord is strung through the eyelets and looped over round-headed screws inserted to within a quarter of an inch of their heads to alternate with the eyelets (3). This method enables you to stretch the screen tightly, and it is easy to unloop the cord from the screws, leaving it strung through the eyelets. Shops which specialize in covering buttons and making belts can put in the eyelets.

The size of the shadow screen depends upon the size of the puppets to be used with it; at least one and a half times the height of the figures should be allowed. It should be approximately twice as long as it is high.

A shadow screen can be used on any stage built for hand- or rod-puppets which has a proscenium. The frame should be **tilted**

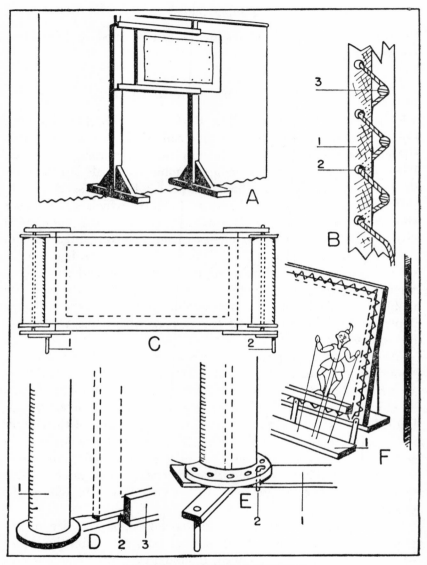

PLATE 35. SHADOW SCREENS

A. Screen and stage
B. Method of lashing screen to frame
C, D, E. Mechanism for continuous scenery
F. Detail of screen and standing ledge

slightly forward, and if the stage has a front curtain, the shadow frame should be so placed as not to interfere with its opening and shutting.

Ledge. A ledge is necessary for puppets built in the Chinese manner (*Plate 1*). After the screen is laced on, the ledge is attached with bolts (*figure F, Plate 35*). Felt or velveteen glued to the top of the ledge and projecting slightly over the side, touching the screen, makes a tight fit and keeps the figures from slipping when they are manipulated. A shelf, also felt-covered, is set some distance below the frame (1), and bolted to it. The distance of this shelf below the frame will depend upon the length of the rods you are using, because its purpose is to enable you to prop characters in place on the screen.

Scenery. If the scenery is to be painted on the screen, each scene will require a separate frame which can be slipped into place (*Plate 35, A*). It may suit your play to have the scene change before the eyes of the audience. This can be done by using rolled scenery. On either side of the screen frame, and attached to it at top and bottom, is a cylinder set on a 1″ dowel for an axis (*Plate 35, C*). The screen is made long enough to accommodate all the scenes and is rolled onto the cylinders by means of cranks (1) and (2). *Detail E* shows the base of the cylinder, the axis rod set into it, and the crank for turning. In order to keep the screen taut, the cylinders must be locked in place. The cylinder is moved until one of the holes in its base coincides with one in the supporting bar (1) then a pin (2) is dropped through. If preferred, a ratchet can be used. *Detail D* shows the cylinder (1) screwed to the base of the frame (2). A ledge (3) is fastened to the bottom edge of the frame and far enough away from it to allow the screen to move freely back of it. A similar arrangement must also be used at the top of the frame or the screen will sag, and it will be difficult to work the figures.

Scenery can be made separate from the screen, pinned to it as needed, tacked to the frame, or set into the space between the ledge and the screen (*Plate 35, F*).

Light. For illuminating a shadow screen, a single light source is best. A photographer's reflector type unit which can be clamped in place is good; it can take a 150- or 200-watt bulb. If the screen is very large, a 500-watt floodlight can be used. The unit should be placed high enough above the screen to prevent the shadows of the operators from falling on it, and far enough back to get an evenly diffused light over the entire screen.

HAND-PUPPET STAGES

Methods of Operation. Hand-puppets can be worked over the top of an upright piano, from behind a table, a large chair, or a screen, but they are much better when acting in their own theatre.

The operator can either stand or sit. Most puppet booths have the stage floor at the level of the puppeteer's head, and he holds the puppet on his upstretched arm. Sometimes the proscenium is made lower—about 4' or 4¼' from the floor, and the operator stands behind a curtain through which he can see the puppet, but which is thick enough to keep him from being seen. The puppeteer's arm is bent at the elbow instead of raised over his head. This method limits the action because the puppet sinks as the arm is bent, and the distance between the backdrop and the front of the stage can be no greater than the distance between the operator's shoulder and elbow. On small stages this is not a great disadvantage, but in medium-sized booths the freer movement of the puppets held above the head is more satisfactory. A low proscenium (about 4') can be used if the operators sit and hold the puppets above their heads. With movable stools (*Plate 45*), free movement can be obtained, but the operators may get in each other's way. This disadvantage is often balanced by the advantage of having a lower proscenium, especially if one is playing on a high stage in a theatre.

Folding Booth. A folding hand-puppet booth, designed by H. V. Tozer, is illustrated on *Plate 36, A.* The size of the stage depends upon the height of the puppeteers who are to work the

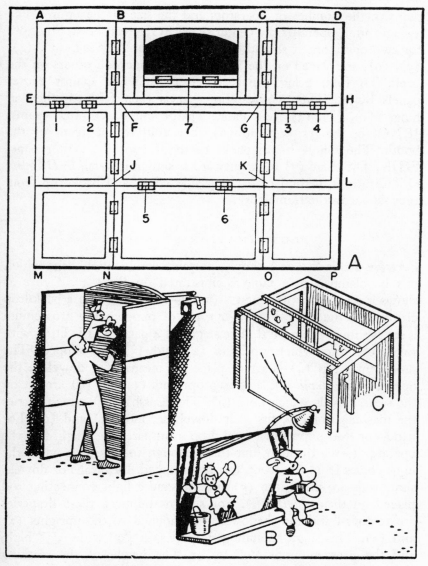

PLATE 36. FOLDING HAND-PUPPET BOOTH
Designed by H. V. Tozer

puppets, the number of operators and the size of the figures. For a single adult operator the center panel FGJK can be 54″ by 30″; for two operators, it should be wider. Hinges (1), (2), (3), (4), (5), (6), are placed on the front of the frames, all others on the back. To fold, bring panels ABIJ and CDKL against center panels BCJK. The two resulting panels then fold together on hinges (1), (2), (3), (4). Panels IJMN and KLOP fold against JKNO; on hinges (5) and (6) they fold to the front of the booth. The whole booth packs to the size of the center panel FGJK. The ledge (7) folds outward as shown in *detail B. Diagram C* illustrates a method of hanging side wings and backdrop from rods set across the framework.

COMBINATION STAGES

Portable Table Stage. A simple, portable combination stage which can be clamped to a table is illustrated on *Plate 37. Figure A* shows it set up for marionettes (string-puppets), with a backdrop clamped to the table. For other types of puppets, the proscenium is set as shown in *figure B*. The stage has 4 parts: (1) is fitted with two slots into which uprights (2) and (3) are slipped. The proscenium top (4) is set in place by means of a dowel in the uprights (see *detail C*). The two uprights (5) and (6) are set on the same dowels which hold (4). The crossbar (7) which carries the masking drapery, fits over dowels set into (5) and (6). For hand- or rod-puppets, a backdrop transparent enough for the operator to see through, but thick enough to hide him when the light comes from the front, can be arranged. By means of dowels, short rods are fitted into (5) and (6) and a light connecting rod placed on them (*detail B*). For shadow-puppets, these draperies are removed and the shadow screen hooked to the uprights (2) and (3). This stage, including draperies, is 4′9″ wide, 3′3″ high, and the proscenium is 2′9″ by 2′. The height of the masking draperies should be adjusted to hide the operators; the above dimensions are best for use with puppets worked from below.

[128]

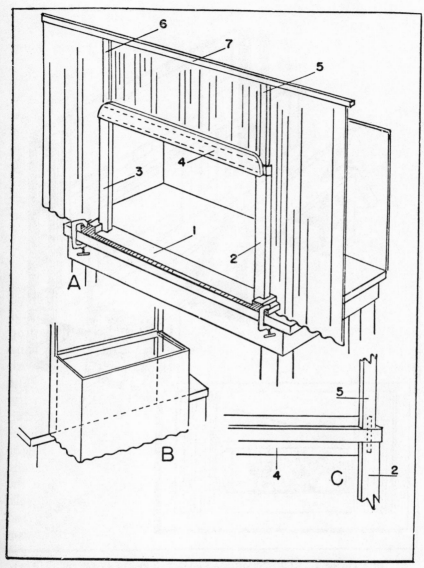

PLATE 37. SIMPLE COMBINATION PUPPET STAGE
Designed by Marjorie Batchelder

PLATE 38. LARGE COMBINATION PUPPET STAGE SETUP
FOR MARIONETTES

Designed by Gayle Michael Anderson

Puppet Stages

Large Combination Stage. On *Plates 38-44* is illustrated a portable combination stage which is large enough for professional shows, but simple and flexible enough to use for all types of puppets. When struck, it packs into sections not exceeding 4'4". It was designed by Gayle Michael Anderson, and has been used successfully in the puppet theatre at Ohio State University.

The basic elements of the stage are two folding towers (*Plate 40, A,B*); two folding frames (*Plate 41, A, B*) which consist of three parts; two folding backdrop supports (*Plate 42, A, B*); ledge (*Plate 39*); two ladders (*Plate 42*); three parallels and bridge floor (*Plates 43, 44*); stage floor (*Plate 44*); leaning rail (*Plate 38*) and various cross braces.

Several different combinations of the parts are illustrated on *Plates 38, 39*. The setup for marionettes (string-puppets) on *Plate 38* shows the towers with the front crossbars in position to form the proscenium opening; the leaning rail; the back bridge and ladder leading to it. In *diagram A, Plate 39* the front towers have been moved outward and to the sides to form light towers for an open-proscenium stage. Draperies are hung between the towers and the scenery to form masking wings on either side. The scenery support shown on *Plate 61, D* is used to support the two flats which form the background. The framework of the stage proper is composed of the folding frames illustrated on *Plate 41*. These are covered by a flat drapery hung by small brass rings sewed to the top hem which fit over screws in the framework. An open-proscenium stage is a complete unit, and can be set up anywhere, with a small screen on each side to hide backstage operations. If necessary, a cyclorama can be used back of this unit, but if care is taken in designing the background scenery, it is not necessary.

A stage with proscenium for puppets worked from below is shown on *Plate 39, B*. Towers, folding frames, and backdrop supports are set as shown. The front crossbar is here set 4' from the floor to form the stage opening. Lights can be hung on the middle crossbar, with a curtain batten just below it. If shadow-puppets are used, the screen is clamped to the front ledge and tilted forward.

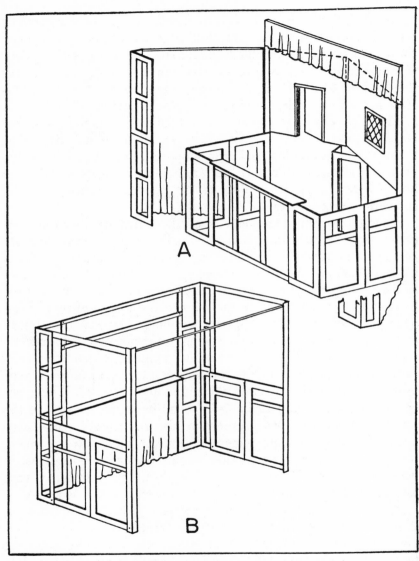

PLATE 39. LARGE COMBINATION PUPPET STAGE
A. Open-proscenium setup
B. Setup with proscenium for puppets worked from below

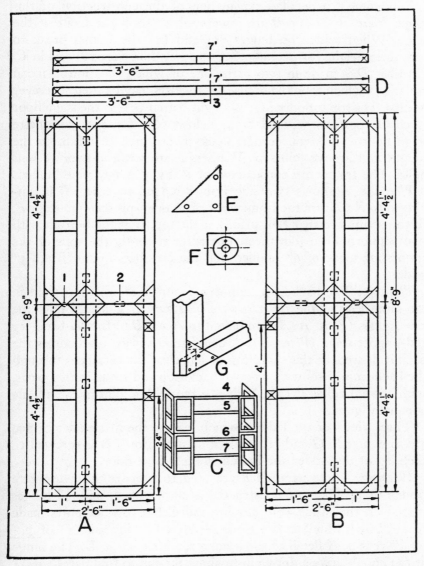

PLATE 40. DETAILS OF TOWERS FOR COMBINATION STAGE

Following is a detailed explanation of the construction of this stage: *Plate 40*. *A* and *B* are towers which form the front of the stage. When folded on hinges (1) and (2) the frames break to half their height for packing. Set up, they fold vertically as in *C*. Crossbar *D* is made in two parts, one of which slips into a metal collar (3) which is bolted in place. Crossbars may be used wherever needed: as a top support (4); as a light batten (5); as the stage floor level for puppets worked from below (6); for the marionette stage floor (7). Metal corner blocks *E* are used to reinforce the tongue and groove joints *G*. Washers *F* are screwed over all bolt holes. The frames are constructed of 1″ by 3″ white pine lumber.

Plate 41. *A* shows two side frames hinged together; *B* is pin-hinged to *A* to form the framework of an open-proscenium stage *F*. In this setup, crossbar *D* is placed at the top, *E* at the bottom with two supports *C* to join them. For extra strength, the tops of the frames are made of 6″ lumber, and the crossbars *D* and *E* are 5″ wide.

Plate 42. The backdrop supports *A* and *B* are made to fold in the same way as the front towers. *Diagram C* indicates how the side frames (*Plate 41*, *A*) are bolted to *A* and *B* to form a hand- or rod-puppet stage (*Plate 39*). A crossbar *D* can be used across the back if desired, or this space can be left clear for entrances through the backdrop. *E* shows a wooden backdrop rod made in two parts, with a metal collar at (3). A pipe batten with a joint in the middle is equally good.

Three views of the ladders which lead to the marionette bridge are shown at *F*, *G* and *H*. A piece of strap iron (4) is screwed to each leg of the ladder and bolted to the bridge floor.

Plate 43. Three parallels *B* are used to support the marionette bridge floor. They are constructed as shown at *A*, with all hinges placed on the inside. The leaning rail *C* has four supports made of 1½″ by 3″ lumber. To these are bolted a kick rail (1) of ¼″ by 4″ veneer. A detail of the leaning rail is shown at *D*. The hinge at (2) should have a draw pin to allow the rail to fold flat. *Plate 38* shows the leaning rail bolted to the supporting parallels, and the

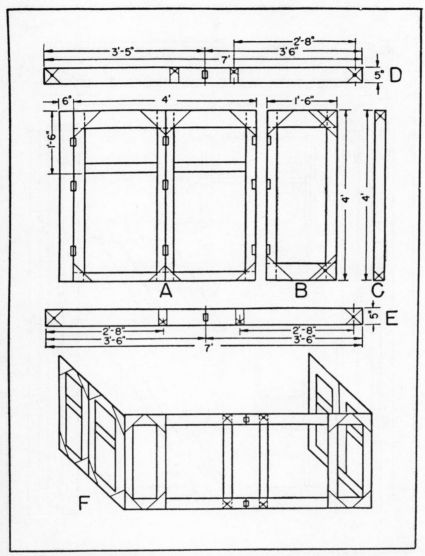

PLATE 41. DETAILS OF SIDE FRAMES FOR COMBINATION STAGE

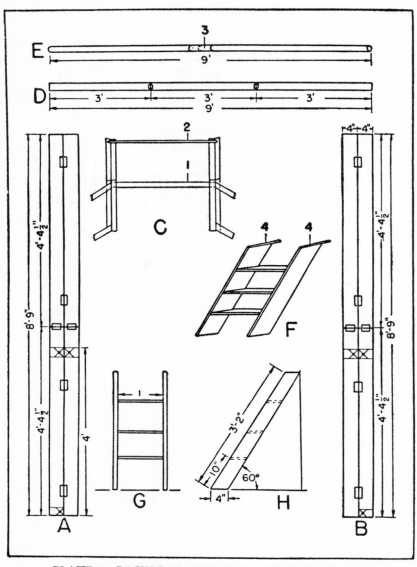

PLATE 42. BACKDROP SUPPORTS AND LADDER FOR
COMBINATION STAGE

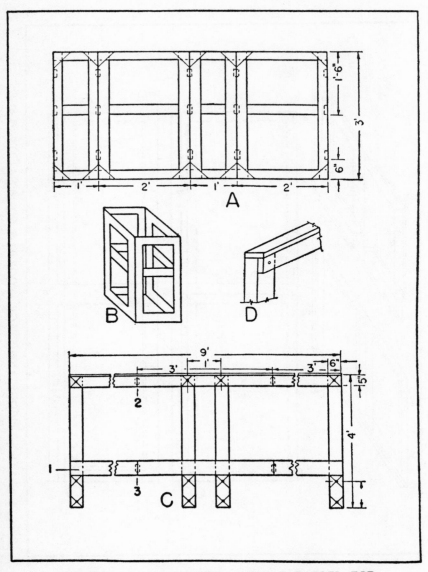

PLATE 43. LEANING RAIL ANND PARALLEL FOR
COMBINATION STAGE

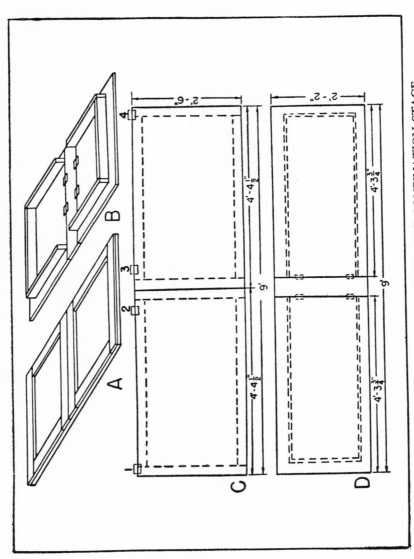

PLATE 44. BRIDGE AND STAGE FLOOR FOR COMBINATION STAGE

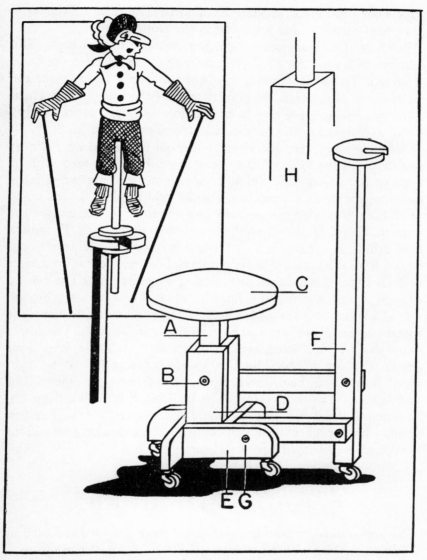

PLATE 45. MOVABLE STOOL FOR PUPPET OPERATOR

stage floor pin-hinged to the rail supports. The front of the stage floor rests on a crossbar set between the front towers.

Plate 44. The marionette stage floor is made in two parts. The framework is of 1″ by 3″ white pine with ¼″ veneer for the floor, *A* and *C*. To deaden sound, a rubber matting is tacked over the floor. *B* and *D* illustrate the construction of the bridge floor which folds up to form a packing box. The floor is of ⅝″ veneer with a 1″ by 4½″ piece in the middle. The framework is 1″ by 2¼″.

Movable Stool for Operators. The stool illustrated on *Plate 45* was designed for use with the above stage. It can be used with or without the pedestal *F*, which is principally for supporting large rod-puppets which are too heavy to be held in place on the stage, or if both hands of the operator are required to manipulate the puppet. *Detail H* shows another variation of pedestal *F*, with a hole drilled in the top in which the center rod of the puppet can be set. This is better for heavy puppets, because there is no danger of their slipping out of the slots during violent action. The central support *A* can be adjusted in height by bolt *B* which passes through one of a series of holes drilled in *A*. The seat *C* is attached to *A* be metal corner braces screwed to each of the four sides. The lower framework of the stool, which is 12″ high, is made from four pieces of 1″ by 3″ stock lumber, and four pieces (*E*) 8″ by 1⅛″ by 3″ into which the casters are set. *A* and *F* are 1 ¾″ square. The seat is about 12″ in diameter. The pedestal *F* is removed by unfastening bolts *B* and *G* which hold the wooden braces. For best results, hard rubber casters at least 1⅛″ in diameter should be used, and they should have ball bearings.

A TWO-BRIDGE PORTABLE MARIONETTE (STRING-PUPPET) STAGE

The professional two-bridge marionette stage designed and used by Rufus and Margo Rose is shown on *Plates 46-53*. When set up, it occupies an area 8′ by 17′ and is 11½′ high; when packed, it fits into a sedan delivery truck.

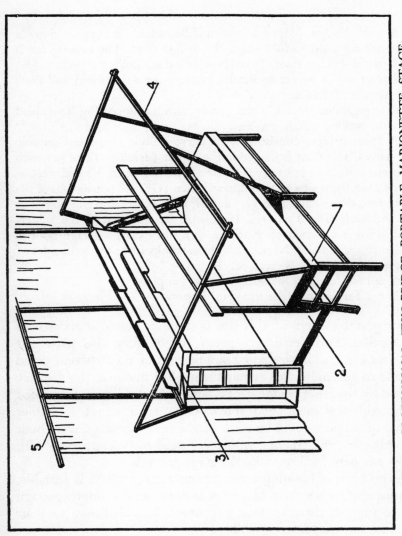

PLATE 46. PROFESSIONAL TWO-BRIDGE PORTABLE MARIONETTE STAGE: PERSPECTIVE VIEW

Designed by Rufus Rose. Drawn by Margo Rose.

1. Back bridge   2. Stage floor   3. Front bridge   4. Puppet rail   5. Masking rail

A sketch of the stage is shown on *Plate 46*. The basic elements are:

1. A back bridge, hinged in the middle, which is supported by a framework designed to fold inside the bridge floor. The leaning rail is bolted to the bridge floor. Flexible wire cables hold the unit steady. See *Plate 51* for construction details, *Plate 50* for a side view, and *Plate 52* for details of folding.

2. A stage floor, hinged in the center with its supporting leg folded inside for packing (*Plate 52, 2*).

3. A front bridge, consisting of a narrow floor supported on two trunk halves. The floor is hinged in the center (*detail 10 Plate 52*) with six stiffeners to hold it steady. Of these, two (G^1) are hinged permanently to the front side to fold upward, two (G^2) are pin-hinged at the back to fold downward, two (H^1 and H^2) are detachable and bolted to front and back (*Plates 48, 49*). Details of the trunks with the ladders folded inside are shown on *Plate 52*, (3) and (4). The stage floor is attached to the ladders. Notice that these trunks form the solid sides of the proscenium, which is recessed.

4. A rail for hanging the string-puppets in place.

5. A rail for hanging the masking drapery.

Any portable stage of this size is more or less complicated in construction. Full details are given for building this particular stage, but changes in size and simplification of construction could be made to suit individual requirements. For instance, the distance spanned by the front bridge necessitates elaborate bracing provided by the stiffeners mentioned above. On smaller stages, a simpler method of support could be used. Likewise, if the stage were built in a permanent theatre, one would not need to be concerned with the devices here used to make the stage portable.

The problem of building a string-puppet stage which is portable, yet adequate to use in a large auditorium, and strongly enough built to support three or four puppeteers is a challenge to your ingenuity and carpentering ability.

Following is a summary of the principal dimensions and the materials used for the main parts of the Rose marionette stage:

Back bridge floor, 2′ by 11′. The floor is of ⅜″ plywood, the frame of 1″ by 4″ white pine.

Back bridge supports, 1″ by 3″ white pine. Height from floor 4′.

Puppet rail, 1″ by 1″ oak.

Puppet rail supports, 1″ by 2″ white pine.

Leaning rail, 1″ by 4″ white pine.

Leaning rail supports, 1″ by 3″ oak.

Stage floor, 3′ by 11′. Frame of 1″ by 4″ white pine, floor of ⅜″ plywood.

Front bridge, 18″ wide, 11′ long, made of ½″ plywood.

Front bridge stiffeners, 1″ by 5″ white pine.

Front bridge supports, (2 halves of trunk), 2′ wide by 6′ long. The face is made of ¼″ plywood, the sides and ends of 1″ by 10″ white pine.

Front bridge ladders, 1″ by 2½″ white pine.

Masking drapery rail, 1″ by 1½″ oak. Supports, 1″ by 1″ oak.

With the exception of the details on *Plate 53*, the construction diagrams are drawn to the scale of ⅜″ equals 1′. The wooden parts of the stage are joined by draw-pin hinges, permanent hinges, and bolts with wing nuts—details of these are shown on *Plate 53*. Following is a detailed description of the construction drawings:

Plate 47. Floor Plan. The relative positions of the main parts are shown here.

Plate 48. Front Elevation. This view shows the proscenium 8′ wide and approximately 4′ high. The front masking drapery hangs low enough to conceal the strip light L. Trunk halves D form the solid sides of the stage. The front bridge stiffeners G^1 and H^1 are held together by draw-pin hinges at (6). The front masking drapery is tacked to the top of rail F, which is hinged to fold into three pieces. At M is the hinged puppet rail support which is attached to D with a spike (see *detail 5, Plate 53*) and to the stiffener G^1 by means of a bent strap iron tongue (a) inserted into hole (b). The stage floor is secured to the front bridge upright D by wing nut and hinge attachments at (7). A metal rod U locks into a hole in support J to hold it in place. Cord tie-offs (8) are used to hold the puppet-rail to its support, and the masking rail support to stiffener G^1.

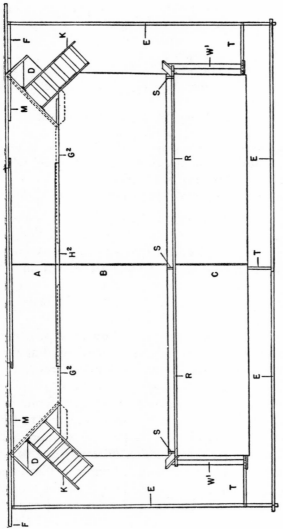

PLATE 47. FLOOR PLAN OF ROSE STAGE

A. Front bridge. B. Stage floor. C. Back bridge. D. Front bridge supports. E. Puppet rail. F. Front masking rail. G². Hinged bridge stiffeners. H². Detachable bridge stiffener. K. Ladders to front bridge. M. Front puppet rail supports. R. Leaning rail. S. Leaning rail supports. T. Side and back puppet rail supports. W¹. Ladders to back bridge.

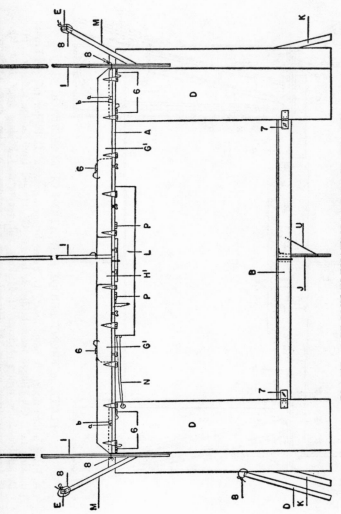

PLATE 48. FRONT ELEVATION OF ROSE STAGE

A. Front bridge floor. B. Stage floor. D. Front bridge supports. E. Puppet rail. F. Front
Masking rail. G¹. Hinged bridge stiffeners. H¹. Detachable bridge stiffener. I. Masking rail
supports. J. Folding stage floor leg. K. Ladders to front bridge. L. Border light trough.
M. Hinged puppet rail supports. N. Light cord. O. Switchboard. P. Hinged attachment
for light trough. U. Rod brace. (6) Draw pin hinges. (7) Wing nut hinge attachments.
(8) Cord tie-off. (a) Strap iron tongue fitted in hole (b).

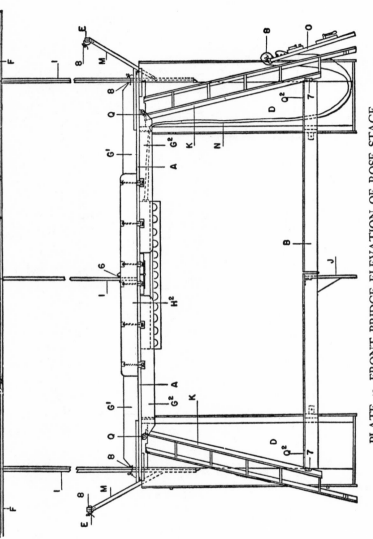

PLATE 49. FRONT BRIDGE ELEVATION OF ROSE STAGE

A. Front bridge floor. B. Stage floor. D. Front bridge supports. E. Puppet rail. F. Front masking rail. G¹. Hinged front bridge stiffeners. G². Hinged front bridge stiffeners. H². Detachable front bridge stiffener. I. Masking rail supports. J. Folding stage floor leg. K. Ladders to front bridge. M. Hinged puppet rail supports. N. Light cord. O. Switch-

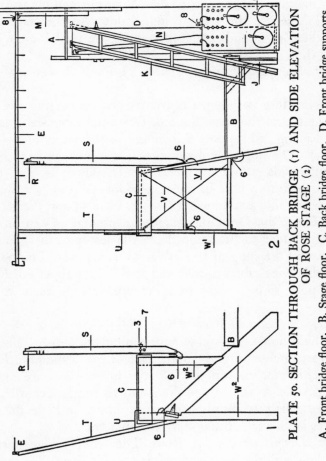

PLATE 50. SECTION THROUGH BACK BRIDGE (1) AND SIDE ELEVATION
OF ROSE STAGE (2)

A. Front bridge floor. B. Stage floor. C. Back bridge floor. D. Front bridge supports.
E. Puppet rail. F. Masking rail. I. Masking rail support. J. Folding stage floor leg.
K. Ladder to front bridge. M. Folding puppet rail support. N. Light cord. O.
Switchboard. R. Leaning rail. S. Leaning rail support. T. Puppet rail support. U.
Metal rod braces. V. Adjustable wire cross braces. W[1]. Back bridge legs and ladders.
W[2]. Back bridge center legs. (3) Bolt holding leaning rail support to bridge. (6)
Draw pin hinges. (7) Holes for wire cross brace attachment. (8) Cord tie-off.

Plate 49. Elevation of Front Bridge. This view shows the stage floor and front bridge from the back. At H^2 is shown the detachable stiffener bolted into slots cut in the front bridge floor. The two stiffeners at G^2 hinge downward. A draw-pin hinge (6) holds the center masking rail support to H^2. Wing nut and hinge attachments at (7) secure the front bridge ladders to the stage floor. Double pulleys at Q and single ones at Q^2 are used for the front curtain cord.

Plate 50. Section Through Center of Back Bridge and Side Elevation.

1. *Section.* Here is shown the framework supporting the back bridge floor C and the stage floor B. Draw-pin hinges are used at (6). The leaning rail support S is bolted to the stage floor (*detail 3, Plate 53*). The puppet rail support T is spiked into the bridge support and made steady by metal rod U, which is bent at the free end to fit into a hole in the stage floor. At (7) is a hole for a flexible wire cable attachment (*detail 8, Plate 53* and *Plate 51*).

2. *Side Elevation.* Draw-pin hinges are used at (6) to hold the back bridge ladder to the stage floor; the leaning rail support to the ladder, and the rung of the ladder to its support. The position of the flexible wire cables is indicated at V. The puppet rail E rests on its support T by means of spike attachments secured with cords (8).

Plate 51. Elevation of Back Bridge. This view shows the cross bracing which holds the bridge and leaning rail steady. The two top cables are anchored on the under side of the leaning rail R, and to the center leaning rail support. The two lower cables are attached to the underside of the bridge floor and to the ladder W^1. The short braces which steady the ladders are shown on *Plate 50, 2*. All these cables are made adjustable by turnbuckles.

Plate 52. Details of Folding Parts. The front bridge uprights, the stage floor, and the back bridge form packing cases for scenery, puppets, properties, and lights.

1. The back bridge is shown with ladders and legs taken apart by removing pins from hinges and loosening turnbuckles on cables.

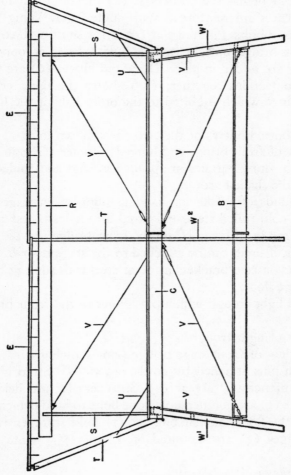

PLATE 51. BACK BRIDGE ELEVATION OF ROSE STAGE

B. Stage floor. C. Back bridge floor. E. Puppet rail. R. Leaning rail. S. Leaning rail supports. T. Puppet rail supports. U. Metal rod braces. V. Adjustable wire cross braces, W¹. Back bridge legs and ladder. W². Back bridge center leg.

The legs are tied in place by cords permanently attached to the bridge floor for this purpose. Angle irons are used at the corners for reinforcement. The box is closed by pin hinges (6) at the ends.

2. The stage floor has the corners at (*b*) cut off to fit in the truck; other corners are reinforced with angle irons. Wing nuts (*a*) are replaced on bolts. Pin hinge at (6) is for shutting box.

3. The front bridge uprights are laid with bases at opposite ends and ladders are folded in place. Draw-pin hinges (6) are used to lock the two sections together; (12) shows the open center section of the hinge which is bolted to the other half of the hinge at (13).

4. Top and bottom views of the two parts shown in 3.

5. Top view of front bridge and hinged stiffener (G^1 and G^2) folded. The front draw curtains are packed in bags and folded in, as indicated by the shaded area.

6. Various kinds of hooks for hanging puppets on stage can be made of ⅜" cold rolled steel, and fitted into holes bored along the leaning rail and in stiffener H^2 on the front bridge.

7. Footlights, if used, can be attached to the stage floor *B*. The light trough rests on two brackets made of steel rods sunk in holes bored in the stage floor.

8. Overhead light trough which pin hinges to the front bridge floor.

9. End view of light trough.

10. Bottom view of front stage bridge floor showing hardware. Pin hinges, with pins attached by cords, are at (6). Strap hinges for attaching stiffeners G^1 are at (*c*). Stiffeners G^2 are held by hinges at (*d*). At (*e*) are countersunk stove bolts to hold detachable stiffener H^1 to the floor. Similar bolts at (*f*) hold stiffener H^2 in place. Strap hinges (*g*) are mounted on 1" by 1½" white pine blocks.

Plate 53. Details of Attachments.

1. Leaning rail and backdrop assembly. *R* is the leaning rail, *S* its support. Backdrop battens of ⅜" by 1½" pine are shown at (*a*). Round rods tacked at the bottom of the drops are at (*b*).

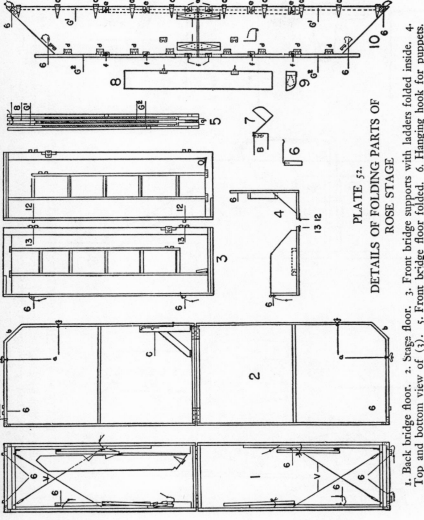

PLATE 52.

DETAILS OF FOLDING PARTS OF
ROSE STAGE

1. Back bridge floor. 2. Stage floor. 3. Front bridge supports with ladders folded inside. 4.
Top and bottom view of (3). 5. Front bridge floor folded. 6. Hanging hook for puppets.
7. Footlight trough in metal bracket. 8. Border light trough. 9. End view of (8). 10. Under
side of front bridge floor.

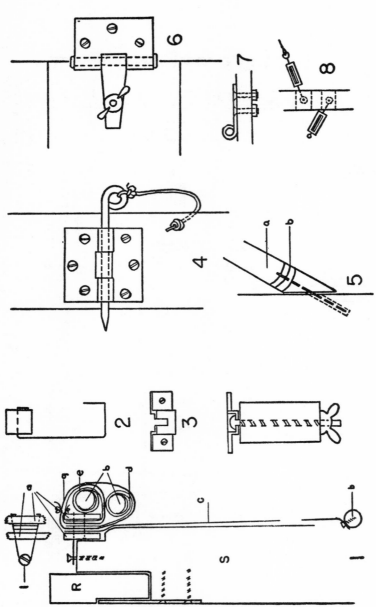

PLATE 53. DETAILS OF ATTACHMENTS FOR ROSE STAGE

1. Leaning rail and backdrop assembly. 2. Hook for hanging puppets. 3. Wing nut and bolt attachment. 4. Draw pin hinge. 5. Spike attachment. 6. Wing nut and hinge. 7. Hinges attached with bolts. 8. Flexible wire cable attachment.

The drop for the first scene is shown in place on the stage (*c*). The second and third drops (*d*) and (*e*) are rolled and tied with cords (*g*) which are tacked to the battens. The whole set of drops is fastened together by a wire run through them, and hooked over a screw (*h*) in the rail as shown in *detail* (*i*). Three such attachments are used.

2. The hooks for the puppet rail are made from heavy coat hanger wire and fastened into the rail at 6″ intervals.

3. Wing nut and bolt attachment of leaning rail supports to back bridge. Bent strap iron pieces with a slot for the bolt head are screwed to the bridge.

4. Draw-pin hinge. Wherever this attachment is used, the pin is anchored by a strong cord.

5. Spike attachment. A spike is driven permanently into (*a*) and a wire (*b*) wrapped around it to prevent splitting. This attachment is used to hold in place the center masking drapery rail support I, the puppet rail supports *M* and *T*, and the puppet rail *E*.

6. Wing nut and hinge attachment.

7. Hinges bolted to framework with the bolts headed over nuts.

8. Attachment for flexible wire cables. One end of the turnbuckle is bolted into a hole bored through the framework.

CHAPTER VI

SCENERY, LIGHTING, PROPERTIES AND SPECIAL EFFECTS

SCENERY

Purpose. Martin Stevens summarizes the purpose of the stage setting when he says: "Scenery should establish the mood and locale of the scene and then get out of the way. If it is so brilliant or so figured or so near the color of the puppets' faces that you can't see the faces—out! If it is so beautiful that after the performance the audience talks about it rather than the show—out! Scenery isn't an exhibit of one person's ability to paint, but an aid to the presentation of an idea."[1] The puppet and its mode of construction limit it to certain typical gestures; likewise the setting should stress only the typical features of the scene. The size and type of puppets used will also influence the scenery—nimble marionettes or very large puppets might have a more detailed background than tiny figures or primitive, crude hand-puppets. In general, puppets can do with far less scenery than the human actor, but what there is must be right in design, color, and scale.

Planning. In planning the set, Stevens suggests making "lots of thumbnail sketches, so you can see how the actors will fit. Plan your lighting as part of your design—its source, its color, and where it's going to hit. Look through the *Encyclopedia Britannica* and *Theatre Arts* to see how the regulars get feeling into their designs. Determine the mood of the scene, and let your pencil hunt for lines and movements that will express that mood. Keep the sketch small; it will force you to make your masses big and to leave out detail."[2]

If you like to work plastically, try juggling small blocks of wood of various sizes and shapes until you get the feeling of the principal masses. Folded cardboard or heavy paper can be used to represent flats, columns, steps, and other units. Consult a book on stage scenery construction (see pp. 266-7) if you are unfamiliar with stock scenic equipment. But don't take it too seriously. On the puppet stage there are short cuts to construction and many possibilities of doing things which you cannot do on the large stage. For example, green velvet laid over small sofa cushions makes verdant hills; rougher terrain can be done the same way by using various kinds of material placed over irregular objects. Use imagination—leave out everything you can, because the puppets will look better on an uncluttered stage.

Plastic vs. Painted Scenery. Puppeteers are divided on the question of painted versus plastic scenery. Painted backdrops with a few set properties are usually more compact to transport. Because the puppet is a three-dimensional figure, there is a closer unity if the setting also is plastic. It is generally harder to make a good-looking painted background than to use a plain one and several pieces of plastic scenery. Great care must be exercised not to make the painting too heavy, too intense, or too spotty. As you experiment with your sketches or model, the best way to construct the setting can be determined. There may be an unobtrusive painted backdrop combined with plastic units. Or you may want a plain sky drop combined with a unit set similar to that illustrated on *Plate 54.* A little experimenting with these screens, columns, steps, and platforms will show how they can be juggled to suggest gardens, terraces, prisons, or throne rooms.

Construction. When you are sure of your design, plan your construction. Scenery should be durable enough to withstand the handling which it will receive. If used only for one performance, you don't need to build it to last a century; if you are going to tour or even move the stage several times, it should be solidly built. At the same time, plan it to be portable and compact so it won't take a whole army to move your puppet show around. Be careful not to build projections which will interfere with the puppet's movements, especially if you are using string-puppets. Take time to

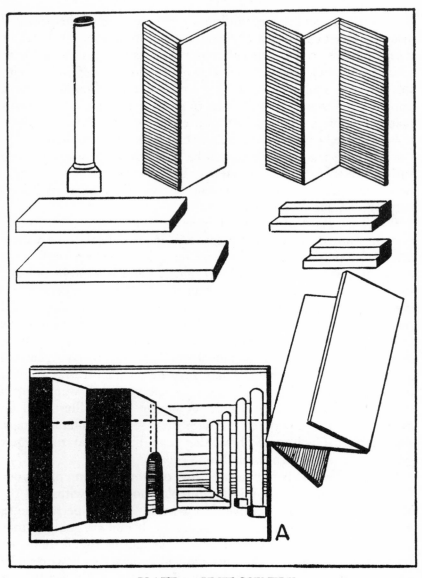

PLATE 54. UNIT SCENERY
By Jero Magon

smooth edges and surfaces so the puppets will not catch their costumes.

Methods of construction will vary to some extent according to the type of puppet you are using. For instance, if the actors are marionettes and they must enter through doors or gates, there must be a gap for the strings to pass through. If the top of the entrance is out of sight, well and good; if not, the door frame can be made in two parts, one of which is set slightly behind the other (*Plate 54, A*). Puppets worked from below have no such difficulties and can dash in and out of doors quite easily.

If the stage is large, some of the scenery may be built in the manner of regular stage scenery—flats, ground rows, set pieces, but on a smaller scale. Books on stage scenery construction will tell you how (see pp. 266-7). However, it is more likely that lighter weight materials will be adequate. Heavy cardboard, corrugated cardboard boxes from dry goods stores, Beaverboard, pressed wood, and three-ply veneer board are usable. Often they need only to be reinforced with a light wooden frame. Imagination in the use of different materials to produce varied textures helps the distinctiveness of the setting. Especially with plastic scenery, one can use wallpaper, wood grain, oilcloth, Craftex, metal, sponge, plastics, corrugated board, stucco, fabrics, tile, sand, straw, oilskin, bamboo, and many other textures.

On the large stage, many irregular forms are built of cloth on a foundation of chicken wire. This (or wire screening) can be used for puppet scenery, with paper substituted for the cloth covering if the piece is not too large. Heavy brown wrapping paper is laid over the wire frame. Use as many layers as are necessary to make a good strong form. Wallpaper or flour paste are satisfactory for binding the pieces together. Carefully modeled forms can be built on the wire framework by using crumpled tissue or toilet paper dipped in paste. Rough or smooth textures can be obtained; for the latter, several layers of brown paper or paper toweling can be used on top of the rough paper. The large cardboard cylinders (obtainable from dry goods stores) upon which cloth is wound

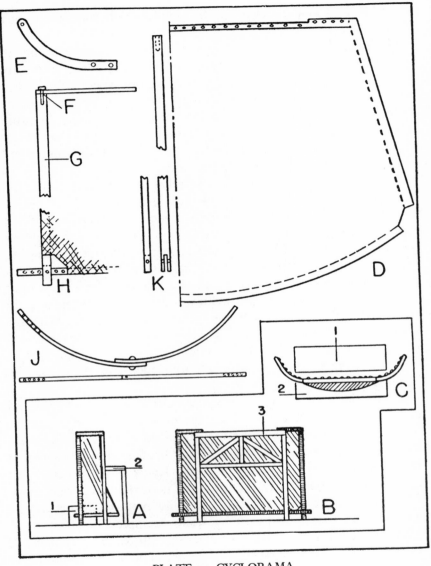

PLATE 55. CYCLORAMA
By William Duncan

are excellent for tree trunks and columns. Corrugated cardboard, which comes in various colors, makes good fluted columns.

Flameproofing. In some places fire regulations make it necessary to flameproof your scenery. Wooden frames should be sprayed before they are covered; finished pieces can be sprayed again, with a mixture of one pound borax, one pound sal ammoniac dissolved in three quarts of water. For delicate fabrics a solution of ten ounces borax, eight ounces boracic acid in one gallon of water will serve. Flameproofing dyed or painted fabrics may cause them to change color, so experiment before you expend hours of effort on a paint job. It is better to use ready-flameproofed fabrics if you can afford them (see p. 283 for places where they may be purchased).

Cycloramas. Some kind of a sky drop is useful to give depth to the stage. It may be a flat blue backdrop hung on battens. For a small stage, a curved cyclorama can be made of Beaverboard which comes in 4′ widths, and in lengths up to 12′. It is somewhat bulky, but is all right for a permanent stage. For a portable string-puppet stage, a cyclorama such as the one designed by William Duncan and illustrated on *Plate 55* is easy to construct and assemble. The same basic principles could be used for a hand- or rod-puppet stage cyc, but the supports would be somewhat different, owing to the lack of a bridge.

The Duncan cyclorama consists of muslin hung by grommets from roundheaded screws set in the leaning rail and stretched tightly with wooden side poles and a curved piece of strap iron at the bottom. The side, back, and top views of the cyc in place on the stage are shown at *A, B* and *C, Plate 55*. The stage floor is at (1), the bridge at (2). *Diagram D* shows one half of the muslin, with ⅜″ grommets set in webbing at the top, and hems for the side pole and strap iron. A ¾″ piece of plywood at *E* is cut to the proper arc and bolted to each end of the rail as at *B* (3). The screws for holding the muslin are also set in these curved brackets. Joint *F* is a ¼″ by 3″ bolt dropped through the bracket into *G*, which is a wooden curtain pole 1½″ in diameter. The strap iron *J* is ⅛″

by ¾″ bent to the proper arc and bolted in the center. ¼″ holes are drilled 1″ apart at the ends for bolting the side pole G (*detail H*). K shows a ¼″ slot 6″ long cut in the side pole to fit over the strap iron, with the bolt hole 4″ from the floor.

To construct the cyclorama, cut the webbing to the right length, insert the grommets and hang on the roundheaded screws. Cut and shape the strap iron and lay it in position on the floor. Cut the curtain poles to length, drill, slot, and stand in the proper position in relation to the strap iron. Make the brackets and fasten them to the rail so that the poles are held vertically. Use a large nail to fasten the strap iron to the poles and raise the center of the strap iron temporarily so that the whole iron is parallel to the floor. Now, pin the muslin to the webbing and around the poles and strap iron, stretching it until it is taut and free of wrinkles. Mark the hems and sew them in.

To assemble, hang the cyclorama by the webbing. Drop the poles through the side hems and fasten to the brackets. Slide the strap iron through the bottom hem and fasten to the poles. If the muslin is not tight and smooth when first assembled, dampen it *slightly* and it will shrink tight.

It will be noticed that this cyclorama curves back under the bridge, leaving space between the stage floor and the cyc for the installation of lights. This cyc could be adapted for use with the Rose marionette stage illustrated on *Plates 46-53* by constructing the bridge and stage floor units separately, and by using a different center support for the bridge.

Gauze Drops. Theatrical gauze can be purchased in various colors, and it is useful for some effects, such as underwater scenes, mists, and transformations. On the marionette stage, drops can be hung just back of the proscenium, or a few inches in front of the backdrop. In other positions they might interfere with the puppets' strings, unless you have a double bridge. For other types of puppets, gauze drops may be placed anywhere. Lighted from the front, gauze is opaque if care is taken not to let a strong light shine directly on the drop. For transformations, a scene is painted on

PLATE 56. REVOLVING STAGE
By Jero Magon

the front of the gauze. When the light is removed and thrown on the scenery back of the drop, the painted scene disappears.

Changing Scenery. In the puppet theatre, waits between scenes should be cut down even more drastically than in the large theatre. Sometimes scene changes are very simple, and involve only a property or two. For more elaborate productions, Jero Magon recommends these three methods:

1. The Revolving Stage. A circular turntable (*Plate 56*) mounted on casters, may either be hand propelled or motor driven. Each setting should be mounted on a semicircular Beaverboard base. While the scene is being played, the next succeeding unit is slipped on the turntable backstage, ready to be revolved into view without a moment's delay.

2. The Sliding Wagon Stage. This requires adequate wing space at either side of the proscenium opening (*Plate 57*). It is advisable to have two platforms, each corresponding to the size of the stage floor, mounted on casters or domes of silence. Setting and prop- erties for each scene are prepared on individual Beaverboard bases. When one scene is concluded, the setting is slid off to the wings and the next set rolled on from the opposite side. The first wagon is then unloaded and the third scene is set.

3. Reversible Scenery. This type can be used to advantage with a semipermanent architectural arrangement of posts, screens or other abstract elements (*Plate 58*). The painted fill-in between the two posts may be a flat with a representation on either side. Just turn it around, lock it in place and you have a new background. If used on a marionette stage, the flat may be pulled upward, turned and slipped back into the grooves (*Plate 58, A*). On a hand- or rod-puppet stage, it would be simpler to use a button lock as shown in detail *B*. To remove, turn the button, lift the flat straight down, reverse and replace.

Other methods of changing scenery are:

The Large Three-Dimensional Setting. A set large enough to contain all the necessary playing areas is built in a single architec- tural unit. During a brief blackout, there is a change of light, a

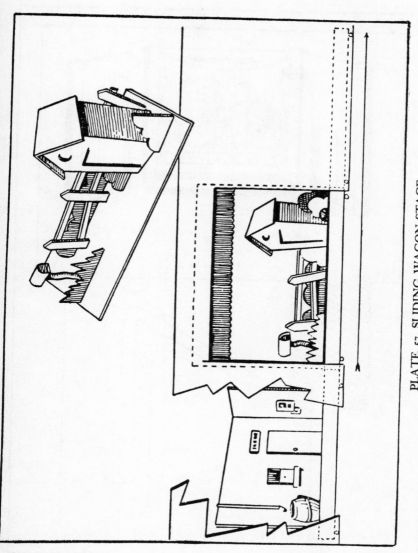

PLATE 57. SLIDING WAGON STAGE

By Jero Magon

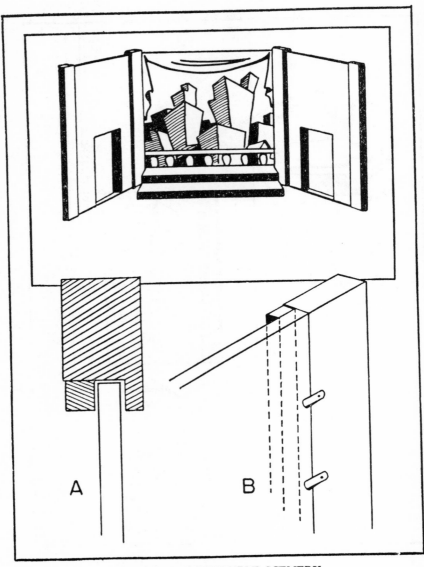

PLATE 58. REVERSIBLE SCENERY
By Jero Magon

shifted property or two, and a new scene in another part of the set is ready for use. This type of stage is particularly good for hand- or rod-puppets, because it is relatively simple to enclose large areas with simple flats, arches, stairways, and doors. You don't have to worry about supporting the puppeteers, because they work on the floor, either standing, or sitting on movable stools. It is not neces- sary to have a proscenium; in fact, the most effective settings of this type are built on open-proscenium stages (*Plate 39*).

Changing Backdrops. If several backdrops are to be used during the play, they can all be tacked to a wooden batten, with scene one on the bottom. The others are rolled, each one separately, and secured by a piece of string tacked under the curtain and looped over a roundheaded screw in the batten. Each drop should be weighted by a light rod in the bottom hem. When the new scene is needed, all you do is unhook the strings holding the drop and let it fall into place. This method is particularly useful on the mario- nette stage (*Plate 53, 1*).

On *Plate 59, A, B* is shown a simple method of hanging scenery in a hand-puppet booth. The valence (1) is cloth, with a hem large enough to admit a rod which is slipped over large hooks screwed into the frame of the booth. Trees (2) which serve as wings, are set farther back, and a third plane is represented by the backdrop (3). Such scenery is easily changed by removing the rods from the hooks and substituting other pieces. The ground row (4) might be a part of the tree, but it could be a set piece cut from Beaver- board and fastened to a cross brace of the puppet booth with an angle iron and picture hook (*Plate 61, B*).

Treadmill. With a large marionette stage, a treadmill can be used for changing scenery if you want elaborate effects (*Plate 60, D*). All you need is a continuous belt about 18″ wide of stout canvas arranged to pass across the stage from side to side and over a roller at each end of the stage. The belt passes under the stage. While someone turns a crank on one of the rollers, the property man places various pieces of scenery on the belt. A character can thus stand in one place and appear to walk through miles of

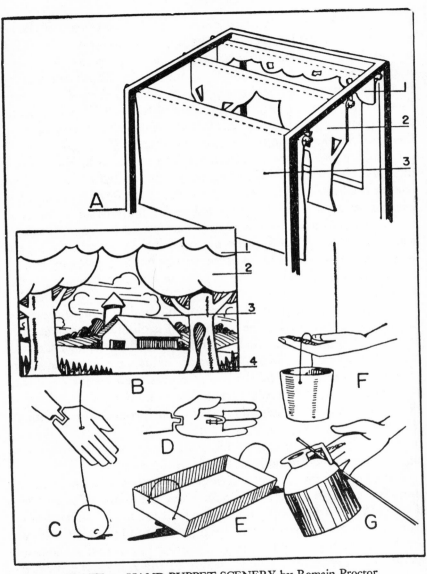

PLATE 59. HAND-PUPPET SCENERY by Romain Proctor
DEVICES FOR HANDLING PROPERTIES

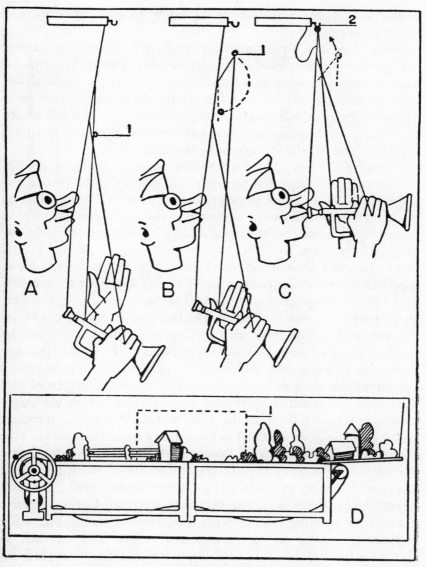

PLATE 60. BUGLE PLAYER by Romain Proctor
TREADMILL

countryside. There must be considerable wing space on either side of the proscenium (1).

You can get much the same effect without a treadmill by having the stagehands slide pieces of scenery across the stage. For rod- or hand-puppets a groove in a board placed across the back of the stage framework can be used for sliding the scenery. The great danger of the treadmill device is that the moving scenery will divert attention from the puppets. There are occasions, however, in which it is legitimate for the scenery to be the chief actor.

Fastening Scenery. There are various ways of fastening puppet stage scenery together and securing it in place. On the marionette stage, the problem is not so great because most of the scenery can be set on the floor; it can be anchored to the leaning rail, supported by a hinged brace, or otherwise steadied if there is difficulty in making it stand up.

The lack of a floor in hand- and rod-puppet stages makes various supports necessary. Suggestions for fastening scenery are illustrated on *Plate 61*. *Diagram A* shows a bolt set in a wooden strip nailed to the back of a piece of scenery. The bolt slips into a slot cut in the support, and is tightened with a wing nut against a washer. In *diagram B* a picture hook socket is screwed in the proper position to receive an angle iron, which can be placed either on the top or bottom of the piece to be supported. In *diagram C*, lengths of ¾" strap iron are fastened by screws wherever needed on the stage. A washer is placed between the wood and the iron so that mending plates or angle irons attached to the scenery can be slipped in. This is an easy and quick way of fastening. A two-fold wooden frame for supporting scenery is at *D*. Built of 1" by 2" stock lumber, it has mortise and tenon joints, or half laps reinforced with triangular corner blocks to provide the necessary strength. Cords keep the frame from opening too far. Such frames are especially useful for supporting scenery on open-proscenium stages. Two methods of fastening are shown at *E*. The flats are held in place by angle irons screwed to their framework and secured to the support by C-clamps. The flats are lashed together by the lash line, which is

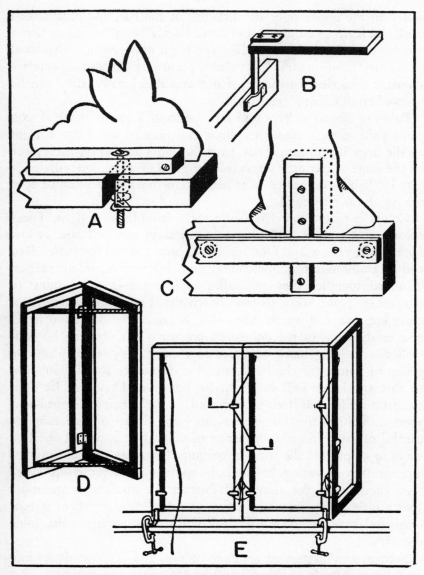

PLATE 61. METHODS FOR FASTENING SCENERY

nailed to the upper right hand corner of the flat, and crisscrossed back and forth as indicated. For small flats, 2" or 3" mending plates can be used for lash cleats (1); for large ones, regular theatrical cleats may be necessary. Lash cleats, picture hooks and sockets are standard theatrical hardware; if not available locally, they can be ordered from Clancy (see p. 280).

Painting Scenery. You will save yourself a lot of work if you paint your scenery under the light you plan to use. Paint it right on the stage if you can; if not, have the lights set and try each piece on the stage at frequent intervals. For good measure, keep the puppets in their costumes close at hand; remember they must be seen against the background.

Colors in pigments behave differently from those in light. Three colors—red, yellow and blue—are primary; mix red and yellow for orange, yellow and blue for green, blue and red for violet. Red and green, orange and blue, yellow and violet are complementaries; if mixed together they neutralize each other—a good thing to remember if you want to tone down that violent red barn. Even more important to watch than color, is value (the degree of lightness or darkness of the color you are using). Value can be controlled by adding black or white to a color. Try to establish one group of values for the background and another for the puppets, so that the latter will show up by contrast. They can be light against a medium or dark background, or dark against a light background. Within this range you can have plenty of variation. Be careful of intensity (the brilliance of colors). It is one of the best ways to emphasize the most important characters or the center of interest of your setting, but don't let spots of color jump out where they should not, for they will distract the audience's attention. Use a little complementary color to gray (or neutralize) a too-bright mixture, or add some black if this will not make the value too dark.

Scenery can be painted with almost any kind of color, depending on what it is made of, how long you are going to use it, and what you have on hand. Show card color on pasteboard, crayon on paper, colored paper cut into figures and pasted on a colored background—although fragile, these will do for a show that stays in one place if only a few performances are given.

More professional and better for touring are the following methods, suggested by Martin Stevens:[3]

Dye on Muslin. Stretch unbleached muslin on a frame. Lay out the design in charcoal. Mix ordinary drug store package dye with water and a little gum arabic to prevent spreading. Paint with it as you would with transparent water color. It leaves the cloth soft and easily transportable. But don't let it get rained on. It will fade in time.

Oil on Muslin. Use the cheapest tube colors, or the colors ground in linseed oil with which house painters tint paint, and gasoline as a thinner. Work it just as you would any dye; stain the gasoline with the oil color instead of mixing the gasoline into the oil. This will give the same flexibility as dye, but without the potential disaster of rain. WARNING! Gasoline is too dangerous to use anywhere except outdoors; try substituting kerosene if you work indoors.

Oil on velvet. Rich effects can be had by this combination. Mix your oil paint thick as heavy cream, and scumble it on across the top of the pile. Don't load it on, just hit the accents. By doing this you get a quality of light unattainable by other means. It is durable, too.

Oil on Window Shade Material. Excellent for transparencies. If you want a magic transformation, paint a winter scene on the front of some white window shade material, using oil paint thinned down with turpentine until it's translucent. Leave a strong light in front of the scene, go behind and paint a blossoming summer scene on the back. Then during performance, if you take the light off the front and put it on the back, cold winter will be banished by radiant summer before your very eyes! Similarly, you can cause visions to appear, or skies to change from dull gray to brilliant sunset.

Scene Paint. Dry color, which may be purchased with or

without a size, is easy to use on muslin, Beaverboard, wood, and other materials. Suggested colors for the regular scene paint are: Danish whiting (white), Hercules black, medium milori yellow, French ultramarine blue, light and dark chrome green, Italian burnt sienna, Italian blue (turquoise), and Chelsea vermilion. The last two are dye colors. If it is necessary to paint over them, the surface must be glazed with a coat of thin glue size to prevent the colors from bleeding through. They mix better if made into a paste with a small quantity of water before using. Scene paints need to be mixed with size to make them stick. White flake glue is standard. Cover the glue with water and allow to soak overnight. Heat in a double boiler (or its equivalent, one tin can inside another) until dissolved. For one part of the dissolved glue add sixteen parts of water and you have size water. For double strength, add only eight parts water. Gelatin glue can be prepared the same way, but use only half as much for the size water.

Many kalsomine companies put out dry, deep colors in one pound packages with the size added. These are more expensive, but are good if only small quantities are needed. Oil, lacquer and metal powders are sometimes useful. The latter must be mixed with bronzing liquid or dextrine. Luminous and fluorescent paints are good for spectacular effects.

Painting Techniques. Flat painting of scenery is often satisfactory on the small scale of the puppet stage, but the various techniques prevailing in the large theatre usually produce better results.

Scumble. For bleeding areas of different colors and grading from dark to light, use two brushes with different colors, and brush one color over the other until all the paint is worked out. A third brush, dry, is used to blend the colors more thoroughly. For rough stone or stucco, lay short brush strokes over each other in all directions, allowing some to blend and others to remain visible.

Rolling. For rough textures like stucco, stone or mottled wallpaper, use a sponge or rag dipped into the paint. Squeeze out surplus paint and roll against the scenery.

Stipple. For medium rough texture touch the surface with the ends of the bristles, changing the angle for each stroke. Sponges, rags, or crumbled paper can be used. It is a good idea to use several colors.

Spatter. By using a number of colors, spattering will produce a surface which takes the light well. Fill the brush and partly drain against the side of the pail. Make the paint come off in drops either by flicking the wrist or striking the brush against the cushion of the thumb and palm of the hand in the direction of the scenery. The size of the spatter can be adjusted by the size of the brush, amount and thickness of paint in it, and force of the motion.

Dry Brush. Effects of wood grain, bark, striations in cut stone or rock can be gotten by draining out most of the paint from the brush, then drawing the tip lightly against the surface of the scenery. For wood, tilt the brush from one side to the other.

Puddle. To suggest depth and richness, or make imitations of old marble and plaster, lay the scenery face up on the floor. Hold brushes at waist height and shake paint on the scenery. Two or more brushes with different colors should be used at the same time. Graduations can be made by adding new colors and leaving out others as you go across the scenery. A wet ground will soften the work.

Backdrop Painting. For painting backdrops, tack the material on a paint frame, wall or floor. If you are using scene paint, put on a priming coat of whiting thinned with size water and allow it to dry. This will stretch the muslin or canvas, and give a smooth working surface. Sketch your design in charcoal. If you are enlarging a small drawing, divide it into squares, then divide your backdrop into the same number of squares. By enlarging square by square you can get an accurate rendering of the original.

Painted Scenery for Shadow Screens. If your shadow screen is made of paper, you can use black waterproof ink and transparent water colors, or washes of oil paint thinned with turpentine. On cloth screens, the same material can be used, if a thin sizing

[173]

(ten cents worth of gum arabic dissolved in a quart of water) is brushed over the screen first. Dye is also excellent.

Projected Scenery. You can paint scenes on lantern slide glass which has been given a thin coating of ordinary clear gelatin. Use the transparent water colors designed for coloring slides and photographs. With a regular lantern, project these scenes onto your backdrop from the rear. This kind of scenery is particularly effective for shadow plays.

LIGHTING

Purpose. Adequate illumination is particularly important in the puppet theatre because of the small size of the stage and actors. Be sure that your puppet actors can be seen clearly; this is much more important than intricate imitations of the time of day, or the creation of vague poetic lighting effects which may be charming to look at but which obscure what the puppet is doing. Mood and time of day should certainly be suggested, but never at the expense of visibility.

It is most important in lighting to bring out the plastic quality of the puppets. The strongest modeling in the faces will flatten out unless the light from the various sources is *unequal*; it may be stronger from one side than another, or a strong overhead light may dominate with other units less intense. Keep the strongest light on the puppets (the most important characters can be spotted) with diffused light on the scenery. While contrast in intensity is desirable, too strong light from one direction creates heavy shadows which destroy the unity of the puppets; this is as bad as flat lighting.

Color in Light. Color is as important as intensity in light. Much has been written about the symbolic quality of different colors and their supposed psychological effect on people. While there is no doubt that a lurid red lighting scheme will produce a different emotional effect from a cool blue one, individual colors cannot be depended upon to convey precise reactions, because individual feeling about color is too variable. You can be sure that bright, cheerful, warm colors (yellow, orange, red) will suggest gaiety and comedy; while somber, dark colors more or less on the cool side (blue, violet, green) are generally depressing. But there are so many variations of each color—light, dark, intense, dull—that the final effect depends upon these qualities rather than upon symbolism. In American and European theatres, there is no standardized color symbolism which is universally understood to indicate social rank or character traits. However, rich reds and purples are usually associated with royalty, black with death and white with purity.

The warm colors tend to advance, the cool colors to recede and create a sense of distance. But it all depends upon where they are placed and the particular variation of the color used. It is impossible to state any set rules about the use of color in light; it is better to experiment with it and relate it harmoniously to the costumes and setting, for it is a part of the total scenic scheme.

Lighting should be designed to harmonize with the style of the puppets and scenery; if highly stylized puppets are used, the lighting can supplement the color of the background or costumes, rather than suggest a natural effect. Sometimes a soft light such as pale straw or pink diffused over the entire stage tends to unify costumes and scenery. Cool light on the background, with clear or warm lights on the puppets, heightens the plastic effect and also suggests distance. Try reversing this device; you may get interesting results. There are infinite possibilities, if you design the light with imagination, and if you don't try to be too realistic. But a word of warning is necessary—avoid heavy intense colors such as magenta, red, and bright green; they are hard to look at except as accents, they kill the colors of the costumes, and make the puppets look like ghouls—all right if the puppets *are* ghouls.

A few suggestions may help in selecting the color for your lights. White light when passed through a prism is broken into the spectrum colors. Blue, green, and red are primary; secondary colors are made by mixing blue and green for blue-green, blue and red for magenta, red and green for yellow. When a given color filter is used on a light unit, certain colors are absorbed and others are transmitted. For instance, place a green gelatin in a spotlight; red and its component colors are absorbed, while green and its components are transmitted. This is important, because a green light on a red costume makes it look black. So also, blue costumes are killed by a yellow light, and green ones by magenta. Flesh tones go sallow under an amber or green light, while under blue, rouge becomes very dark. A little pink cast to the light always helps give life to faces—even painted puppet faces. An easy way to find out what happens to colors under specific lights is to make sketches (or just daubs) with colored chalk and place them under different colored lights. Or you can use textiles of varied colors; this is even better because material of shiny texture does not look the same on the stage as a dull fabric of the same color. All this should be a dire warning to plan the color scheme of your costumes, scenery, and lighting at the same time, and in relation to each other.

Color slides for your lights are best made of gelatin manu-factured especially for the purpose. Stage lighting equipment companies offer about seventy-five shades, of which the following will give you a good range of color: light flesh pink, medium pink, light magenta, rose purple, special lavender, light purple, light sky blue, special steel blue, medium sky blue, dark sky blue, moonlight blue, light blue green, light green, medium green, light lemon, light straw, medium straw, amber, light scarlet, fire red. A descriptive booklet with samples of gelatins can be obtained from some companies (see p. 280).

For some units, notably strip lights, it is sometimes easier to dip the bulbs for the desired color. Transparent color comes in red, amber, pink, frost, straw, green, purple, moonlight blue and dark blue. Buy what you need by the pint or quart from your nearest stage lighting equipment company; about 400 60-watt lamps can be dyed with one quart.

If you can't get dye or gelatin, try colored Cellophane, paper or cloth placed far enough away from the lamp to prevent burning. Even so, you have a fire hazard.

Kinds of Light Units. The number and type of light units necessary for a puppet stage depend on its size and the kind of puppets. A large marionette theatre may need units like those used on the stage for human actors, while a string of Christmas tree lights may be enough to light a small table stage. Except for the smallest stages, the lighting should consist of a number of spotlights, several strips, and a flood or two, all fitted with grooves for gelatin slides to provide flexible color arrangements.

The following list of usable light units is suggestive rather than exhaustive; other ideas will occur to the ingenious electrician.

Christmas Tree Lights. These do not provide enough light for any except the smallest stages.

Gooseneck Desk Lamps. Two of these with 100-watt bulbs will give enough light for a puppet booth—one clamped to the inside of the framework, the other outside to light the puppets when they lean over the ledge. They can be used in other places where general illumination is required, but it is hard to get color effects with them.

Light Bulbs with Flat Tin Reflectors. These are somewhat makeshift, but can be used successfully for general illumination. The light tends to spread because of the large reflecting surface.

Photographic Reflectors. These are useful especially for shadow screens. One powerful light source, such as a 150- or 200-watt bulb, is best for this purpose. Because they can be clamped into position, this type of light has many uses. By setting wire hooks into the edge of the reflector, gelatin slides can be used for color effects.

Bird's-eye Spot. This is a spotlight bulb which can be screwed into an ordinary socket to give a concentrated light. For the puppet stage, it is well to have the socket mounted on a flexible base so that the direction of the beam can be controlled.

Commercial Stage Lights. On large puppet stages, baby spots or small portable floodlights can be used. Consult the catalogues of the lighting equipment companies listed on p. ooo, but don't buy a lot of commercial lights until you see what you have at hand, or can make.

Home-built Lighting Units. See *Plate 62. Diagram A* shows a hanging strip light with a tin reflector bent to hold a gelatin slide. The divisions are ⅜" thick wood, to which the reflector is nailed or screwed. Any number of compartments can be made, and their length is determined by the size of the bulbs to be used; for a 60-watt bulb 6" is all right. In *diagram D* three views of another strip light are shown. This unit is designed especially for background lighting. The casing is of three-ply veneer board, with a piece of bent tin (1) to form a color slide groove. The porcelain socket is attached at (2), and (3) indicates the position of a tin reflector inserted into each section. At (4) is shown the top view of this reflector, (5) and (6) are the wires, and (7) is a 25-watt T bulb. For larger bulbs the size must be increased. Strips can be wired in three circuits for different color effects if desired. The unit should be made entirely of metal if possible. It is well to learn the fire regulations of places in which you plan to play, in order to be sure your equipment can be used.

Diagram B is a spotlight made from a one-pound coffee can, with a round hole cut in the top for the spot and tin grooves for color slides. A porcelain socket made in two parts which screw together, is fitted into the bottom to receive a 100-watt spotlight bulb (G type). The bottom of the can is left for a reflector, but the rest of the inside should be painted with flat black to avoid unpleasant reflections. Blackboard slating with an alcohol base is good for this purpose. A yoke and pipe clamp of galvanized iron are attached with small bolts and wing nuts to allow adjustment in all directions. Another yoke made from three angle irons is shown at (2). This can be used with a picture hook socket (*Plate 61, B*). A color wheel (1) can be bolted to the unit. This is generally less satisfactory than individual slides, if these lights are used above the proscenium on marionette stages,

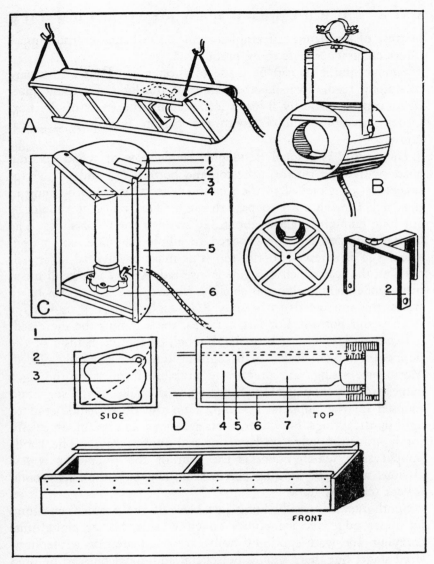

PLATE 62. HOME-BUILT LIGHTING UNITS

A, D. Strip lights
B. Spot
C. Flood

because of the danger of tangled strings. On hand- or rod-puppet stages color wheels are more practicable.

Similar spotlights can be made of sheet metal bent into square or oblong forms to make the casing of the light. Focusing spotlights can be made by using a lens set into the front of the box. Other variations will occur to the person skilled in electrical knowledge.

Diagram C is a small floodlight. Semicircles of wood covered inside with sheet tin form the top and bottom (1) and (6). A tin reflector (5) is tacked to the top and bottom, with an opening in the back for the cord to pass through. This reflector should be cut long enough to allow about ¼" overlap for color slides. The bottom wooden piece is grooved to admit the slide, and a spill shield (4) is screwed to the top; this must be pivoted so it will open all the way when the slide is inserted. At (2) is a small metal piece under which the spill shield is slipped. For a lamp up to 75 watts, this unit needs to be only 8½" high, with a 3" radius for the top and bottom. For larger lamps, the size must be increased.

Placing Light Units. In general, much of the mechanism of the puppet can be concealed if the lighting units are carefully placed. Marionette strings are practically invisible if most of the light comes from spots placed overhead or on the sides of the stage and focused on the puppets. Footlights, on the other hand, tend to light up the strings. However, foots are sometimes useful, especially for lighting the ledge on hand- or rod-puppet stages. The hand-puppet sack which conceals the arm of the puppeteer is less obvious where the lighting comes from above, if the background is kept relatively dark.

Spotlights are usually hung just back of the proscenium along its upper edge and sometimes on either side. Six or eight units carrying 100-watt spotlight bulbs are adequate for a medium-sized stage, but there should be several additional ones to be used in other positions when necessary. Strips are useful to light backdrops, to place outside doorways or windows or to give general diffused light to supplement the spots. Small floods serve a similar purpose where less light is needed.

Switchboards. Whatever types of lighting units are used, they are most effective if they can be flexibly controlled, each by its own switch. Commercial switchboards are too bulky and costly for the puppet stage, so you might as well construct your own. You will find one illustrated on *Plate 63*, which was designed by Vivian Michael. This board is planned for twelve units; any number could be used by adding more receptacles to the top of the board. Twelve are adequate for the average puppet stage. The switchboard is 12″ by 21″ by 3″, with a cover to fit over the front to protect it, and a handle for carrying and hanging in place on the stage. The inside of the box is lined with sheet asbestos, glued into place. In addition to the twelve single receptacles, there is a double one to be independently connected. This is for music, microphone or P.A. system when a dimmer is used with the switchboard.

The materials needed are: Radio toggle switches, standard receptacles (thirteen singles, one double), sheet asbestos, friction tape, screws, inlet cable, screen door hooks, metal carrying handle, bolts for handle, one piece white pine for box front ⅞″ by 12″ by 21″, two pieces ¼″ plywood 12″ by 21″ for back cover, ¾″ by 2″ white pine strips for sides of box, ⅞″ by ⅞″ strips for sides of cover.

To construct the switchboard, arrange the metal receptacle plates on the front of the board, leaving ⅛″ between the top and bottom of the plates, ½″ down the center, and 1″ for the border (*Plate 63, A*). Draw accurately around each plate, and around the circle in the center of the plate. Fit the radio switches snugly to the inside of the plate about ¼″ from the corner. Determine where the hole is to be drilled for attaching switch to plate. Drill holes to fit the switch. *Diagram D, Plate 63* shows a detail of the opening to be cut in the board to accommodate switch and receptacle. The metal plate on the front of the board is shown at (1), the switch at (2), the receptacle screwed to the board at (3), and the opening in the board by the heavy line at (4). Use a ¼″ drill to start, and an open blade jig saw to cut out the opening. Both switches and receptacles vary in size; the

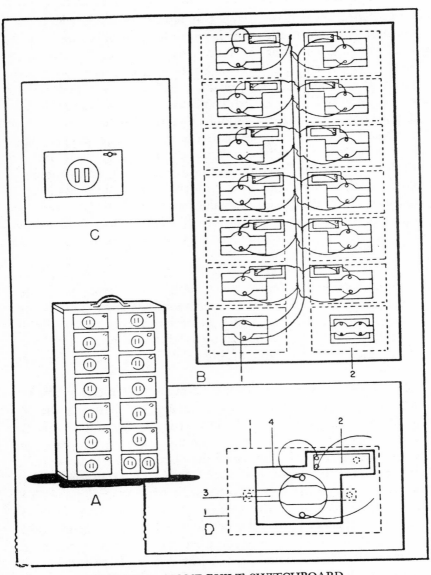

PLATE 63. HOME-BUILT SWITCHBOARD
Designed by Vivian Michael

directions given here are for a receptacle plate 2⅝" by 4½", and a 2" toggle switch. Before cutting all the openings, try the receptacle and switch in one of them for accuracy.

Lay the board face down and place all the switches and receptacles in position. Wire according to the diagram on *Plate 63, B*. When the wiring is complete, turn the board over and screw the switches tightly to the plates, adjust receptacles so that they fit the plates when the latter are in place, and fasten receptacles to the board. Screw the plates onto the front of the board. Fasten to the back of the board a frame made of ¾" by 2" strips to form a box. Cover the back with ¼" plywood, fastened with screws so that it can be easily removed. The cover is made from plywood and ⅞" by ⅞" strips, the same size as the box, and fastened to its front with screen door hooks. Bolt a heavy metal handle to the top of the frame.

This switchboard is made to operate on a 110-volt current; be careful if you are playing in a theatre not to connect it with a 220-volt circuit.

Theodore Fuchs in his *Home Built Lighting Equipment* (see p. 267) shows several diagrams for portable switchboards which could well be adapted to the puppet stage. Full directions are given for the construction.

Dimmers. If you want subtle lighting effects, you will need a dimmer. There are a number of slide dimmers and ring type rheostats which can be used on small stages. The regular plate dimmer used in most theatres can be purchased in small sizes suitable for larger puppet stages. Addresses of companies which supply dimmers can be found on pp. 281-82. It is a good idea to write to one of these companies when you are planning your lighting equipment. If you know the wattage of the individual units you wish to control by your dimmer, as well as the total wattage of the maximum number of units you plan to use, you can get advice as to the best kinds of dimmers to buy.

Anyone who understands his ohms can make his own dimmers, but it is not an easy job. Fuchs, in the above-mentioned book,

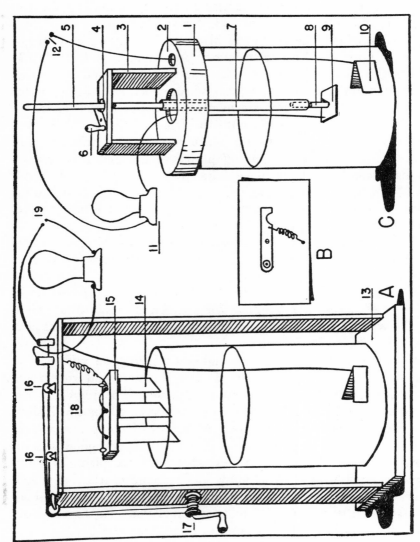

PLATE 64. HOME-BUILT DIMMER
By Lemuel Williams

gives directions for making slide dimmers of 250- to 1000-watt capacity, which would be usable for the puppet stage.

For small stages, you might find one of the models shown on *Plate 64* adequate. In C, a large glass jar is fitted with a wooden ring (1) cut from ⅜″ or ½″ plywood. A top (2) of ¼″ plywood is fastened to the ring with waterproof glue, reinforced with screws. The frame (3) is made of ½″ material. A 1″ hole is drilled in the top and a ½″ hole in the frame. The wooden stop to hold the ½″ dowel (5) in place is ½″ by ½″ by 3″ (*diagram B*). It is screwed to the top and a small spring is used to hold the stop against (5). At (6) a small handle is placed. A piece of garden hose (7) is fastened to the end of (5), and another short dowel (8) serves to hold the electrode (9), which is made of sheet copper. A second electrode (10) rests on the bottom of the jar. One wire is soldered to (9), carried to the light (11) and thence to the switch (12). The other wire is connected as shown.

The solution may be made of one teaspoonful of ammonium chloride to three quarts of water, or one-eighth of a cup of salt to the same amount of water.

In *figure A* a similar glass jar is set on a wooden platform (13) which has two uprights and a crossbar fastened to it. Sheet copper electrodes (14) are fastened to a wooden block (15) suspended by ropes which lead over pulleys (16) and connect to a crank (17). The electrodes can be lowered into the solution; the closer they approach the electrode on the bottom, the brighter becomes the light. A spring (18) is connected to one terminal of switch (19); this allows the wire to stretch as the electrodes are lowered. This same wire connects the three electrodes. In both these designs, a three-way switch can be used to cut out the dimmer and feed the current direct to the lights.

PROPERTIES

Once again the importance of scale must be stressed. If each piece of furniture and every prop is right in size, the audience will soon accept the puppets and settings as human size, and the appearance of a human being on the stage will bring gasps of awe, for he will look gigantic.

Go easy on furniture and accessories; they are lots of fun to do, but unless reduced to a minimum they will clutter the stage and distract the spectators' attention. If you have to use a period setting, study interiors, furniture, and decorative details until you have the feel of the period. Work for general lines and masses which are characteristic, and leave out most of the detail, which will not be seen from the audience anyway. If they are to be used constantly, properties ought to be solidly built of wood, Plastic Wood, or heavy papier-mâché. Cardboard or Beaverboard do well enough for a performance or two, but they are sometimes as much trouble as wood and far less dependable. Keep alert to the possibilities of plastics—you have a gold mine if you have access to the Plexiglas scraps from an airplane factory. Chloroform is a good solvent and adhesive for this particular plastic, which can be tooled like wood and bent into various shapes when heated in water (see p. 285 for notes on plastics).

Furniture. George Cole makes these suggestions: In building furniture the same scale as that used in constructing the puppets should be followed. One third or one quarter life size are common reductions for puppets. Measure the dimensions of the full size piece of furniture you want to adapt for the puppet stage; if you can't find it, try a mail-order catalogue which usually lists over-all dimensions of standard pieces. Make a working sketch to puppet scale, and you are ready to build.

To make furniture sturdy, use screws and dowels if possible; if not, nails strengthened with furniture glue are all right. If you can, design the piece to fold, because furniture is bulky and awkward to pack if you are touring, and space consuming if you are not. Table *A* on *Plate 65* has a pliable strip of wood (1) screwed to the center. This has just enough flexibility to be lifted and thus allow the hinged legs to fold flat against the table. When open, the strips holds the legs solidly in place. A folding bed is illustrated at B, *Plate 65*. The headboards and footboards are hinged. *Detail C*

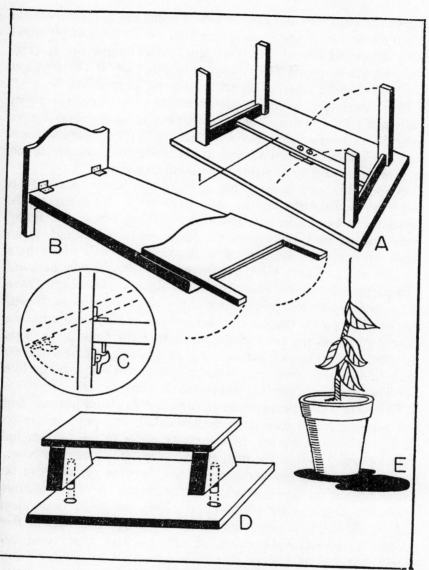

PLATE 65. PUPPET FURNITURE
By George Cole

shows the cupboard door catch which holds the parts in position when the bed is set up. Folding furniture can be built of plywood with the pieces hinged with very small brass hinges. For storing, the pins are removed from some of the hinges; if the pins get lost they can be replaced from the nearest pincushion.

It is important to finish all furniture smoothly to prevent costumes from catching. On the marionette stage, special care must be taken to avoid elaborate carving or overhanging parts which might tangle with a string. If there must be some projection or prongs, run a wire or string from point to point.

Puppet furniture is often too light or top-heavy to stand up properly, particularly on the marionette stage. To correct this, weights can be put in the bottom by drilling a hole and filling with nails or lead. Sometimes the lower parts of a stand, piano stool, or lamp can be cast of lead, which is easily done in a wooden mold. Spikes made of phonograph needles can be sunk into parts of furniture which touch the floor; often weights have to be used in addition. Thin sheets of plywood or heavy cardboard can be glued to the bottom of the furniture and covered with the same material as the floor cloth, or painted the same color. This is useful for groups of pieces, such as a piano and bench. You can't fold up the furniture, however, unless you use a device like the dowel-and-hole method illustrated on *Plate 65, D*.

There are a few peculiarities of furniture for hand-puppets and rod-puppets which should be mentioned. If rod-puppets are to sit comfortably in chairs, there must be a slot in the bottom for the supporting rods of the puppets to fit into. They can, however, sit on narrow benches without any slot, because the rod can be passed behind the bench. Hand-puppets cannot sit very well, but this movement can be suggested if chairs are made bottomless and turned slightly away from the audience, or shown in flat profile. Hand-and-rod-puppets of the Michael type need no special adaptations, except that benches should be narrow from front to back.

The various methods of fastening scenery illustrated on *Plate 61* are also useful in setting furniture or other properties on hand-puppet stages. Most pieces of furniture need a plywood base which can be bolted, clamped, or otherwise secured in place. The folding furniture pictured on *Plate 65* can be so used, if the legs are fitted with dowels which stick into holes in the base (*Plate 65, D*).

Handling Properties. With puppets, handling properties is somewhat tricky, and must be carefully planned. Don't let your playwright load the script with complicated actions such as picking up, laying down and transferring objects from one puppet to another. Many of these actions can be suggested rather than actually performed, but occasionally they must be done. Hand-puppets are the most adroit in handling objects, because the operator can actually grasp them in his fingers if the puppet's hands are made of some flexible material. Punch constantly picks up and lays down his stick, clowns juggle balls, puppet stage hands come in and change the scenery.

There are various ways marionettes can pick up things. A string is run from the object through the hand, long enough to disguise the fact that there is any connection between the object and the puppet (*Plate 59, C*). Then the puppet brings his hand over the object, the string is pulled, the hand raised—and your puppet has gallantly picked up the lady's handkerchief, or drawn a dagger to stab his enemy. Many interesting things can be done if a hook is attached to the puppet's hand and appropriate loops or handles are fitted to the object to be lifted (*Plate 59, D, E*). Marionettes can lift things like pails if the string is tied to the palm of the hand as in *F, Plate 59*. A small magnet imbedded in the puppet's hand will allow it to pick up light metal objects. If it has to set them down again, try using a steel core wound with very fine wire. Run the two ends of the wire to a small flashlight battery strapped to the controller. When contact is made, objects can be picked up and held as long as the circuit is closed.

Rod- and hand-and-rod-puppets can pick up some things directly with their hands, or carry bundles, bouquets of flowers, plates of tarts, and set them down (*Plate 59, G*). Other things, such as telephone receivers and musical instruments can be fixed on rods so the operator can keep them under control. Shadow-puppets can also handle properties attached to rods.

Musical Instruments. Sometimes you can buy the instrument you need in a toy shop or the ten-cent store, but it is likely to be the wrong size and you will have to make it yourself. Wood, Plastic Wood, plastic, metal or whatever suggests itself and is sufficiently durable, may be used. For instance, a concertina can be made of a tube of silk with small rings or wire squares sewn inside. The ends can be of light wood or stout cardboard; one end should be weighted, the other can then be moved by the puppet. If made of lightweight paper, hand-and-rod or rod-puppets can manage a somewhat more substantial concertina. Pianos, xylophones, drums, and other instruments played with hands or mallets are relatively simple for puppet performers.

Romain Proctor's stringing for a marionette bugler who places his hand in position, raises the bugle and sounds reveille is shown on *Plate 60.* The strings are shown at *A.* To manipulate, the puppeteer grasps the ring (1) in his left hand and pulls. The first pull *B* brings the puppet's hand into place. The second pull *C* brings the instrument to the lips; the ring is then placed on the hook (2) and the bugle is held in place.

Pictures and Tapestries. If you cannot find just the right picture for your living room wall, daub a few spots of color on a piece of cardboard and paint a gold band around the edge for a frame. An added strip of cardboard or very thin wood will give thickness to the frame. Handsome tapestries can be made on unbleached muslin with poster paint put on in small strokes to suggest the weave. Wax crayons can be used in the same way.

Dishes, Pots, and Pans. When you can get them, small wooden dishes, which can be painted as you wish, are less breakable than china. All kinds of small pottery figures, vases and bowls can be found at the ten-cent store. Small cognac bottles are useful for bars; candy jars for store counters can be made from one-ounce tempera paint jars filled with dry scene paint for candy. Unglazed pottery can easily be made from ordinary potter's clay; it is not very durable unless fired, but will do for a show or two. It is a good idea to glue small properties in place, to avoid having them knocked over by the puppets.

Lighted Lanterns and Glowing Torches. Marionettes can easily carry lanterns, lamps, torches (*Plate 66, E*). If these are to be lighted while the puppet is on stage, a small battery should be fastened to the controller with the ends of the wires from the bulb arranged so that the circuit can be opened or closed at will. You can rig up a small switch, or one wire can be soldered to a thin piece of sheet copper which is slipped between two similar pieces secured to the controller (*Plate 66, C*). For flashing dragon eyes, the same device can be used; you can make the copper pieces to fit around the forefinger or thumb.

The switch and bulb (or a small flashlight) can be installed in the lantern or lamp and turned on before the puppet makes its entrance, if it is unnecessary to turn the light on or off while onstage. For hand-puppets this is better anyway, since it is more difficult to arrange a battery than with marionettes. For rod-puppets, the same mechanism used for marionettes can be reversed, with the battery fastened to the main control rod.

Transformations and Magic Tricks. Some tricks are performed in full sight of the audience. The growing plant shown on *Plate 65, E* is typical. The string to which the leaves are attached should be weighted to give the plant stability as it grows. With puppets worked from below, the same trick can be done by attaching the leaves to a steel measuring tape, which is run up slowly through a hole in the bottom of the jar. The tape is particularly good, because the puppet can appear to break the plant by bending the tape, and such a plant can sway from side to side with considerable animation.

Excellent tricks of magic can be performed with the magic table pictured on *Plate 66, D*. The table is an ordinary one, covered with a cloth which touches the floor on the two ends. (1) and (2) are mirrors placed at such an angle that they reflect the side draperies

PLATE 66. PUPPET PROPERTIES

A. Transformation
B. Container for smoke cartridge
C. Metal switch for controller
D. Magic table
E. Lighted lantern

in a straight line at the bottom. The audience sees merely a draped table. Actually, the mirrors allow room enough for an operator to push objects up through a hole in the table top, thus making them appear to grow suddenly from the box. Or the puppet can reach into the box and pull out objects. The hand must have a hook in it; the operator below simply hangs the various objects on the hook.

Most transformations take place during a brief blackout, or a flash of light (made with photographic flash powder) which momentarily blinds the audience. The general methods of doing transformations are the same for puppets, properties, and scenery. One easy way is to have one object covering another. By pulling a string, the outside object is whisked off. Sometimes the object may be turned over by the pull of a string to change its appearance. Another method is to have the final transformation laid flat on the floor, to be pulled up by a string when needed. For instance, a C-ration tin could be changed into a delicious layer cake with a lighted birthday candle (*Plate 66, A*). Cut the cake (1) from flat cardboard or thin plywood, and fasten a three-dimensional C-ration tin (scaled to proper size) to the back of the cake. Lay the latter flat on its face on the table to show the ration tin (3). Pull a string, the cake is revealed, with the C-ration hidden behind (4).

By using springs you can do various kinds of transformations, based on the principle of the Jack-in-the-box; you open the cover and out pops Jack. The arrow shooting contest in *Robin Hood* can be done successfully this way. The arrows are laid flat in grooves in the target, held in place by small springs. As the contestants shoot, a string is pulled to release a pin holding the spring in tension, and the arrow straightens up. Many other devices work the same way. Hiding one object inside another, like the bean vine in the pot (*Plate 65, E*) is still another way of doing transformations. It is frequently simpler to remove one object and replace it by another during a blackout than to worry with various mechanisms.

The tricks suggested above are done on marionette stages and worked by strings. With the floorless stages used for hand-puppets and rod-puppets, various adaptations have to be made, but most of the principles mentioned above are workable. The magic table on *Plate 66, D* can be worked with any type of puppet. Strings to release springs can be pulled downward instead of upward; rods can push things up from boxes which have a hole in the bottom; a flat object can be pulled into position from below as well as from above, if it is anchored at the base. For the C-ration-to-cake change described above, it would be necessary to hinge the base of the dish to a platform, and attach the string to the ration box in order to get enough leverage to raise the cake into position.

In the end, you will probably have to depend upon your own ingenuity to solve specific problems in the construction and handling of props. Just be sure they work easily and do not hold up the action; if they don't work throw them out.

SPECIAL EFFECTS[4]

Many puppet plays call for special effects, and their accurate suggestion helps to give reality to the performance. They must not be overdone. Let it rain long enough to suggest rain, but not for the audience to discover that it is really only Cellophane strips in motion.

Thunder. A piece of tin or galvanized iron 3′ to 4′ long, 1′ wide is suspended. Shake it to produce rolling thunder. For single crashes strike the tin in the center with a rubber hammer, a tennis or rubber heeled shoe.

Lightning. Flash white light on and off. If you want to see an actual flash, cut appropriate openings in a backdrop, cover with gauze, and paint the whole drop. A light flashed back of the cuts will do the trick.

Breaking Glass. An old piece of window glass in a sack is dropped on the floor.

Crashes. Fill a wooden box with broken glass and a few stones, then nail the top on. By dropping or tipping the box end on end, various kinds of crashes can be produced.

Horses. Two half coconut shells clapped on a wooden board give the sound of horses walking or galloping on a hard road. For hoofbeats on a soft road or turf, use wallboard.

Running Water. A wooden box 1′ by 2′ and 2″ is fitted with tin on the bottom and ends. Finishing nails are driven into the bottom and ends in a 1″ diamond pattern. Place a small amount of lead into the box, tilt, and the sound of running water is produced.

Trains. Place small wire nails or shot inside a flat cigarette tin, move back and forth and you have a train chugging along. Sandpaper, or wire brushes on metal will also give the effect, when done in the right rhythm. (See rumble cart for wheel noises.)

Gong and Chimes. For the former, use a commercial Chinese gong or a 4½′ to 5′ length of water pipe suspended by a rope. Tubes from an old brass bed (or water pipes) can be cut in various lengths for chimes. Cut off half an inch at a time and test for tone. You can get a fair scale if you work carefully. Strike with a rubber mallet, a tennis or rubber heeled shoe.

Airplane. Knot one end of four 6″ leather thongs and attach by the other end to the pulley of a small electric motor. Allow the knots to strike the head of a snare drum—you can get various sounds by changing the position of the drum.

Wind. A cylindrical drum made of two circular wooden ends about 2′ in diameter joined by slats set 2″ apart is mounted on a frame as shown on *Plate 67, A.* Heavy canvas is stretched tightly against the drum which, when rotated by the handle, produces the sound of wind. A wind whistle can be purchased from novelty or toy shops, and is adequate for some shows.

Rain. Fill a tin biscuit or cookie jar one third full of dry peas or beans. Rotate slowly. On *Plate 67, C* is a rain machine made from a large tin can with cleats placed inside at intervals. After the peas or beans are put in it, the top is soldered on, a handle is run through the center, and the can is mounted as shown.

Roars and Creaking Doors. Make a hole in the bottom of a large

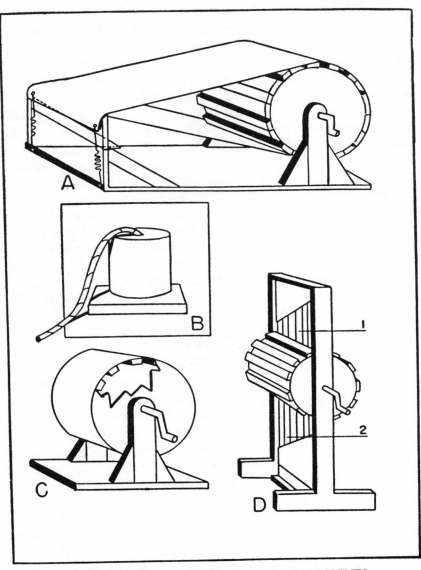

PLATE 67. SPECIAL EFFECTS: SOUND MACHINES

By Lemuel Williams

A. Wind
B. Roars and creaking doors

C. Rain machine
D. Crash machine

tin can, put a cord through it and knot it securely, then fasten the can to a board. Powdered rosin is put on a piece of cloth or a canvas glove worn by the operator. He then pulls up on the cord. The pitch is varied by the tautness of the cord (*Plate 67, B*).

Crash Machine. Hardwood slats are placed in a frame as shown in *D, Plate 66*. A cylinder with wood strips nailed lengthwise and a handle to turn it is placed to strike the ends of the slats (1 and 2) for the sound of breaking wood or a crash.

Rumble Cart. Figure *C, Plate 68* shows a box with a hole in the center and a flange (1) screwed to the floor. A handle, consisting of two short lengths of pipe (2 and 3) and two elbows (4 and 5), is screwed into the flange. Casters are screwed to the corners of the box. A platform, shown in *figure A*, has a smaller flange (6) set in the middle, with a smaller pipe attached to it which fits into the larger pipe of the handle on the box. Strap iron or wooden strips are secured to the platform. The dotted line (7) shows position of box *C*. As the box is turned, the rollers passing over the strips produce a rumble.

Shot. Snap a yardstick or a thin board on a hard, flat surface, or fire a cap pistol.

Miscellaneous Sounds. There are many sound effects which can be purchased from novelty, music, or ten-cent stores—bird, train, boat, siren, police, and slide whistles are the most common. You can also get dog barks, cow moos, and razzberries. Small sirens of various types can be bought at bicycle and hardware stores. A doorbell, push button, and two dry cell batteries mounted on a wooden base make a useful machine for ringing telephones and doorbells. If you can't find these effects, don't despair—the human voice can imitate many of them successfully.

Recordings. For a list of places where you can buy recorded sound effects, see p. 288.

Smoke. Hydrochloric acid and ammonia placed in bottles as illustrated on *Plate 68, B* are sometimes used for smoke, which is produced by blowing through the glass tube in bottle (2). A rubber tube leading to the stage is attached to bottle (1). This

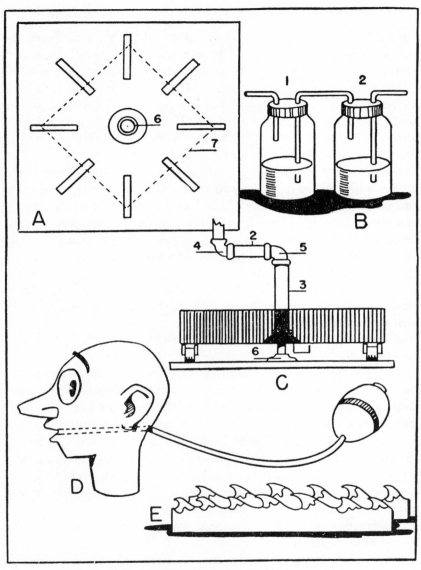

PLATE 68. SPECIAL EFFECTS: MISCELLANEOUS

By Lemuel Williams

A, C. Rumble cart
B, D. Smoke
E. Waves

apparatus is dangerous to use, for it will explode if the two chemicals are mixed; besides, it is difficult to transport, and is likely to asphyxiate the puppeteers.

If you get a lusty smoker, cigarette smoke may be blown through a rubber tube with good effect. Incense may be used in some cases, or melting dry ice, but the vapor from the latter tends to sink rather than to rise. A bulb with powder in it will produce a small amount of smoke (*Plate 68, D*). Smoldering string produces a good smoke, too.

F. L. Brant has this formula for a smoke cartridge: "Mix one measure of saltpetre (potassium nitrate) in nine measures of water (10 percent solution by volume). For four or five cartridges you will need about one tablespoon of saltpetre to nine tablespoons of water. When dissolved, dip paper towel into the solution (wet thoroughly but don't let it get soggy) and then hang it up to dry. While still slightly damp, roll it into cartridge shape as tightly as possible. This is best done by laying it on a flat board, turning one edge and rolling it with the palms of the hands pressing against the board. Continue to roll for some time after cartridge is completely rolled, in order to compress and make it tight. Wrap with string and set away to dry."[5] The best way to use this cartridge is to take a large tin can of several gallons' capacity (*Plate 66, B*), cut a hole (1) in the top large enough to admit the cartridge, and cover with a heavy metal top (2) to which a wire for holding the cartridge has been soldered. If the smoke leaks out, friction tape or adhesive around the top will seal it. Two rubber tubes should be fitted into the can, as illustrated. The cartridge is ignited, suspended inside the can about midway between bottom and top, and the lid is set in place. If you light the cartridge some time before you need the smoke, there will be plenty of it when you blow through the tube at the bottom of the can—and the dragon will belch forth clouds of smoke.

Volcano. A cigar or cigarette butt placed in a metal container in a tin can will simulate a smoking volcano, chimney, locomotive— or what you will (*Plate 69, E*).

PLATE 69. SPECIAL EFFECTS: FIRE

By Lemuel Williams

A, B. Flickering flames   E. Smoking volcano
C. Raging flames   F. Burning walls
D. Flash of fire

Waves. Cut two or more strips the length of the stage as shown on *Plate 68, E.* These are then moved back and forth in opposite directions. Another method is to fasten silk strips loosely to a frame so that a small fan placed below will cause the silk to rise and fall in billows.

Fire. For a simple, glowing fire, place a red electric bulb behind a set piece of miniature logs. This effect can be augmented by a red spotlight. Flickering fire is made by a simple machine consisting of a painted drum of celluloid (be sure it's the noninflammable variety) constructed as shown on *Plate 69, A.* The heat from the bulb sets up an air current which rotates the drum by means of the rotor blades at (1). *Diagram B* shows the machine in position. Raging flames can be made by fastening flame shaped pieces of red, yellow, and orange silk to the guard wires of a small electric fan. This trick makes an effective flash, but, like all trickery, is hard to sustain. It works best in front of a dark background (*Plate 69, C*). A flash of fire (*Plate 69, D*) can be made by throwing photographic flash powder on an electric hot plate—an excellent effect for supernatural appearances, such as the arrival of the Devil.

The above effects can be combined to make a spectacular fire scene. Starting with a red glow, smoke and flickering light, a burst of flame engulfs a building. The walls finally crash, showing charred timbers as flames continue to rage. For details of crashing walls, see *Plate 69, F.*

Snow. Small pieces of white paper fanned off a flat box top will give a snow effect; moth flakes or Christmas snow can be dropped from above. A revolving wheel of special gelatin purchased from a theatrical supply company can also be used.

Rain. If you must be realistic, try drilling small holes in a pipe about ½″ apart, but be careful in arranging the trough to catch the water, since it is easy to have a flood. In fact, the trick is probably more trouble than it is worth. Fine Cellophane strips with a small fan blowing on them can be used for driving rain;

a slight agitation of the strips will give gentle rain. Tiny Cellophane pieces can be worked like the snow effect.

Sky Writing. For the "handwriting on the wall" or magic writing in the sky, cut out the message from thin plywood or metal and back it with a box in which electric bulbs have been set. Cover the writing with a continuous strip of friction tape, and place the box close to the backdrop or wall (which would need to be made of a translucent cloth to allow the writing to show through). At the proper time, turn on the lights inside the box, pull off the tape slowly, and the message will appear.[6]

CHAPTER VII

PLAYWRITING AND PUPPET PLAYS

HOW TO CHOOSE A PUPPET PLAY

When you select a puppet play or write one yourself, your choice should be influenced by the type of puppet you want to use, the purpose of your performance, the talents of those who are to participate, and the kind of audience which will see the show. Not all puppet plays are suitable for acting by all types of puppets. Hand-puppets are excellent as comedians and satirists. Let them carry, embrace, pull and push, fight, dance together, go in and out of doors. Leave to rod-puppets serious drama; they can be very dignified, and even create a religious atmosphere. They can also be convincing fighters with sword, lance, or fists. Hand-and-rod-puppets lend themselves to many different plays; they do satire well, but they can also reach the heights of tragedy. String-puppets are excellent for climbing, swinging, rocking, and most forms of aerial movement. Tricks, dances, and acrobatic stunts are traditional string-puppet material. Shadows are somewhat unreal in quality and are good for fantasy, dreams, and processions; they can dance and do tricks so long as these are kept within the two-dimensional limitation of the screen. It is wise to experiment with puppets to learn what each type can do before choosing the play, or at least to study up a little on puppet construction.

Why are you giving your show? Is it a dramatic experiment likely to interest only a limited audience? Do you want to make money and entertain people? Or just entertain? Is the show supposed to sell something, promote a cause, or educate the

[203]

audience? Determine the purpose of your show, for it will influence your choice of play.

Think about your audience. If you are playing for children, that implies one kind of performance. Adults in different groups enjoy different types of programs; you could do things for a night club revue which would be inappropriate for a church entertainment. A few puppeteers have a repertory which pleases everybody—a rare but happy situation. For mixed groups avoid touchy subjects such as sex, religion, and politics; for special groups they may be just right. Because they are so impersonal, puppets can sometimes carry off situations which would give offense on the stage of human actors.

Consider also the participants when you choose your play. Maybe they are convalescents; if so, they ought to enjoy the show and their part in it, for this may be part of their rehabilitation program. Even the show which is to go on tour with paid puppeteers is better if those who have built it and those who run it are pleased with it.

CHARACTERISTICS OF A GOOD PUPPET PLAY

You have plenty of choice in selecting a puppet play, but there are certain basic qualities which it should have. In general, it should be the kind of play which puppets can do better than human beings. Plays requiring actions which can be performed more convincingly by puppets are good: Dragons flying through the air, skeletons dancing and coming apart, transformations, and tricks of various kinds. The whole world of fantasy in which anything may happen, and superhuman accomplishments are everyday occurrences, is ideal for the puppet stage. Plays based upon caricature, satire, or broad humor are excellent, for puppets by their very nature are ironical. The puppet stage is a good place to present plays which for various reasons would be impracticable for human actors because of elaborate staging, costuming, or mechanical effects— but don't do them unless they are really good puppet material in themselves. Plays with animals are fun to do because such characters have a plausibility difficult to achieve on the large stage, and they provide endless amusement. Don't put the puppet at a disadvantage by requiring it to imitate human beings or animals too closely. Avoid forcing it constantly to perform difficult actions like picking up and handling objects (unless you are using hand-puppets), or climbing in and out of confining spaces like closets, boxes, chimneys. One of the joys of the puppet theatre is the degree to which you can use your imagination; why exert all your time and effort on a realistic puppet in a realistic play when the puppet theatre offers so much beyond the capacities of a mere human being?

At least your first play should be a simple one. Have only a few characters, a plot which does not demand tricks but which gives a chance for the puppet to show what it can do. Work on this simple play until you have become proficient, get your co-workers to share your enthusiasm, send your audience away charmed— then you can begin more pretentious shows. Many a puppet group has become discouraged and given up long before the complicated puppets and script for an overambitious show have ever seen the footlights. Comedy is safer for a first venture than a serious play, for a slight mishap may turn your tragic hero into a buffoon.

SUGGESTIONS FOR WRITING PUPPET PLAYS

Maybe you can find a play ready-written which you will like; there are all too few good ones, and most of those are for children. There is a list on p. 267-69. Probably you will have to write your own. Amusing or semi-tragic things happen around us every day; science makes a new discovery; politicians bicker and the taxpayer boils. You can make puppet plays from such material. If you don't like the present, there is the whole realm of folklore, fairy tale, mythology, and fable to explore. There is the puppet revue, which can surpass its human counterpart in extravagant dance or exotic song (and give your musician a chance to compose to his heart's content). A list of source material is included on pp. 269-77.

Having made your selection of piece, check and be sure it is not subject to royalty. Authors of stories retain their rights no matter what you do in dramatizing the plot. While many things are copyrighted, there is much free material. Just be sure the proper arrangements are made, either for the payment of royalty, or for permission to use a story, play, or song.

When you are ready to write the play, consider the following suggestions which are summarized from the opinions and writings of leading American puppeteers. The following excerpts from Clem Easly's talk at the Cincinnati Puppet Festival admirably sum up the general principles of play writing:

"Nobody should speak with too much assurance on the subject of writing puppet plays. There is no sure-fire 'how.' What is a good script? It should be thought of first not as dialogue but only a series of actions. It will follow the formula: 'Who, aided by whom or what, is going from where, opposed by whom and what, through what circumstances, wither?' We might call this recipe the 99 W's.

"Start making notes early in your planning of the play. Answer the above W's concisely. Next, identify the climax—the highest, fastest point in the story. The climax is not necessarily of major importance to the characters of the play, but it certainly is the most tense period for the audience. Decide everything that the audience must know in order to participate fully in that climactic moment; then, working backward, plant these vital bits of information.

"Clearly define all relations between characters. Do not confuse or mystify the audience. They must share in everything that goes on upon the stage.

"Take care to develop all important facts. Do not produce decisive events suddenly, as a magician draws rabbits from his hat. Suspense is better than surprise. If you are going to use a revolver in the last scene, let the audience know early that it is hidden in the table drawer. They will remember it is there and will almost die of suspense when in the last act the villain backs slowly toward it. Will he reach it before the hero stops him? He must not! He does not!! In this way the audience participates in the actual sensations of the play.

"Emphasize conflict. Remember among the 99 W's that portion which runs: 'opposed by whom or what.' Conflict is the keystone of a play. Conflict of man against man produces comedy or melodrama; conflict against convention, the problem play; conflict against the superhuman, tragedy. And remember, too, the hero must win, or if he loses he must lose nobly and admirably.

"This hard-set rule brings before us an axiom in the theatre: The audience reaction must be 'yes.' If at the climax of the play, the leading lady is to shoot her mother, the audience must be wanting her to do it. They must have been saying for some time, 'If that girl would only shoot that woman I could go home and get a good night's rest.' Juggle your material about until such an arrangement can be achieved. If it cannot, the material is not dramatic; it may make an excellent novel, or essay, or poem, or encyclopedia, but it will not make an audience-gripping play.

"Now, as regards the actual mechanics of writing: start with an action outline (the 99 again). Write each important development upon a separate piece of paper. Arrange the slips in an intelligible and interesting sequence. Decide what characters must be on stage to successfully present the idea of each scene. This will lead you to detect superfluous characters and save you making unnecessary puppets.

"Choose for the opening of your play that scene at which development action is noticeable—when things of greatest moment are about to occur. Everything prior to this may be classified as contributory and explained later. Don't drag it all in at the beginning, with two servants dusting the furniture and gossiping. Action should give birth to the conversation; and if two characters are about to engage in mortal conflict, get them at it and let the remarks fall where they may. Speeches should be as short as possible, fully in character and leading toward the next action. Be lucid. If you happen to write, 'Oswald felt strangely as though through saffron clouds he had witnessed the rising of an orchid moon into a verdant sky,' cross it off immediately and substitute, 'Oswald was ill.' "[1]

Besides having a plot with sustained interest, and opportunities for good puppet acting, a well-written play should call for characters and scenes which offer the designer a chance to exercise his talent. The play, even though it be a simple one, ought to be substantial enough to give everyone concerned in its production a sense of accomplishment.

In addition to these general hints, one needs to consider some special problems. As Martha Hargrave says: "Just as writing for the motion picture, radio, or legitimate theatre demands a specialized technique, so does your puppet, and you must keep his limitations and capabilities constantly before you if you are to avoid production embarrassments later on. A puppet is not a human being. While he can perform many actions impossible to ordinary mortals he can also fail in carrying out some of the simplest movements." Furthermore, the puppet play is a concentrated form of drama stripped to essentials. This does not mean that it cannot be a rich dramatic experience, but it does imply that what happens must be straight to the point. Martha Hargrave continues, "Simplicity should be your criterion in character and story plotting. Just as the puppet does not easily adapt himself to heavy drama he also fails at a subtle or complex characterization. Puppet villains should be blackhearted brigands; heroes, the epitome of gallantry and goodness. Like most rules, this one has outstanding exceptions but it takes a skilled performer and a gifted writer to ignore the taboos, and the beginner should study his medium thoroughly before he attempts either a complex puppet plot or a complex puppet character."[2] One of the greatest charms of the puppet play is that it usually lacks the verbosity of the large theatre; one is not submerged in an avalanche of words.

At this point, we must re-emphasize the importance of *action* as the basis of the puppet play. Upon whatever other points they may disagree, all puppeteers maintain that action comes first. The *kind* of action largely depends upon the type of puppet you are using; hand-puppet movements are quite different from those of marionettes. Sue Hastings and Dorcas Ruthenburg remind us that "puppets cannot make the minute gestures with which human actors give nuance to a line. Don't call for any action beyond the capacity of the cast you have in mind. If the puppet producer says to you, 'Look, I've invented a puppet that can smoke a pipe, swing a lariat, and climb a tree,' by all means invent a situation calling for all three. On the other hand, don't, as one writer did, require your wooden artists to adopt 'cynical and startled expressions.' The best operator in the world cannot coax a puppet to intimate by a glance that his sister is sick in Singapore. Puppets don't insinuate; they say things."[3] Meaningful speech linked to appropriate action should be the puppet playwright's aim.

Don't give the puppet long speeches, unless you can interrupt them by remarks or bits of action from other characters. If you need an introduction, keep it short and light. Rhyme and song are useful here, as well as for breaking the tension of a dramatic scene. Use verse or prose or whatever combination suits the kind of play you are writing. So long as you allow for plenty of action and write with clarity, any amount of literary charm can be introduced.

How long should the puppet play be? Again, that depends upon the number and type of puppet used, the audience and the occasion. As a general guide, the play can be as long as the puppets can provide varied action and hold the audience's attention. A couple of dancing hand-puppets may run the gamut of their particular movements in two minutes; add some dialogue and they may be good for ten minutes; use some additional characters and you have a fifteen-minute show. Maybe you can have enough actors doing enough things to interest your audience for an hour and a half, but remember that a lot more has to happen during that time in the puppet theatre than would happen in the large theatre.

Be careful about intermissions in the puppet theatre. On this subject Remo Bufano says, "An intermission must be like a dramatic pause in a scene or dialogue. If held too long it breaks the connecting thread. When circumstances demand an unusually long intermission you must bridge the gap with appropriate music or a monologue before the curtain by one of the puppets, or by means of some other ingenious device which may suggest itself. You must never under any condition plan your show so that the intermissions are longer than your scene. I have seen that happen time and time again. And I must say that nothing is more annoying to an audience. It shows bad management and lack of showmanship."[4] The people enjoy a chance to talk with their neighbors during one or two short intermissions, but they came to see a performance, not to gossip. The puppet play is concentrated drama; reduce intermission time in the same proportion you would reduce the length of your scenes as compared with those of the large theatre.

It is important to remember in writing a puppet play, that each character must be controlled by a human operator. Think three times before you demand mob scenes with hordes of puppets milling about the stage. Don't assume that the puppeteers can work it out somehow. It is better to find out before you start how many operators will be available to present your play, or, if you don't know this in advance, be on the safe side and plan the action so that a minimum of puppeteers will be needed. One person can present a hand-puppet show if he is adroit (Walter Wilkinson's performances are ample proof of this); two will give you far greater opportunities. For hand-and-rod shows, an operator is required for each character, except in some cases where extra puppets can be set in place. The same thing holds for rod-puppets. If the right kind of controller is used, one person can manage two string-puppets for simple movements, and groups can be arranged by hanging the figures on hooks. But remember that completely static puppets tend to look dead. Unless they can be given an occasional bit of motion while fixed in place, get rid of them, and leave the stage to whatever number of characters can be properly animated.

The play can often be made more interesting by introducing dances, acrobatic turns, and various tricks. But characters not essential to the development of the plot should be used with discrimination, and they should advance the story, even though slightly. At the beginning of scenes, or during expository passages, or as accessories to build up the excitement of climaxes, incidental characters are useful, but they should never slow down the action, just to perform their turn.

Musical interpolations such as songs or the playing of various musical instruments might be incorporated in the script to utilize the talents of specific people. If you have a bassoon player who wants to contribute to your show, make a place for him if you can. On the other hand, it may be fun to construct a tuba-playing puppet, but not practicable if you cannot find suitable music to be played backstage for him. Phonograph records are sometimes usable, but it is not always easy to find what you want, and the number may be more trouble than it is worth. Try not to write into your script any elaborate tricks unless those who are making the puppets are capable of constructing workable figures. There is nothing worse than a trick that doesn't come off.

In addition to the general notes given above, there are some hints about specific kinds of plays and methods for building them, which are helpful.

PLAYS ADAPTED FROM STORIES

When you have found a story you like, study it carefully to see if it can be interpreted in terms of puppet dialogue and action. Material which is effective in narrative form may not be suitable for drama. Even tales which are essentially dramatic usually need considerable change before they become effective puppet plays. Decide first what type of puppet is best suited to act out your story. Make an action plot, and group the major developments into scenes, with a climactic action at the end of each, and the final climax at the end of the play. This action plot should tell the whole story before you even begin to write the dialogue. A list of essential characters will be part of the action plot. Write down the principal character traits, costume, and physical appearance of each person in the play as well as any special dialect or speech peculiarity which would help in building the puppet and interpreting its character. If the story has too many characters to be practicable, you can probably combine actions and speeches in order to eliminate some of them. Many good stories have too many changes of scene; these may prove a fine challenge to the scenic designer, but it is usually better to combine and rearrange. Remember always that drama is essentially *conflict*; if your story does not lend itself to such interpretation, put it aside and look further.

PLAYS FOR EDUCATION OR PROPAGANDA

There are occasions upon which a puppet show may be a lively method of advertising something, or presenting educational ideas, or stimulating interest in a "cause." Harry Fowler makes the following analysis of this type of show:

"The show may be for propaganda or advertising, in which case it is little more than an animated poster where light, color, action and the novelty of the puppets attract the crowd for a three- to ten-minute skit. Probably the audience stands, for the show is usually given several times a day in a store window, an exhibit hall, or a display booth at a fair. This, the simplest of educational puppet shows, presents its message with direct, sledge-hammer subtlety. It is nearly always successful.

"The second type of educational show is often seen in schools, colleges, settlement houses, or museums. The audience is given a picture of the manners, costumes, background, and customs of another country or period of history. The attempt is made to create a visually accurate production with colors and forms as nearly authentic as possible. The script is based on a fairy tale, classical literature, drama, or music. In art museums, such shows are often correlated with current exhibits and sometimes actual art objects are used as properties or settings. These shows usually run from forty-five minutes to an hour, and are presented in an auditorium.

"The third type of educational puppet show is the one which is too often poorly written and presented. Sometimes a message will be tacked on to an otherwise good show, or a good script is written for a show which is artistically bad and mechanically poor. For example, an ordinary show becomes a so-called health play by the simple addition of dancing fruits and vegetables.

"The script of a good educational puppet show should be written so that the teaching content or (propaganda) is carefully balanced with humor, interest-holding action, and climax-building scenes. Laughter is timed to fit into the script often and strategically. As much audience participation as possible is used, for it helps to clinch the points. Action and business are planned so that a device appears only once, and constant variety keeps the show fresh and surprising. No one action is allowed to go on so long that attention is lost, even though the action is basically good. The language is simple and direct, speeches are short, and pantomime is used as much as possible.

"The audience should leave the show with a glow of pleasure and sympathy for the characters, and never with a feeling of having been preached at, but with their ideas knowledge, or habits variously modified."[5]

IMPROVISED PLAYS

If you have some puppets, but no play and no playwright, don't be discouraged. Improvise. Hand- or hand-and-rod-puppets are best for this purpose. Select a small group of people you think will be good operators, give each of them a puppet, and let them try to find a suitable voice and manner of speaking consistent with each character being manipulated. Conversations between the various characters will naturally begin; a dramatic situation will soon present itself and before long a play will be in progress. Further development of the plot will be suggested as the operators continue to work with the puppets, and the conflict will eventually be resolved. After a few rehearsals, the good lines may be written down, the whole plot made clear and consistent—and you have a play![6]

Improvisation is also an excellent way to learn the acting ability of a group of people. It can be combined profitably with the usual tryout for specific parts, or puppets can be distributed, and you can watch to see what people do with them. Quite a lot can be learned about an individual's rhythmic response to a puppet; this is important because it will tell you whether or not he is likely to be a good manipulator.

It is traditional in the puppet theatre that audience and puppets be closely associated. The puppet is small, intimate. It can talk directly to specific individuals, and draw a response from them. Audiences enjoy this, for then they feel a personal interest in the performance; it is not just something seen objectively, like a movie. The script may be arranged to allow for some improvisation. Through a slit in the masking curtain, the operators can watch the audience, single out different people for the puppets to talk to or discuss. It is always startling when a puppet turns to the audience, looks directly at someone with its staring eyes and proceeds to call him by name; not only the person addressed, but the whole audience at once becomes alert.

To a small group of people who have worked together for a long time—where there is a minimum of time in which to write new plays, build new puppets and new scenery—the improvised play becomes the answer to the demand for a continuous change of repertory. A group of stock characters forms the basis of the puppet acting troupe (see p. 4). Hand-and-rod puppets are an excellent type to use because their costumes and heads can be easily changed. For improvised plays an action outline with appropriate climaxes is worked out in advance; the words are filled in as the show progresses. It may vary from performance to performance according to the audience reaction, the inspiration of the puppeteers, or references to current happenings. All this makes for aliveness in puppet production, but it must be done by people who have a good sense of rhythm and know how to build climaxes and bring the play to an exciting conclusion.

PLAYS BUILT FROM
CHARACTERISTIC PUPPET ACTION

Another way to develop puppet plays is to work for a considerable time with whatever type of puppet you have in order to find out what actions it can best perform. Walter Wilkinson has demonstrated the value of this method for building hand-puppet plays; in the following excerpt he suggests its use with all types. "Perhaps the last thing a puppet should do is to speak. Its unique value seems to be in the way it moves, does things, performs—in a word, acts! And as for speaking, the words should be shaped to time with the action, and be in character with the movements of the puppet. No harm can be done if manipulators (especially beginners) would work out their scenes, numbers, or plays by the movement alone, without using any words—work out a pattern of movement that flows with a rhythm, with a pattern that builds up to dramatic points and accents. The movements should be like music—slow, quick, or agitated according to the dramatic sense, but they should all be related to a basic sense of time.

"A puppet is not a human being. Although the puppet may suggest human action, at the same time it should move freely in its own way. A puppet scene should be built up from the natural movement of the puppet. In the beginning, it is better to build simple scenes on what the puppets will do easily and effectively in the space allotted to them and with the means of acting at their disposal. If attempts are made to impose the tricks of human actors upon them, or the conventional action of the large stage, nothing but a chronic, ineffective muddle is likely to ensue, or else something very dull and meaningless, something very inferior to the stage work you are imitating. Never imitate anything—imitation is always weak."[7]

By emphasizing action before words, it is not meant to imply that one can be substituted for the other. The time invariably comes when the puppet must speak, unless its role is simply that of a trick performer or dancer. Suitable words are just as hard to provide as suitable action, but a thorough knowledge of the latter will give a sound basis for dialogue.

DRAMATIZED POEMS AND SONGS

Even the simplest problem in playwriting may seem difficult for the beginner. Dramatizing Mother Goose rhymes or favorite nursery songs may solve the problem of simple shows for children. Ernest Lawrence Thayer's *Casey at the Bat* was produced by Douglas Anderson with a group of adults at a WPA training center. The poem was dramatized for hand-puppets. The lines were spoken by a choral speaking group which was supervised by one instructor while another took charge of the construction of puppets and scenery. Turned heads, cutout hands and basic costumes were prepared in advance because time was limited. The whole production was built in seven hours. This poem is a good one to use when there is a large group involved, because the grandstand which forms part of the scenery can accommodate any number of spectators.

Even professional companies would find a wealth of fresh material for their variety acts in folk songs, ballads, or nonsense verses. Think of the brilliance and color of a Gilbert and Sullivan potpourri done with Vinylite plastic shadows, or the nostalgic cowboy songs done with a marionette horse and rider.

Some musical compositions, such as Prokieff's *Peter and the Wolf* have been effectively dramatized, and there are others which may be interpreted by puppets. However, care must be taken not to select music which is too long, because the puppet actors will not be able to provide enough variety of action.

Collections of folk songs, ballads, poems, and other material from which puppet shows can be built are listed in the bibliography on pages 269-77.

CHAPTER VIII

PRODUCING THE PUPPET SHOW

PROGRAM PLANNING

The production of a puppet play involves planning, building, rehearsing, advertising, and finally the performance. Methods of organizing a production will depend largely upon its size and type, as well as the number of people involved. If you are your own playwright, builder, press agent, and sole performer, the problem is quite different from that of a therapeutic or educational show in which the purpose is to interest as many people as possible. A full-length puppet play requires more time and preparation than one or two numbers designed as spots in a variety program. The suggestions offered here will have to be adapted to your own problem.

The Theatre. If you have any choice in the matter of the theatre in which your show is to be given, select an auditorium or room which is longer than it is wide, because it is difficult to arrange the stage settings for good visibility on the sides. If the theatre is small, have one block of seats with aisles on the sides in order to make the best use of the center space. A raked floor is a great advantage, but if you do not have this, arrange your stage on a platform high enough to make the puppets visible to everyone. It is especially disconcerting when you have to view a puppet show by peering between the gigantic heads of the persons in front of you because the puppets by comparison look even smaller than they are.

For adequate lighting effects, the auditorium should be one in which a complete blackout is possible. If you have a permanent theatre, there should be a green room where the audience can see sketches and models of your productions, past and future; where you may mingle with the guests and perhaps overhear useful criticisms; where the audience may be served refreshments upon occasion. A workroom reached by a door from backstage is a great asset.

Puppets are best when they can establish intimacy between themselves and the audience. A small theatre (seating between fifty and three hundred persons) where the detail of the figures is not lost and the audience does not have to strain to see what is going on, is far better than a huge hall where the puppet stage is seen as a small patch of light set in a great void. One of the unique qualities of the puppet theatre is its relatively small size and its ability to function successfully in places where a large theatre could not. To place it in competition with the latter is both unfair and inappropriate. Several plans for studio-theatre homes are illustrated in *Puppetry 1942-43*, while drawings for a community puppet theatre are included in *Puppetry 1931*.

The Producing Company. The puppet producing company may consist of one or two people or a large number, depending upon the kind of show and the reasons for its presentation. Sometimes puppetry is a recreational project, as in the *Sokols* of Czecho-Slovakia, to which many persons contribute their various talents. Presentation of plays is as much for the benefit of the participants as for the entertainment of the audience. This plan works well if an efficient, well-co-ordinated performance is not essential. Too many people connected with a puppet show usually complicate rather than help it. After all, one advantage of the puppet theatre is its freedom from too much human temperament. If you are going to have as many people around as it takes to run a play in the theatre of human actors, you might almost as well do a regular stage show. Professional companies may employ several specialists to do scenery, costumes, construction or other jobs, but they keep the number of operators to a minimum, and select them for their versatility. This is principally for economic reasons, but it is obvious that two or three people working closely together can achieve a closer harmony than large numbers of operators. If it is necessary to interest and provide duties for many people, a number of separate projects is often more practicable than one large production. Each unit can be designed to suit the interests of the individual or small group working on it, and if desired, a program can be made up for presentation from these separate acts or short plays.

Types of Puppet Shows. Several types of puppet shows are commonly used: Variety, floor show, groups of short plays, and full-length plays. In choosing a program, the available resources should be considered. Are there sufficient funds to buy costume materials, lumber, and lighting equipment, or must you depend entirely upon your ingenuity in making something out of nothing? Unless you can mount it appropriately, don't attempt an elaborate production, but try something simple. The play must be related to the dramatic abilities of those who are to speak the lines—unless your production is designed for therapeutic purposes. Children's high voices would be inadequate for a performance of Maeterlinck's tragedies. Furthermore, both audience and participants should be considered, as suggested above (p. 203).

The most flexible program is the variety show in which you can incorporate practically anything you have or that anybody wants to do. Tricks, acrobatic performances, dances, short scenes, improvisations, songs, ballads, anecdotes and jokes, feats of magic, and prize fights are among the possibilities. You will find more listed on pp. 279-80.

The selection of variety numbers is too often unimaginative. Timeworn pieces are presented in the traditional manner, with no fresh interpretation to bring them up to date. Practically every company acquires a puppet pianist done in the tradition of Paderewski and long flowing hair. If you *must* have a pianist, study the mannerisms of contemporary performers (Rudolf Serkin could inspire a whole new set of movements) and build your caricature upon them. The mention of a circus brings up pictures of puppets performing upon trapezes or walking the tight rope. For a change, it would be fun to build a performer to bounce on a net. The classical ballet has received ironical comment at the hands of puppet ballerinas. An amusing variant of the number is Esther Cheatle's Scarlet O'Feather, a pink bird with a long neck and legs which can outdo any human dancer. Closer observation of the entertaining characters around us would be a far richer source of inspiration than imitation of current vaudeville numbers. With so many possibilities to be really creative, why pilfer from the past or from our fellow puppeteers?

Although variety acts may be simple or complex, they need as careful preparation as a play. The difference is that a variety program can be worked up more or less independently by a number of individuals, whereas a play takes synchronized group work.

A puppet program based upon movement, song, tricks, and easily understood pantomime is excellent for diverse groups of people whose background and language vary, because such acts transcend time, place, and nationality. In the last century, Walter Deaves took his whole family on a seven year tour around the world, playing in the East Indies, China, Japan, South America and in many other places where the puppets were always enjoyed and understood.

The floor show is similar to variety, but is somewhat more exacting. At night clubs or on the movie vaudeville circuit, puppet numbers usually fit in with other acts, hence they must be carefully timed, the puppets must work to perfection, and the operator must be completely sure of himself. Because floor show acts are usually performed with the operator in view of the audience, "the personal appearance of the puppeteer, of minor importance in a show masked by drapes, is a factor for success. One is seen perhaps only when entering and taking a bow; but whether or not the audience likes the looks of the puppeteer influences the reception of the puppets. His make-up cannot be exaggerated, yet cannot be dispensed with. Clothes are important; they must not distract from the puppets, yet must catch the eye as the puppeteer enters. They should be appropriate to the place and time of day."[1]

Programs of separate numbers are sometimes given continuity

[220]

by a master of ceremonies. He should not be too talkative, but an occasional remark addressed to the audience helps to create intimacy. In arranging the program, alternate songs with dances, tricks with bits of dialogue, and end up with your best number.

Groups of short plays chosen for variety make good programs; by omitting one or two, the length of the program can be adjusted to suit any time schedule. Suggestions for writing your own plays are given in Chapter VII, and source material is listed on pp. 267-77. The principal difficulty with a group of plays is in the number of puppets and amount of scenery they may take. Often the total equipment needed is greater than for a long play. However, there are many combinations of plays and short turns which are satisfactory.

Permanent puppet theatres which play regularly need a larger repertory than those which go on tour or play only occasionally. The building of new shows often taxes the producer. He might find it practical to use a set of stock characters as the basis of his repertory. Most of the successful popular puppet theatres in the past were built upon such a scheme. The nucleus of the puppet company was a popular character, such as Hänneschen, Casper, or Punchinello, who appeared in a variety of dramatic situations. This favorite character was generally a personification of success. He was always able to overcome opposition, but not without many adventures and a final violent combat, which provided continuous amusement. The popularity of Charlie McCarthy is a contemporary example of this type of character. If he uses words instead of a cudgel, his opponents are no less vanquished, and his audience is equally amused.

For a children's theatre, you could use a set of stock puppets designed to perform fairy tales: The prince, the princess, the wicked fairy, the good fairy, the king, and so on. Special characters needed to play certain stories could be added when necessary. For adults, characters depicting everyday modern types such as the rich banker, the college professor, the office girl, and the clubwoman, could be used in an endless variety of situations, with only minor changes of costume or accessories to suit the occasion. Each puppet theatre could have its favorite character which everyone would associate with that theatre, and whose adventures would be followed as we follow the exploits of Superman or Mickey Mouse. For this kind of repertory, the hand-and-rod-puppets described on pp. 45-49 have been found particularly valuable because changes of costume are easy to make. This can be done just by changing the puppet's head or adding a new accessory. By making new heads and costumes, a set of bodies can soon be transformed into a completely new cast, with a minimum of construction.

The modern audience, particularly an adult one, usually demands novelty, so it would be necessary to supplement your stock company with variety numbers frequently changed.

DANCING IN THE PUPPET THEATRE

Music and dance are invaluable for all types of puppet shows. Louise Martin discusses puppet dancing: "There are some kinds of dancing for puppets which are not successful, but other kinds, though they would never pass the rigid test of human technique, are fun for audiences and interesting to the puppeteer. Puppets cannot dance as human beings dance, just as they cannot move as human beings move, but in the attempted imitation of human beings there is nearly always humor, and frequently satire. You have often heard it said, after a performance by a puppet ballerina, 'I can never look at a flesh and blood ballerina again and keep a straight face.' The little stiff-legged puppet with its jerky movements and unperturbed calm has cast a kind of dead-pan aspersion on the human ballerina doing difficult and physically unnatural movements with her serenely smiling face which denies the energy and strain of the muscular exertion.

"But there are other kinds of dancing besides the classical ballet, which puppets attempt with varying degrees of success depending upon who is doing the handling and how much knowledge he has of human movement, as well as of puppets. Set forms, patterns and figures are difficult if not impossible for puppets, but they can jump up and down in time to music; move to the right and left, forward and back; kick their feet, and move their arms in a kind of imitation dancing which lends liveliness to any scene and points the music.

"Another kind of dancing is the floating-fairy kind. This, of course, rises above the realm of mundane human beings and gets into the field of fantasy where you can go as far as the imagination and invention of the puppeteer will allow.

"The Oriental dancer is a favorite. The puppet is made with a very flexible waist and strung at the hips so that the puppeteer can produce deep backbends, a waving midriff and 'bumps.' The fixed, uncoquettish expression of the puppet, combined with the torrid movements, always brings hilarious mirth from an audience.

"These types of dancing are suitable to puppets controlled from above with strings. When the puppet is controlled with rods the possibilities for exact and controlled movement are greater. One pair of American puppeteers achieved a unique dance routine by attaching to the feet of a string-puppet little rods projecting from the heels. While the puppet was seemingly handled from above in the usual fashion by one puppeteer, another one worked the feet from behind a curtain, and gave the puppet the positive accent of the tap or clog dancer."[2]

Rod-puppets can twirl easily. The center rod is rotated at different speeds, while the arms, legs, and skirts fly outward by centrifugal force. Incidental movement can be had by setting the head on a spring, and using smaller springs for the arms. Twirling puppets are limited in movement, but are effective as background for a more flexible solo dancer, or for quick passing back and forth across the stage. Chorus groups, with three or four figures set on a single crossbar with a handle for supporting it, are easily worked and are suitable for short routines. Legs and arms can be made of springs, or controlled with rods and strings (*Plate 15, E*).

Another type of rod-puppet dancer is based on the simple puppet

THE PUPPET THEATRE HANDBOOK

illustrated on *Plate 11*, *E*, in which movement is concentrated in the head and arms. The former does no more than turn from side to side, but the latter can be moved in intricate and precise patterns which are excellent when combined with simple turns and sways of the body. In other dancers, movement may be concentrated in the legs, with the upper part of the body rigid and the arms either hanging freely to move outward with centrifugal force or set on springs for incidental movement. The Yaqui deer dancer shown on *Plate 15*, *A* is one of the best liked performers in the Mexican puppet theatre El Nahual. The figure is supported by a rod fitted into a belt worn by the operator. Wires on the heels control the legs, and the arms swing freely on springs. The waist is articulated, and the dancer bends forward when in a normal position. A wire secured to the small of the back is pulled to straighten the puppet and to produce the up-and-down bend, characteristic of Indian dances. Rattles held in the puppet's hands, bells on its ankles and wrist augment the chanting of the puppeteer. Further movement is given the figure by the puppeteer's body. In another Mexican dance, two skeletons, one dressed as a cowboy and the other as a woman, are worked by rods which form their legs. With plenty of room on the stage to work them, these puppets are remarkably lively, although their movement is limited. The mechanism of these dancers is illustrated on *Plate 15* and described on p. 58.

The Russian hopak and the hornpipe can be danced by flat rod-puppets, if the legs are strung like the puppet illustrated on *Plate 11*, *B*. Again, movement is concentrated in the legs, but the arms can be given incidental motion with springs, or they can be strung to move with the legs.

With rod-puppet dancers, the principal problem is one of support because one hand of the operator has to hold the figure in position, and the other has to perform all other movements. Both hands can be freed if the puppet is fitted into a pedestal attached to a movable stool (*Plate 45*), held by a second operator, or set in a belt worn by the operator as for the deer dancer (*Plate 15, A*).

Hand-puppets have certain movements which can be well

adapted to dances. They can do all kinds of turns and bends; dance together in waltz rhythm or swing; dip, sway, and bump. With long full skirts they can suggest many Spanish rhythms; if they cannot imitate the exact steps, at least they can dance with gay abandon. No special mechanism is necessary to accomplish all this. You need only a sense of rhythm and plenty of practice.

Shadow-puppets can also dance. While their action is confined to the two-dimensional plane in which they perform, a skillful operator can invent lively dances. Front view figures, with rods on hands, head and hip can be clowns, hornpipe dancers, or animated jumping jacks (*Plate 2, A*). Animals, lady bareback riders, and other circus acts are quite possible with shadows, and are especially effective if they are done in color. Shadow ladies with swaying hips can perform seductive dances.

With all these possibilities before us, it is obvious that, as Louise Martin points out, "the field of dancing by puppets has by no means been exhausted. It has, in fact, been scarcely touched. It is conceivable that someone with some dance experience, a knowledge of the possibilities and limitations of puppets, with taste and imagination, who is willing to apply concentrated study and make extensive experiments, might evolve something not yet thought of, quite beyond the present somewhat limited achievements along this line."[3] A number of books which would help in designing the movement of specific dances are listed on pp. 271-72.

MUSIC IN THE PUPPET THEATRE

Music in puppet shows is much used, but it is not always too well done, and little has been written to help the puppeteer in this important aspect of his production. David Gibson offers the following suggestions:

"The puppet showman can use original music especially composed or select existing works. The music can be played by a pianist or orchestra or through recordings. With a public address system at his disposal, he can choose from a wide variety of available recordings, including discs of foreign folk song and dance music.

"Music must never overshadow the drama. Only in opera and ballet is it as important as the action itself. Then it must be outstanding as music; nothing mediocre will do. In drama when the actors maintain silence, or between scenes, music can carry the action forward 'on wings of song.' But it must end the moment that important action or dialogue resumes. Music in a continuous undercurrent loses its effect.

"Theatrical music falls into these catagories: background, which paints moods, points scenes, and heightens action; atmospheric, which sets a scene before the curtain goes up; accompaniment, for a dance or song; and incidental, unconnected with what happens on the stage, as in a gay interlude between numbers of a variety show, or a song thrown in to pad out the entertainment.

"Short fantasies can be charming with just a piano background, but major drama requires more. We have become so accustomed to a symphony orchestra in the films that it is taken for granted. The worst thing in the world is a pianist thundering away at an orchestral extraction, trying to create the illusion of a whole orchestra. But a well played, well written piano background is vastly superior to a jumble of tunes from scratchy records on a bad P. A. system.

"You don't have to stick to one composer or period. A flexible background score can be drawn from whatever supplies the right music for the moment.

"During the overture the music reigns supreme. For a puppet show it should last no longer than four or five minutes and should be played after the house lights are out and the footlights up. This allows the audience to start concentrating on the business at hand. Here is your opportunity to set the mood of the production. The music should suggest the atmosphere of what is to come. The moment the curtain is up and the actors start speaking, the music should fade to the background or conclude on some final chord; fading to a cut in the middle of a phrase is sloppy. Overtures for later acts are selected in the same way. A few bars may suffice to regain the audience's attention and prepare it for the rest. In opera or ballet the music flows from overture to act with a smooth juncture during which the curtain rises.

"Try to avoid music which is so trite that your audience groans after hearing the first few bars. And do not use something familiar like Beethoven's *Fifth Symphony* which is recognized to have an entity of its own. For intense drama the music should augment the performance and blend with it—highlighting and clarifying key scenes and speeches. Under no circumstances should it tower by itself—three miles from the drama. Great drama does not predicate great background music. The former can stand by itself, but appropriate music will not detract from it.

"Music cannot convey a definite story unless the listener knows the scenario. It is an art which *presents* and does not *represent*. It appeals to the ear directly, without intermediary of the intellect. Listen to a Respighi tone poem to see if you can follow its program without having read it first. But 'pictorial' music is excellent in the theatre, for the action makes its meaning clear.

"A radio station which must depend upon recorded backgrounds rarely lets you recognize the strain of a familiar work. Music is considered only for its emotional effect. It can be soft and romantic, restrained and calm, tempestuous and fiery, gay and lilting, tinkling and brilliant, sad and heavy, dreamy and confused, or pious and other-worldly. A record must be selected to suggest a definite mood. If you are not familiar with too many of the titles in the catalogue, pick what looks as if it might serve and try it out. Don't buy something which 'might work.' Be certain what you want before you buy. Ask for suggestions from those who know music better; they can save you hours of listening in a stuffy little booth.

"Much ideal background music comes from tone poems. As these are constructed from rambling themes, they have concert hall associations for few. In them you can find unfamiliar leit-motifs for your own purposes. But don't overdo these tags or they'll become ludicrous, like the ominous fanfare of the villain's entrance in an old-fashioned melodrama. In Richard Strauss is a treasure trove of background music. Some Wagner (*not* the *Ride of the Valkyrie*) is excellent for puppets. The *Siegfried Idyll, Rhine Journey, Fire Music, Liebesodt,* and *Venusberg* music have very usable parts. Wagner was one of the greatest co-ordinators of music and drama. The Respighi tone poems, Mendelssohn concert overtures, and Ravel noctures are just right. Hazy themes with emotional power are to be found, particularly in the works of Borodin, Stravinsky, Rimsky-Korsakov, and Moussorgsky.

"If you use a symphony for a background, select only the less remembered passages. In Beethoven's *Second, Third, Eighth,* and *Ninth,* in any of Sibelius' except the *Second,* in Tschaikowsky, the second movement of Dvořák's *New World,* such parts are to be found. The second movement of the classic symphony is an *andante.* The other movements, varying in tempo and color, may have tricky sudden changes, but since a lot of dynamic music is in them, they should not be overlooked.

[Be careful that your puppet show music is not too heavy. Recordings of string quartets, trios and other combinations are often appropriate. Eighteenth-century composers such as Bach, Haydn and Mozart provide a wealth of music with excellent rhythms for the puppet stage; their orchestrations are simpler than those of later composers.]

"Choose a theme which lasts out all the speeches it is to accentuate. A dreamy string passage may burst into full orchestra strength and scare the audience out of its wits if the record watcher dozes. Blending, mixing, timing, and volume are elements to be watched carefully. Never drown the actors' voices by having volume up too high. Though a gradual crescendo is natural for a climax, the voices, too, must build up, but should not be forced to howls and screams. Timing is all important; nothing is worse than music which enters and leaves at the wrong time. Blending requires one hand on the volume control; the music is started almost inaudibly and held there till the cue draws near, then it is brought up, merely coloring the voice—singing behind it or through it—then, gradually, it is diminished so that the audience feels it hasn't heard any music at all, save the music of the play. Any abrupt opening or closing startles and calls attention to the music, away from the drama. Mixing is the blending of sounds from two or more turntables. You must decide which sounds are to predominate and at what times.

"A musical finale after the curtain is down is generally an anticlimax; after the lights are up, and the audience is readjusting itself to the scale of the normal world, it tends to be confusing. With a variety show the custom is, of course, to play something gay to send 'em out humming a tune.

"This is how you can play parts of records: Place a very thick old needle in the phonograph arm, and while the record revolves, guide the needle crosswise over the grooves in a spiral from the end of the last passage chosen to the end of the disc. Then the record will play only what you want, with pauses between passages. Experiment on old records before trying it on a good one. This may seem a waste, but it gives you peace of mind and enhanced efficiency. [A more economical (and more efficient) way is to have the various sections you want to use in a show recorded on one or two discs, with adequate spaces between. This saves your expensive album from mutilation.] Otherwise, you can mark pieces with white cloth or adhesive tape. On pieces of such tape on the record, mark in black ink the exact passages with act and scene numbers, as 'Act 2, Scene 1, and Act 3, Scene 2: ominous motive: murder.' Thus, no matter how shuffled the records may become, you can always find what you want. And they do get shuffled, with both sides of a record used several times during a performance! Records which are used constantly should be kept apart from those which are used only once. They are easier to locate.

"If one musical number succeeds another in a variety show, the records can be marked simply in numerical sequence. A rack with a small light should be built to hold the records, so that they can be handled one by one, played, and returned to their places. If there are elaborate musical or sound effects throughout a performance, they will keep one person busy, and should be assigned to a special operator. He can help set up the stage, pack and arrange scenery, run the light switchboard, and keep backstage visitors at their distance."[4]

Other phases of the music problem are suggested by Sue Hastings and Dorcas Ruthenburg. They recommend simple, substantial lyrics rather than subtle or sophisticated rhymes, and they believe folk tunes and old-fashioned melodies are usually more effective than musical-comedy scores. The advantages of a piano are pointed out: "One is almost always available and has greater flexibility than recorded music. While a phonograph is often employed, records are usually too heavy to be really appropriate, and you have the added disadvantage of being unable to improvise. On a piano, when a string breaks or a puppet head flies off, you can, by ad libbing, go a long way toward making a catastrophe look like intentional drama, whereas a record grinds on with inexorable candor. If you don't play the piano yourself, suborn someone who is not only a performer but who can do a bit of improvisation as well. He will add greatly to your productions if he is able to create music to fit the mood and requirements of a play, or ripple on in emergencies.

"If you are going to add a second instrument, choose one that provides rhythmic background. A banjo, guitar, or accordion lends contrast as well as pointing up dance routines.

"As to the choice of vocalists for your company, select for versatility and showmanship in preference to vocal virtuosity. Good voices are less essential than the ability to project a personality and sell the lyric content of a song."[5]

There is one great advantage of music composed especially for the puppet show—it can be designed with the same compactness and emphasis upon essentials that dominates the play and underlies the design and character of the puppet. Too often excerpts from existing music, even though they are skillfully arranged, are not completely unified compositions and lack the force of the puppet play. Writing music for the puppet stage is just as specialized a technique as writing it for the dance or any other theatre form.

Care must be taken that the music is not too long. Puppets are more limited in movement than human beings; a puppet dancer performing to the music of a phonograph record may be able to show everything it has during the first minute and be forced into tiresome repetition for the remainder of the number. It would be much better if the variety of action of which a puppet is capable could be related to a specially written musical accompaniment, instead of forcing the puppet to follow the pattern of music too intricate for it. Various attempts have been made to use puppets to illustrate opera played on phonograph records. Some of these have become popular, but the puppet show is reduced to an animated picture, and the actors to automata which repeat the same movements over and over again. They cannot match the subtle variations and changes in the music. If you want to do opera, try to find a composer who can write one in terms of the puppet actor's capabilities.

DIRECTION AND REHEARSAL

The Director's Job. A director is as necessary for a puppet show as for any other theatrical production. The simplest dance routine is better if someone stays outside and tells the puppeteer how the puppet looks. The director must supervise not only the puppet's action on the stage but he must also give suggestions to the person who is working the puppet, because puppeteers are likely to get in each other's way. He must also keep all the parts of the production co-ordinated. Scenery, lighting, costumes, dance, and movement pattern have to be properly related to each other, and the director is the person to do it. Any changes which have to be made in any of these parts should be done at the request of the director, for he is best able to see the show as a whole. If the scenery is the wrong color, it may have to be repainted, or the light changed. If the music is too loud or of the wrong type, if a puppet's joints stick, if the rain doesn't sound like rain, the director must see that these defects are remedied.

For a play of any magnitude, it may be necessary to have some assistants to the director: A stage manager, an electrician, a property man, and a wardrobe mistress. Such division of labor will provide jobs for a number of people, and it works well for some productions, but the usual professional company combines these jobs with that of puppeteering. Each operator is assigned certain technical duties such as pulling the curtain, setting props, changing scenery, working lights and music. This simplification makes for closer unity in the production and is, of course, more practical for touring.

Tryouts. The first job of the director is to assign parts. A good way is to assemble everyone interested in the production, read the script to them and discuss it. Then tryouts can be held. The casting is done in terms of voice (volume, flexibility, richness, and variety) since that is the puppeteer's chief tool. It is a good idea to let the potential operators handle a puppet or two before assigning them parts. Improvising with puppets (see p. 214) is a practical way of learning whether a person has the rhythm and co-ordination necessary to be a good operator. Dancing the puppets to music also helps. Potential ability is as important as a creditable performance at the tryout; keen interest is essential, and a co-operative attitude imperative.

Production Plans. The director should plan the show carefully, and make a tentative action plan for the play. If there are several scenes, it helps to make a scale diagram of each, with scenery, props, and lines of action indicated. Another aid to directing is the prompt-notebook, in which the script is pasted on sheets of paper large enough to leave generous margins. Sketches, diagrams, notes, can be written down and remembered. The book is handy if you want to repeat a show at a later period.

Tact and patience are necessary for a good director, especially if he is working with inexperienced operators or volunteers. Opportunity should be given the puppeteers to contribute suggestions and to bring some creative interpretation to their roles, though the director should be the final judge of the effectiveness of the action on the stage. Choice of a director should fall upon the person best versed in knowledge of the theatre as a whole, and who has enough leadership to hold together all the loose ends of a show.

Rehearsals. In the puppet theatre it too often happens that the construction of the figures and scenery consumes so much time that there is not enough left for adequate rehearsals. Usually, every moment must be used to the fullest advantage, although if the puppet show has been carefully organized, a balance has been established between construction and rehearsal. At any rate, whatever rehearsal time is available should be planned.

All puppeteers agree that lines must be learned if the persons who are to speak them are also going to work the puppets. Sagging puppets and meaningless jiggles are the certain result of trying to read the lines of the script from a paper tacked to the stage. Until you know lines, the puppet cannot be moved with any precision. Everybody should know everybody else's lines because the next bit of action can be anticipated and prepared for. Frequently a puppet show does not have the luxury of a prompter, so each person should know the play thoroughly in order to be able to improvise if necessary.

Different people have different ways of learning lines. Some find it easier first to learn the content of every speech, then work for precise lines and cues. Having someone read the other speeches is helpful, because saying the lines aloud gives practice in expression as well as memorization. Line rehearsals with all the puppeteers save time in the end, for lines usually vanish completely when the puppets are first taken in hand. Whatever line learning methods are followed, each individual will have to spend some time in quiet, concentrated study, for the difficulties of combining lines with manipulation makes complete mastery of the part essential.

In some productions, delivery of the lines and manipulation of the puppets are done by different groups of people. For proper synchronization of reading and manipulation, the readers should be able to watch the puppets, and the operators should be familiar enough with the text to "suit the action to the word." Often the readers are seated below the stage floor in string-puppet shows, and watch the action in a mirror. For hand- or rod-puppet shows, they may watch from the wings.

It is impossible to say how many rehearsals should be held, because they depend upon the type of show and previous experience of the operators. Every puppeteer should have confidence in his part before the show is given, and enough time should be allowed for the completion of scenery, lighting, and other details. In very simple shows with one or two operators, only a few rehearsals might be necessary (though puppet shows are never over-rehearsed) while it would take six weeks of spare time, or four weeks of full time rehearsals for a full length puppet play. In situations where limited time is available for a show, the type of puppet and play must be carefully chosen so that the necessary technical work can be done and rehearsals will not be slighted. Rehearsals over two hours in length are impracticable on the puppet stage because of the fatigue involved; it is better to have shorter rehearsals every day than longer ones at greater intervals, until the play is ready to be rehearsed in its entirety.

After the preliminary reading of the play, rehearsals begin in earnest. Ellen Van Volkenburg describes her method of conducting them: "At first the play was rehearsed precisely as an ordinary play is done—that is, with the puppeteers minus puppets. When the acting rehearsal was over for the day, we had what was called a 'mechanics' work-out; that was when a puppeteer became acquainted with his puppet—walking it about, seating it, turning its head. There was no formality about it and everyone worked on his own. After a few days' friendship with his puppet it was amusing to see how much the puppeteer looked and walked like him in rehearsals. This procedure went on until the entire script was in hand—all lines letter-perfect, and characterizations well established. Then, and not until then, the puppeteers mounted

the bridge of the stage and began the work of transferring themselves—dramatically speaking—to their puppets. Much time was
spent in these first bridge rehearsals in establishing stage positions,
entrances and exits—where to put the puppets offstage, and so
on. The problem was twofold, because not only must the puppet
be manipulated and achieve his life, but the puppeteer's huge
human body must learn to squeeze in beside other huge bodies
on the small bridge in such a way that his hands and elbows are
free to handle the puppet control. This double task was quickly
learned—thanks to good groundwork. Having worked long enough
on the floor to know their puppets' characterizations and in-
dividualities, the matter of bridge mechanics became only a detail
which did not interrupt the main business in hand—the creating
of living creatures in a known situation."[6]

The above suggestions apply especially to string-puppets. For
other types different methods may be necessary, but whatever
can be done to help the puppeteer feel the action in his own
body and then transfer it to the puppet is valuable.

Because the director has to direct the operators as well as the
puppets, it is sometimes useful to have the first few rehearsals
without the masking draperies on the stage. Both puppets and
manipulators can be seen and difficulties ironed out. However, if
your puppeteers are shy and the purpose of having them in a
puppet show is to give them confidence in their acting, you would
defeat your end by removing the curtains.

If the show is a play with several scenes, each can be rehearsed
as a unit and finally, all together. Difficult bits of manipulation
should be rehearsed separately, either with the director, or by the
puppeteer alone with his puppet and a mirror to show him what
the figure is doing. Too much dependence upon a mirror is not
good, because attention is focused on the image and not upon the
puppet and its relation to other puppets on the stage.

During rehearsals, various jobs such as placing certain props and
pieces of scenery should be assigned to specific persons. Plan
places for keeping everything necessary to the show, and see that

the puppeteers get in the habit of replacing objects correctly. Train the operators to examine their puppets before the beginning of each rehearsal for worn strings, loose rods, broken joints, unsewed costumes, or other irregularities which might cause accidents. Then they will be likely to remember this important detail on opening night.

Even though it is very simple, the operators should practice striking and setting up the stage and scenery; these details are as important to a smoothly working show as good manipulation. If the stage is an elaborate one, and the play has a number of scenes, be sure to practice enough so that changes will move smoothly. A list of jobs to be performed by each person for each scene change should be posted backstage for reference.

Final rehearsels should be complete ones, whether the show is a ten minute scene or a three act play. Although they may take less co-ordinated rehearsal, variety shows need a goodly number of "dress" rehearsals to bring all the parts into their proper place. As far as possible, these last rehearsals should be uninterrupted so that the puppeteers can get a sense of the whole show; the best time for the director to make corrections is just after the action has been established, but before it has solidified. During this time he can stop at the end of a scene or act and make suggestions. If the same errors occur frequently, the action may be stopped and the correction made. In general, don't interrupt too much, because continuity is destroyed when you do.

The farther in advance you can plan your rehearsal schedule the better. If your actors are doing nothing else, it does not matter so much if you call sudden rehearsals, but with volunteer casts there are usually other duties which must be considered. Of course, in professional companies, the puppeteers' entire time is at the disposal of the director.

PUPPET ACTING

The Actor-Manipulator. Those who operate the puppets are really actor-manipulators. Puppet acting is a combination of the voice of the actor, his ability to communicate to the puppet the necessary motions, and the puppet's flexibility in responding. Characterization is based on the puppet's design, but the actor-manipulator must add voice and movement to harmonize with the physical appearance of the puppet.

The Importance of Voice. The importance of good voices has already been suggested. Adequate volume is necessary because the voice is partly muffled by the masking drapery or screens of the puppet stage. String-puppet operators should be careful to talk down through the proscenium opening; if they stand erect and speak into the drapery the sound is absorbed. Puppeteers working below stage level need to project their voices up and out for the same reason.

More often than not, each operator has to speak for several characters. As far as possible, it is best to have the puppet operated by the person who speaks for it, but sometimes you will find yourself having conversations with yourself, changing rapidly from character to character. This is one of the most difficult jobs of the actor-manipulator, for each character must be distinct. Bruce Inverarity says: "There are many tricks used to change the voice, and I have taken up to twenty-one different parts at one time. There were five manipulators and I did all the talking, sitting in front of a microphone and talking away to myself like an idiot. Pitching your voice at different levels, speaking into a tin can, holding your nose, juggling your Adam's apple, assuming an impediment in speech, speaking with an accent, and all sorts of devices can be used so that you may play more than one character. You will have to practice, because it is a terrible thing when you are supposed to be speaking for one character to find that you have slipped into the wrong voice and some other puppet is gesturing wildly on the stage."[7] You don't usually play twenty-one parts, but it is an asset if you can.

For character interpretation, Perry Dilley suggests that you "choose for the character in question a single and appropriate vocal mannerism, or a peculiar tempo in the delivery of lines. This may be a sharp, snarly way of speaking for an ill-tempered puppet; a high, nasal intonation for an old man; a sweet, thin, delicately-modulated intonation for a princess; a heavy, slow, loose-mouthed manner for a stupid puppet. Puppets' voices should be conventional and grotesque, but not in the least strained. A strained voice does injury to the operator's vocal apparatus; worse, it sounds most disagreeable 'out front.' "[8]

Clear enunciation is so important that the director must keep one ear especially tuned and stop the actors every time they slur important words. See that they end every word; unless they are imitating a Virginia drawl, let the final *g's* sound distinctly. If they persist in saying "edjikashin," conduct a few exercises in precise enunciation until you hear "ed-you-cay-shon"; work at it until the words flow easily but clearly.

Vocal Exercises. Hastings and Ruthenburg suggest a few exercises which will help to develop good speech. "If you have had no training, if your voice doesn't carry, if it tends to gargle and squeak, a few lessons from a voice teacher will help you out. If yours is just an average voice, breathing exercises and practice in careful enunciation even without lessons will be of help.

"Standing erect and relaxed, breathe deeply. Put your hands on your ribs to make sure they expand. Try to get your breath well down below your chest into the bottom of your lungs. Let it out slowly and evenly. Vocalize, trying to produce a substantial tone. It is this long, free column of breath, molded by the teeth, lips, and tongue, which makes speech. Repeat the exercise at intervals during the day.

"Hum. Try to feel the vibration of the tone. Try to place the tones of the scale, arching the tone so that it is lifted out of your throat and into your head. Sing the vowels—AAAAAAAAA . . . EEEEEEEEE...IIIIIIIII...OOOOOOOOO...UUUUUUUUU —trying for a smooth round, sustained quality, listening to yourself to be sure the sounds are pure. Try at various pitches. Hold your head slightly bent, relax, and try to project your tone.

"Select the more difficult consonant combinations. Make up nonsense for yourself filled with them. Practice repeating them glibly without a flaw. 'Dentists, obstetricians, and basilisks seldom startle the stratosphere with unseemly utterances.'

"Cut one word neatly before beginning the next. Read aloud. Make the words sing even if you have to exaggerate the vowels. Keep them light and free and winged, as they will be if you are breathing as you should. Try for tone color suitable to the sense. Try for a variety of pitch in bringing out the meaning and emotion of the text.

"Good books on diction will help, particularly if you follow their reading with a few lessons from a good professional."[9]

During the past few years, many professional puppeteers have found it necessary to play in large auditoriums where they could not be heard without an amplifying system. Of this practice John Houghmaster says: "I don't think that mechanical amplification of the voice, particularly with children's audiences, solves the problem of being heard. The hills and valleys of interest and expectancy along which children ride are lost with a public address system; everything is flattened to the dullness that they hear at the movies. Only rarely is an auditorium so big or accoustically bad that a loudspeaker is needed. And you can't get the illusion of reality into puppets without the natural resonance and timbre of the human voice."[10] Ideally, puppets should never be required to perform in large auditoriums for huge audiences, yet this cannot always be avoided, and it is certainly better to be both seen and heard, even though it means amplification. But avoid it if you can.

Puppet versus Human Acting. Puppet acting differs from human acting to the degree that the puppet is constructed differently. A hand-puppet actor moves less like a human being than a string-puppet, because the latter more nearly resembles the human form. Yet the most perfectly constructed puppet is still a mechanical figure and so can never completely imitate human movement. Although it walks with its legs, bends its arms at wrist, elbow and shoulder, and makes other motions more or less like a human being, the puppet is not just a miniature version of one.

Each type of puppet construction presents individual possibilities for acting, and these variations should be used to their best advantage by the operator. It is as futile to try to do with hand-puppets the same things one can do with a string-puppet as to expect a shadow-figure to create the same illusion of three-dimensional reality as a rod-puppet.

Puppet Movement on the Stage. Because the puppet cannot employ subtle gesture and facial expression, it is not always easy to tell which character is speaking unless the other characters are kept relatively still. If the speaking puppet's gestures are quiet, others should be devoid of movement. In more animated scenes, they can display some motion so long as there is plenty of contrast between them and the puppet holding the stage at the moment. With this limitation, it is sometimes difficult to create a sense of relationship between the various characters on the stage and make them look as though they are following everything with intense interest. Rod-puppets which are set in slots or string-puppets which have been hung in their place on the stage tend to look segregated unless they can be given some animation. As on the large stage, there should be some reaction from the puppet actors. Heads may shake or nod in negation or agreement; a slight tap of the foot may suggest impatience at another character's long-windedness; startling revelations may evoke sudden movement in the listening puppets, or they may lean forward to suggest suspense.

Scenery and actors together should form pleasing stage pictures. The puppeteers watch the grouping of their puppets, and try for variation of movement, while the director checks from out front. Many puppet stages are small, and have little depth, but full advantage should be taken of what space there is. Too often, puppets give the impression of being rooted to one spot—they may sway on their feet like flowers waving on a stem, but seem reluctant to move to another part of the stage. It is well to have the center of action move from one part of the stage to another. In scenes where there are a number of puppets, avoid having them lined up like a chorus; place them in groups, with some upstage and others downstage. The kind and number of puppets used will influence the possibilities for stage composition. A simple hand-puppet show with only two characters on the stage at a time will allow fewer variations of position than a rod-puppet or marionette production with a large cast.

Timing and Pace. Puppet actors, like their human counterparts, must learn timing. They should wait just the right interval for laughs, make their entrances and exits at the right moment, pick up their cues promptly, pause long enough for dramatic effect but not so long as to suggest a lapse of memory. The tempo or pace of the performance also needs to be sensitively felt by the puppeteers and controlled by the director. Different characters will speak their lines with a speed appropriate to their age or character, while gay scenes will move faster than quiet ones. Variation in tempo is important; it should increase as climaxes are approached, and diminish as they are past.

PUPPET MANIPULATION

Puppet acting is so closely allied to manipulation that ability to control the puppet is a requisite of a good actor-manipulator.

The eye should be constantly kept on the puppet while it is on the stage. String-puppets will sag at the knees and look like rags, shadow-puppets will pull away from the screen and become fuzzy, hand-puppets and others worked from below will gradually disappear from sight as though sinking in a quagmire, unless the operator is always alert. He must be equally careful not to let any part of his anatomy show, for the audience will see a suddenly revealed hand as the hand of a giant, and the illusion of human scale will be at once destroyed. You will soon learn where the strings or rods are, and need not watch the mechanism.

The puppet can pretend to do many actions which are difficult or impossible actually to perform. Don't worry too much about elaborate mechanisms—maybe you can fake the movement. Transference of small objects such as coins can be suggested quite adequately.

Variety in the puppets' actions is as important as subtle differences in its manner of speaking. Ways of doing this are listed by David Gibson: "You can vary the speed with which the puppets move about the stage; the length of the stride and the gait of the puppets can be as colorful as you choose to make them; general animation of the entire body or the lack of it can introduce a kind of variety—but don't go too far and burlesque everything. You can vary the speed with which the puppets respond to stimuli—the speed and manner in which the head is turned, or the movement of hands and arms; you can use obvious physical mannerisms such as limping, nervous twitching, heavy bodily sighs, silent sobs, stooped shoulders; you can get differences in the carriage of the head and body. All of these are good in their place, but you must be economical with puppet movement; a figure should not be twitching or fretting without reason. The same mannerisms, if repeated too often, will bore people."[11]

Puppet gestures should be definite. Unskilled string-puppet operators are likely to keep the puppets' hands sawing up and down in rhythm to the speech; this should be avoided because it is monotonous and soon loses any chance of pointing the speech. Hand-and-rod-puppets tend to hold their arms aloft as though surrendering to any enemy, until the puppeteer learns to manage the rods. Hand-puppets wave their arms meaninglessly, and shadows jiggle spasmodically unless the gesture pattern is planned for variety and contrast.

Because the puppet is on a smaller scale than a human being or animal, gestures should also be kept in scale, unless exaggeration is desired for comedy or melodrama. The rapid speed with which hand-puppets can move through space is one of their charms, although it is completely out of scale with human movement. Quick nods of the head, very deep bows, leaps into the air are typical movements which can be exaggerated to good effect. Remember that puppet action need not be realistic, but it must be controlled so that a swing of the arm does not sweep the puppet offstage.

Each type of puppet involves certain problems of manipulation. These are quite different from one another, and skill in operating one kind of figure does not imply equal skill with any other type.

Shadow-Puppet Manipulation. Shadow-puppets require delicate and precise manipulation. They often have as many joints as a string-puppet, but only two or three rods to control them. Too violent movement of the control stick will set the figure into pendulumlike action which is both meaningless and out of scale. On the other hand, with two to four control sticks, you can get both subtle and positive movements which suggest haughtiness, dignity, servility, coquetry, or gay abandon.

The script for a shadow play must be carefully arranged so that the puppets will not have to cross each other while on stage. Care must be taken not to block exits; usually the figure which comes on first goes off last. Don't let your hand or head come between the light and the screen. The rods should be held loosely in the hands; for ordinary figures, the head rod can be held in one hand, the hand rods in the other. By placing the rods loosely between the fingers, a figure can be controlled in one hand.

With a front view dancing figure like the one shown on *Plate 2, A* flexible movement can be produced if you hold the hip and left hand rods in your left hand, the head and right hand in your right. The incidental movement of the legs can be partly controlled, and arms or head can be moved independently, provided the rods are held loosely. By transferring the left hand rod to your right hand, you can make the puppet do all kinds of hip movements.

Shadow-puppets can be turned around on the screen if the control rods are correctly placed. If the figures are made of parchment in the Chinese manner (*Plate 1, A*), they can be turned partly around and look over their shoulders. Reverses should be made as quickly as possible, because the figure will disappear for an instant as it is turned. This is not particularly disturbing because shadow-puppets are not realistic anyway. In some shadow theatres, such as the Javanese and Balinese, opaque perforated figures are used, and the image is sharp or fuzzy depending upon the distance they are held from the screen. Large, hazy shadows will suddenly be clarified into sharply defined shapes as they are brought close to the screen. Shadow actors can disappear, only to reappear somewhere else, if you jerk them quickly away or lower them out of sight. For most of the action, however, the figures should be held closely to the screen.

Hand-Puppet Manipulation. A combination of the operator's finger, wrist and arm movement gives a great deal of varied action, from small gestures done with the fingers, to broad sweeps of the arm causing the puppet to dash about with superhuman speed.

Walter Wilkinson gives these suggestions for practicing with hand-puppets: "Move the puppets simply, turning them from full face to profile not just mechanically, but as if they were looking from one thing to another. Make them look up, and look down; make them pick up an object at one end of the stage and carry it to the other end, setting it down and arranging it as if the puppet were interested in what it is doing. Make one puppet hand objects to another, shake hands, embrace—in short, just make the puppet move about the theatre doing all the ordinary little movements you can discover, and do them deliberately, clearly, as if you were showing them to an audience. All this is the basic technique of manipulating a hand-puppet."[12]

Bessie A. Ficklen also recommends practicing the simplest actions first, and when these are perfected more elaborate ones can be tried. The puppet can "march to music, dance, thrust out his chest, then his head, twirl his club; make the 'odiously vulgar sign,' finger to nose; play *'Peas-Porridge-Hot'*; wash his face; fan himself and others; eat, drink, shake his fist, hide his face in his hands and weep. You will find the simplest action can be made important. Then pass on to the action of two puppets together, one on each hand. Let them dance, *vis-à-vis*, and then together; embrace, curtsey; chase each other around, dodging and jumping over furniture; sit down and converse; weep on each other's shoulder, fight! When they talk be sure the talker nods and gesticulates as talkers do, and that the listener *listens* and responds, by nod or by protest."[13]

Perry Dilley gives some good hints to the hand-puppet manipulator: "The figures are hanging, head down, from the 'puppet-rail' in front of him. He slips his hand into the costume, getting his forefinger into the neckhole, his thumb and second finger into the wristcuffs, and clamping the remaining two fingers around the bag [*Plate 5, C*]. He disengages the puppet from the hook, shakes the costume into order, maybe pulling it into shape with his teeth if his other hand is occupied, and sets the puppet up into the wings ready to 'go on.'

"The hole in the neck is stuffed to allow the finger to enter to—or sometimes a little over—the second joint; consequently, most of the weight of the head bears on the top of the finger. It is not necessary that the finger fit *tightly* in the hole; a little *looseness* allows secondary movements. Each puppeteer makes these adjustments for himself; they vary also with each puppet.

"As a general practice, it is best to hold the figure up above the head at full arm's length; this is less tiring than holding it with the elbow partially crooked, and it gives the puppeteer more freedom in turning and moving the puppet about the scene. When the puppet is 'downstage' the operator can rest his arm against a bar or narrow shelf provided for the purpose. This shelf has another use, too. The puppeteer can establish the proper height of the puppet in the scene at the beginning of rehearsal by noting where the bottom edge of the costume comes in relation to this shelf. When the puppet moves 'upstage' he should be raised gradually until he is about two inches higher at the backdrop. This is necessary in order to accommodate the upward slant in the audience's line of vision. If this rule is not observed, the figure will appear to sink slightly as he goes back.

"It is an inexcusable fault to allow puppets to drop below their established height, even for a moment, at any time during a performance. They have a strong tendency to drop on making exits.

"Bending the forefinger causes the puppet to nod, acquiesce; to make him shake his head, expressing objection, turn his whole body by rotating the forearm. The operator's wrist is the puppet's waist; by bending it he can make the puppet lean over to pick up things, etc. By throwing the arms wide and the head back suddenly, the puppet shows amazement or fear. Joy can be expressed by clapping the hands and jumping up and down excitedly. If the head and arms are drawn tightly together into a mass and the operator's wrist is doubled in a right angle to his arm, and the whole rigid mass given sharp, convulsive jerks, the puppet will be weeping beautifully. Excessive grief should not be too realistic in its vocal aspect—conventionalize it. A plain 'boo-hoo-hoo-hoo-hoo' started on a high note and coming down the scale is effective.

"When the puppet talks, a slight accenting movement should be given the head, a hand, or sometimes the whole figure in time with the speech. This is 'synchronization,' a first principle. It creates, when done finely, the illusion of speech coming from the puppet. Excessive bobbing of the puppet's head becomes tiresome—the more subtle and varied the accents, the more charming and alive the puppet will be. *Restraint* is important. For instance, avoid carrying an action or stunt to the full limit of the audience's appreciation of it; better to stop abruptly just short of that point and begin building the next action."[14]

Bessie Ficklen points out that "the fist puppet is especially strong on still-motion or slow-motion effects—gazing and staring, pointing, bowing, weeping, hiding his face in a pillow and peeping out, taking a long drink, or any of the slower, more cautious or thoughtful actions. But the natural impulse of whoever first gets a hand on him is to hop and wriggle him about spasmodically. This lightning activity is impossible for the eye to follow, and very tiresome to watch."[15]

Hand-puppets excel in fighting, but, as Bessie Ficklen warns, "it must be a real fight, not the makeshift scramble of the unskilled puppeteer, which is seldom more than a butting contest—very bad for the puppets' noses—or a writhing about of the two warriors so tightly clinched together that nobody can see what is going on. A fight should be a spirited and dramatic engagement, with variety, and with surprises. The tactics must not be mixed, but each mode of attack kept separate—wrestling, boxing, whacking, dodging, dancing, kicking; with clubs hammering or thrusting like rapiers. Sometimes one, sometimes the other fighter will be knocked down or will be on top. It should mount in a climax and at the end should leave no doubt as to who is the victor."[16]

A hand-puppet walk is quite unnatural, even though the figure may have legs. A reasonably good suggestion can be given by rotating the wrist slightly from side to side, at the same time moving the puppet up and down. The different speeds with which these synchronized movements are made will determine the style of walking.

Of all the types, hand-puppets are the most adroit in handling properties. The operator should use his thumb and middle finger, and the puppet's hands should be of some flexible material if there is much carrying to do. Walter Wilkinson, the famous English puppeteer, is so skillful he can make two puppet clowns simultaneously toss sticks into the air—the puppet on the right hand catches the stick tossed by the one on the left hand, and vice versa. One of the oldest bits of hand-puppet action is the wielding of the cudgel. Mr. Punch and other puppet heroes have risen to fame via their skill with a club. They pick it up, lay it down, take it on and off the stage, thwack people over the head, use it as a lance. One puppet will take it away from another only to have it won back again. Hand-puppets can carry onto the stage anything which is light enough and built so that the operator can grasp it between his fingers. Beds are brought in, made up with blankets and pillow, slept in, and taken out. A bicyclist rides in, collides with a lamp post, breaks up the bicycle. He proceeds to put it together again, but isn't a very good mechanic, and the machine is quite unlike a bicycle when he gets it together. He tries again, aided by a policeman, and is finally successful in making an arrangement of parts which works more or less satisfactorily.

Take advantage of all these movements which the hand-puppet does so well, for no other type is so good in this respect.

Hand-and-Rod-Puppet Manipulation. Much of what has been said about hand-puppet manipulation applies equally to hand-and-rod-puppets. The principal difference is in the arm movement. Because they are longer and articulated at the elbow, wrist, and shoulder, more flexible movement is possible. The hand rods should be held loosely in the operator's hand, with the ends resting on the palm. The four fingers hold the rods, with the thumb free to push them apart if the puppet has to fling wide his arms, or move one hand independently of the other. One rod may, of course, be dropped when the puppet's arm is hanging naturally at its side. With some practice in the various twists of the control rod, you will be able to make the puppet gesture in many ways: Pat its head and stomach (but not simultaneously!); clap its hands, raise one hand to bless, threaten or caress; scratch its back; pray; peer between the covers of a book and so on.

Control over the arms is less direct than with the hand-puppet, consequently hand-and-rod-puppets cannot pick up and carry things quite so easily. However, aided by loops on objects to be handled, or hooks set in the hands, they can perform many such movements well. In carrying things by means of loops, the puppet's hands must be held high in order to keep them from slipping out and dropping their burden onto the floor. Sometimes a rod is attached to the object to be handled. If so arranged, a puppet can place his hand on a telephone, lift it to his ear, talk into it and replace it. The trick is to be sure you have a good grip on the telephone rod before you try to lift it from the cradle, otherwise, it may swing out into space with no relation to the puppet's ear. With an umbrella rib fastened to the puppet's hand as illustrated on *Plate 59, G,* your actor can pick up a small jug, dip it into a well, raise it to the lips and drink, afterwards replacing it. If performed deliberately, such actions are convincing and lifelike.

Inexperienced operators of this type of puppet have a tendency to hold the puppet's hands high above its head. While a good gesture in itself, this is hardly appropriate for ordinary scenes. Usually, one hand can hang at the side with the other raised slightly, when the puppet is entering or during passages in which it is not speaking. Watch the hands when the puppet sits down— too often the manipulator forgets to lower the arms at the same time, and the puppet is seen sitting with its hands in the air. Careful co-ordination of the hands with other movements is necessary at all times.

If the forefinger is thrust into the puppet's head as illustrated on *Plate 9, A*, the movement is similar to that of a hand-puppet. You can make it nod, but there is not much side movement. With the detachable head shown in *B*, the head turns easily from side to side, but it is difficult to make it nod unless the hole in the shoulder piece is much larger than the neck rod. With the mechanism shown on *Plate 10, A*, much more flexible action can be obtained. By pulling the string the head will nod, and by twisting the neck rod you get side-to-side motion.

Hand-and-rod-puppets built like those on *Plate 9* can walk, sit, and lie down much like hand-puppets. By bending the wrist forward a little, the puppet can appear to half sit on a couch or a chair; it can sit better on a chair with no bottom, turned with its profile to the audience.

With the fully articulated puppet shown on *Plate 10, C, D*, sitting is as easy as with any other type of puppet. To do this, the operator stands the puppet in front of the chair or bench, bends the figure forward, passes his arm behind the chair, pulls downward, and the puppet sits. Be sure to keep both hand rods in front of the puppet as it sits, or awkward positions of the hands may result.

Hand-and-rod-puppet movement may be either comic or serious. The type was first used in Russia for tragic scenes, and was successful because of the powerful feeling of reality which the puppets conveyed. Efimova sums up the qualities of her tragic figures: "They are free from the jerkiness of marionette gestures, whose construction compels them to drop their limbs heavily downward. Puppets with draped rods [Efimova's name for this type] have every appearance of passionate flaming life. Their gestures are unmistakably those of real flesh and blood. One of our tragic actors, a Japanese, draws a sabre from under a broad train, regards it pensively, and carries it to his lips. Pointing it to his breast he drives it in, throwing it away from him immediately afterward. Shuddering, stretched out on the floor, he gazes around for the deathly weapon, fumbles with his arm over his head, lays the sabre on his breast, and dies, expressing spiritual and physical torment. This Japanese has only one foot to be managed; it suffices to suggest leg action. Had there been two feet they might both have dangled lifelessly. Firmly bending the knee (the silk skirt folded), the Jap falls forward and suddenly (everyone sees this) grows pale—an effect suggested entirely by the power of his pose."[17]

The hand gestures, plus the turns and bends of the body, make the hand-and-rod puppet capable of more varied movement than any other type. Long speeches, which would tax the string-puppet or hand-puppet can be delivered with enough varied action to avoid monotony.

Rod-Puppet Manipulation. Because they vary so much in size and method of construction, the manipulation of rod-puppets may be quite simple, or it may require as much practice as string-puppets. The puppet shown on *Plate 11, A* can do no more than move back and forth and up and down to suggest walking, lean forward from the ankles, and reverse. The witch at *B* can move both arms and one leg simultaneously. The speed can be varied, but the limited action is best displayed in a quick passage across the stage. Dancers can be made to twirl with arms flying outward from centrifugal motion (*Plate 11, C*). Combined with the twirl, which can begin slowly and rise to a crescendo of movement, simple bends from side to side or front to back can be made. With a group of such figures, the revolutions may be reversed at intervals with good effect, or various groupings can be formed.

In animal rod-puppets, most of the weight is ordinarily carried by a center control stick which is held in one hand, with the subordinate rods operated by the other. For the worm illustrated at *E, Plate 14*, the two ends are held in one hand, while the center one is moved up and down to produce a crawl. The puppeteer needs to be skillful in managing the rods according to what he wants the puppet to do. For instance, if the worm is to do expressive things with the head, one hand should be used for the head rod. The tail can be moved in a similar manner. The cat (*Plate 14, A*) has only two rods, but a great many movements can be worked out with them. If you happen to have some ducks or chickens constructed like these on *Plate 14, C*, the animation will be limited to what you can do by shaking the control stick in order to set the springs in motion.

Rod-puppets which have important acting parts are usually given a more elaborate articulation such as the ones shown on *Plates 12, 13*. They are capable of performing nearly all movements. Skill in manipulation consists in learning what the puppets can do and then in making them do it with surety. You will find that the larger and heavier the puppet, the slower and broader the movement will be; small lightweight puppets can make much quicker motions than large ones, such as those supported on a movable pedestal (*Plate 45*). Manipulation technique must be varied accordingly.

For most plays, a sufficiently convincing walk can be suggested by rotating the central control rod from side to side, thus swinging the legs and moving the puppet up and down. If the figure has leg strings (*Plate 13*), a more precise walk can be obtained.

Rod-puppets can sit easily and gracefully if the furniture is properly constructed. To seat a puppet on a bench, bring it close, bend it forward and pass the control rod back of the bench, pull down and the puppet will sit. If the figure is to sit on a chair, sofa, rock or other object, the central control rod is slipped into a slot big enough to admit it easily. A downward pulls seats the puppet.

To make a rod-puppet kneel, rest the feet on a platform, move

[251]

the control rod toward the front and pull down, thus bending the puppet's knees. When in a kneeling position, the control rod may be moved backward, and the puppet will bend forward in a reverent attitude.

In rod-puppet combats, the weapon is best fastened to the hand. For foils, swords, or daggers a hole can be drilled into the hand and the weapon inserted. A separate rod on a long weapon such as a lance allows exact movements. Don Quixote can deliver a mighty thrust, and when it is all over, place the lance at rest in a socket attached to his saddle. Such motions as sweeping and hoeing can be effectively performed if the broom or hoe is run through both hands and securely fastened. The regular hand-rods are then used for manipulation.

Rod-puppets excell in situations where one puppet must be handed to another; a child climbs into its mother's lap; a baby is handed from one sister to another; the cat climbs upon the old man's shoulder and rubs against his ear.

Although they are not quite so flexible as some other types, rod-puppets are solid and convincing; they have less physical distortion than most other puppets. Their best movements are the dignified, sweeping gestures of serious drama, or the controlled, carefully timed parries and thrusts of combat. However, with the fully articulated figure like the one shown on *Plate 13*, subtle, as well as broad movement can be obtained. The rod-puppet proves a sensitive actor for many types of drama.

Marionette (String-Puppet) Manipulation. Marionettes are perhaps the most flexible of puppet types, but they are generally the most difficult to manipulate well. There are very simple figures which are not hard to operate, but they are usually as limited in movement as any other simple puppet. A string-puppet which has the potentialities of a good actor is much more difficult to control than, for instance, a well-designed hand-and-rod-puppet.

In practicing marionettes, Sue Hastings and Dorcas Ruthenburg offer this suggestion: "Relax. Lift and drop your wrists as if preparing for a piano exercise. Lift your arms above your ears and let them fall. Lie down if you need to in order to let go. Breathe deeply. Say to yourself, 'My wrists are loose; my fingers are loose; my arms, elbows, shoulders are free, easy, filled with delight,' and so on for as much of this type of monologue as you can invent and endure, until you are thoroughly hypnotized."[18] Then begin working the marionette. Try to locate the position of the strings so that you can keep your eye on the puppet instead of watching the controller. Use a mirror, or have someone watch, so you will know when the figure is erect. Don't let it sag at the knees. Keep it from walking with bent knees as though it were sitting on an invisible chair. Make all gestures definite and expressive; some should be large and others small.

You will find walking to be the most difficult movement. A marionette which may otherwise give a near-imitation of life often betrays its mechanical nature when it walks. Some puppeteers believe that a completely lifelike walk can be obtained if the mechanism is sufficiently perfected, but others accept the peculiar gait of the marionette and make it part of the characterization. Oliver Wendell Holmes in an essay, "The Physiology of Walking," points out that man is like a wheel, his legs corresponding to spokes and his feet to sections of tire. As he walks, he rolls successively on the pieces of tire from heel to toe. This is a pendulumlike movement which the marionette operator must try to approximate. If the marionette walks badly it may be too flexible in the legs, or wrongly weighted, or manipulated without the sure, quick jerks on the leg strings which cause this pendulum movement.

R. Bruce Inverarity suggests that too much of a side-to-side sway can often be counteracted by twisting the controller in the opposite direction to the puppet's swing. Hastings and Ruthenburg note that "the whole movement of a puppet is based on the 'marionette swing,' the rhythm of walking compensation. If you will try walking across the room, you will notice that the right arm swings as you move your left leg, the left arm balances the motion of your right foot. The great difficulty with most amateur shows is that the puppets fail to walk convincingly. The knees move in front of the body without relation to the rest of the puppet.

"Stand on the bridge, or if that isn't available, pick yourself a good substantial chair. Hold the puppet erect. Without walking it, let it mark time in a swinging, exaggerated motion till the simultaneous dipping and rolling of the controller in one hand and the foot bar in the other produces simultaneous and enlarged commotion in opposite leg and arm. Keep this up until the habit of the movement is automatic with you. Start walking the puppet. Notice your own balance. If your knees make a lap of your thighs as you walk, you will fall down. Keep the puppet's body erect; swing it forward as fast as his knees go. If his feet are sufficiently weighted, they will cling slightly to the floor and tend to hold the puppet upright."[19]

Don't confine all marionette gestures to the hands during conversations. Use slight turns of the head, a step or two forward, a bend of the body, or any other movements which will give variety and save you from the unforgivable error of "sawing the air" continuously with the puppet's hands.

In manipulating a marionette dancer or trick figure, practice until the action can be done without a flaw. Don't keep the dancer on the stage after it has been through its gamut of movement; if you can't get enough variety to last through a given piece of music, cut the music and end the dance. What often passes for marionette dancing is no more than aimless jigging; design your routine and stick to it, once it is properly timed. Uncertain dancers and tricksters whose tricks come off haltingly can ruin your show. If you don't have time for adequate practice, don't do them at all.

Marionette manipulation is complicated by the possibility of tangled strings which can be avoided only through the ease and surety of movement acquired by practicing until you are thoroughly familiar with the puppets. When not hanging on the puppet rail, the strings of marionettes should be carefully wound around the controller to keep them from tangling. Sometimes it helps to tie a string tightly around the puppet strings as near the controller as possible before winding. Dust bags tied over the puppets will keep them clean.

THE BUSINESS END OF PRODUCTION

Unless you are producing a show in a school, hospital, or in some other place where the purpose is not to make money, you will have the problem of finances. Perhaps you can pay for the materials necessary to construct the puppets and stage, but must depend upon engagements to pay the puppeteers. The latter may work with you and be willing to share in whatever can be made from the show, all on a voluntary basis. It may be that the production you plan calls for resources which you cannot furnish; then you must look for a backer to advance the necessary funds with the expectation of a share in the proceeds—perhaps 25 per cent. You may play exclusively in your own town in a permanent theatre, or you may go "on the road."

Selling the Show. If the show it to make money, it must be sold. It is better, if possible, that this job be given to someone who is not trying to build puppets or to direct. A general publicity man could plan the whole advertising campaign, as well as book engagements. A booker should have enthusiasm for the show he is selling, be a good talker, with a pleasant voice and personality. He should be provided with good photographs of the show, a press book containing notices about the production, and a number of well-written stories about it for the local press. How the booker goes about his business depends upon his own personality, but the price should not be mentioned too soon. Whip up the prospective customer's interest and curiosity before this delicate matter is broached.

Booking should begin well in advance of the opening date of your show in order to give committees time to deliberate. To establish a reputation, it is a good idea to play in your home town, trying to find for your first sponsor someone with prestige. The following list of possible sponsors was compiled by Hastings and

Ruthenburg: Men's luncheon clubs; schools, parent-teachers associations which are trying to raise funds for some civic enterprise and might sponsor a benefit performance; women's clubs; department stores (especially around holiday seasons); wealthy hostesses who might want to celebrate their children's birthdays with a private party; social-service institutions, and colleges. Circulars and personal letters may be sent to nearby towns, followed by personal calls. The local chamber of commerce can usually supply the names of club presidents and others who might be interested in a show.

Touring. If, finally, you decide to go on tour, the principle of booking is the same, except that the booker may have to travel much farther afield. Work from your home base and gradually extend your radius. Be careful about engagements at great distances—if there are no dates in between, the trip will be expensive and likely to absorb all your profits.

A flat guarantee plus a percentage is usually the best arrangement; if you can't get both, a guarantee is preferable. When the terms are agreed upon, the contract should be signed by a person in authority. The booker should always have his blanks on hand so that sponsors can sign before they change their minds.

For transportation, any vehicle which will accommodate the equipment and puppeteers can be used: A station-wagon, a lightweight delivery truck, a passenger car with a trailer or just a car. Care should be taken to keep the auto in good repair, since breakdowns delay you and may cause you to miss an engagement. A list should be made of all the puppets, scenery and properties, and one person should be assigned to check these each time the show is given. It is somewhat embarrassing to arrive at your theatre and find you have left the leading lady at the last place!

Advertising. Advertising is essential, unless the audience is a ready-made one in a school, club, or hospital. Contacts should be made with the local press and radio; the more the better. Spot news giving the facts of the performance is usually run in the daily papers; longer feature articles about the puppets and the personnel of the show can often be run in the Saturday afternoon or Sunday editions. Even the society page will often give you some space, if your sponsor is socially prominent, or members of your company have interesting "stories." Editorial comment and letters to the public-forum department are all to the good. Get all you can. The sponsor should always be provided with several stories about the show and the puppeteers. Half a column (about five hundred words) is the average length. Paragraphs of fifty to one hundred words, with the least important information last, are best, because the last part of the article may be cut. The stories should be double spaced and mimeographed.

Good photographs, the larger the better, are imperative, both for the booker in selling the show and the sponsor in advertising it. For reproduction in newspapers, glossy prints are necessary. Some small papers will not use a photograph unless you furnish a coarse screen half-tone cut of it. Sometimes a mat instead of a cut can be used—this is a negative made by pressing the cut into a sheet of damp paper pulp which is then dried. Be sure and include a proof of either a cut or mat, with the description of the picture, name of the company, and any other necessary information. The photographs should be labeled in the same way. "Under-lines"—identification of the people shown in the picture—should be typed and pasted to the bottom of the photograph or proof.

Posters, handbills, and window cards are additional aids with which to publicize the show. Unless they are really distinctive, a poster will not attract too much attention because so many are seen everywhere. If it has a picture (a zinc etching or woodcut or even a linoleum cut), a handbill will be much more effective. Window cards, although similar to posters, are usually more effective and should be supplied generously to the sponsor. They can be printed with the information about time, date and place left vacant, and the sponsor can attend to filling them in.

If an announcer is used in the show, programs are not usually necessary, especially for children's shows where they frequently end up as airplanes soaring through space. For adult audiences, however, programs are an added attraction. If a printing enthusiast is at hand, souvenir programs decorated with woodcuts can be made and sold for a small sum—but also have plain ones to be distributed free.

Considerable money is often spent for direct mail advertising. According to Edward Mabley it isn't very effective. "I believe that 80 per cent of the circulars go into the wastebasket. Perhaps 10 per cent of those receiving them will write for terms. Half of these, upon receipt of this information, will drop dead. Of the remainder, you will be lucky if 1 per cent of the total finally arrive at the point of signing the contract. I should specify that this applies merely to new prospects. Many return engagements can be booked by mail.

"This does not mean, however, that you can dispense with printed circulars. At least one copy should be left with each person whom you interview. He expects it, and it is useful to him if he has to present the matter to a committee, as often he does."[20]

A mailing list is essential to any puppet company. In a given community it can be compiled from school directories, club membership lists, society columns, and so on. Any printed matter may be sent third class, but more attention is gained by sending it first class. A personal word or two on the circular helps. When you have built up a clientele, various announcements of special programs, the season's list of productions, and similar items may be profitably sent out by mail.

Another way to stimulate interest in a show is to conduct some kind of contest—the more widely advertised in the press and by radio, the more successful it will be. Designs for puppets, settings, stages, original plays, or music can be asked for, with a suitable prize for the winner. Particularly if the contestants are children, it helps to insure attendance at your show if you can exhibit all the entries, and not just the winning pieces.

It is a mark of distinction if you have an insignia for your company, which identifies your show and which can be used on your letter heads, posters, and playbills.

Producing the Puppet Show

The Professional Touch. Even though it may be only a simple show, make it as professional as possible. Create that feeling of pleasant anticipation which the audience at any theatrical performance has a right to expect. Give the impression that everyone connected with the show knows exactly what he is doing, from the ushers to the switchboard operator. Have the house lights on in plenty of time so the first comers will not have to enter a dark auditorium. Dress up the ushers and make an occasion of it if you can. Don't let the puppeteers talk backstage, hammer things, or play with the lights—all this should be done beforehand. Ask the ushers not to seat people during the first scene; if there are a number of late comers, give them a chance to be seated at a convenient place in the program.

Puppeteering Clothes. The puppeteers should keep out of sight and not run about the auditorium, especially if they are wearing their work clothes. These, incidentally, should be comfortable and cool—it is always hot backstage in a puppet theatre. Shorts with shirts which have no buttons to catch on strings are good for marionette operators. Carpenter's aprons with pockets are useful to save wear and tear on your clothes and to hold things. Operators who sit on movable stools should wear shoes with rubber soles or heels, in order to propel themselves about the stage. In general, avoid anything which is likely to become entangled with the puppets.

Check Before the Show. Everything to be used in the show should be carefully checked before the performance; sets, properties, lights, and puppets. Marionette strings should be examined and replaced if there are worn places which might break during the performance. If you are using rod-puppets, the link of chain joining the rod to the puppet should be checked and tightened with a pair of pliers if it has worked loose. Costumes should be watched for places which might have come unsewed. Be sure everything is in its proper place, including a tool kit in which are all the items you might need to replace: Strings cut the approximate length and threaded through needles ready for use; extra light bulbs and other electrical equipment; assorted nails, pins, wire, glue, cord, adhesive tape, screw eyes, jack chain, scissors, pliers, drill, and hammer. Paint and the necessary materials for repairing scenery should also be included. Try out the auditorium for acoustics. If you have a P. A. system, check the volume necessary to use for audibility, but avoid blaring.

Audience Reaction. The puppeteers should be on the alert for audience reaction. Sufficient time must be given for laughs, or the words will be lost. Vary the tempo and action if you are not getting the response you expect. Audiences differ, and what goes over with one may fall flat with another. Do all you can to keep the puppets and spectators *en rapport*; direct conversations are the most effective way, but there are more subtle ways, too. Sometimes a puppet can, by a glance or a bit of action, take the audience into its confidence. Watch the volume of your voices; if the audience is too silent, perhaps it is not hearing the lines, if it is too noisy, the same thing may be true.

Train your puppeteers to cover any accidents which occur, and do not ring down the curtain unless everything is hopelessly confused. Almost all situations can be handled by clever ad libbing. Even such disasters as dropping a marionette controller can be minimized by reference to the gods above who pull the strings.

Finale. Some puppet companies end their show, particularly if it is performed with marionettes, by having the puppeteers come onto the stage with the puppets. This sudden appearance of a human being is always a shock; it destroys the illusion of scale which has been built up during the show and forces an abrupt realization of the inanimate quality of the puppets, which up to that time had appeared imbued with life. If you want the final reaction to your show to be an astonished gasp, well and good, but if you want your audience to carry the mood of the show away with them, don't let any human beings come into the picture.

Bibliographies

〰〰〰

BOOKS ABOUT PUPPETS

Bibliography

RANSOME, GRACE GREENLEAF. *Puppets and Shadows, A Bibliography.* Boston: F. W. Faxon Co., 1931.

History

BEAUMONT, CYRIL W. *Puppets and the Puppet Stage.* New York: Studio Publications, Inc.
An excellent collection of photographs of contemporary puppet work, with some historical notes.

BOEHN, MAX VON. *Dolls and Puppets.* Trans. by Josephine Nicoll. London: G. G. Harrap & Co., Ltd., 1932.
The second half of the book has many illustrations and a fairly full text.

CUETO, LOLA and LAGO, ROBERTO. *Mexican Folk Puppets.* Puppetry Imprints, 155 Wimbleton Drive, Birmingham, Mich., 1941.
A brief history of puppets in Mexico with sketches of toy-puppets and hand-puppets.

EFIMOVA, NINA. *Adventures of a Russian Puppet Theatre.* Puppetry Imprints, 155 Wimbleton Drive, Birmingham, Mich., 1935.
A stimulating account of this puppet theatre which began during the Russian Revolution. Construction details and puppet theory are also included.

JOSEPH, HELEN HAIMAN. *A Book of Marionettes.* New York: The Viking Press, 1931.
A good general history of puppets.

MARTINOVITCH, NICHOLAS N. *The Turkish Theatre.* New York: Theatre Arts, Inc., 1933.

[261]

One section deals with the Turkish shadow theatre and the adventures of its hero Karagoz.

Technique (General)

BUFANO, REMO. *Be a Puppet Showman.* New York: The Century Co., 1933.
A book for beginners, with construction methods for marionettes and hand-puppets.

FLING, HELEN. *Treasure Chest of Marionette Hobby Craft.* New York: Treasure Chest Publications, 62 W. 45th St.
Four booklets with construction methods amply illustrated.

HASTINGS, SUE and RUTHENBURG, DORCAS. *How to Produce Puppet Plays.* New York: Harper & Brothers, 1940.
Construction details and notes on production, advertising, touring, rehearsals, etc.

INVERARITY, R. BRUCE. *A Manual of Puppetry.* Portland, Oregon: Binfords and Mort, 1938.
An excellent technical manual for the beginner, with notes on production and puppet history.

McPHARLIN, PAUL, Ed. *Puppetry, a Yearbook of Puppets and Marionettes.* Puppetry Imprints, 155 Wimbleton Drive, Birmingham, Mich. Published annually from 1930 to date.
Photographs, technical articles, historical sketches, list of producers, book reviews, international news notes. The official yearbook of *The Puppeteers of America.*

MILLS, W. H. and DUNN, LOUISE M. *Marionettes Masks and Shadows.* Garden City, N. Y.: Doubleday Doran and Co., 1928.
An introductory book especially useful for educators.

PAYANT, FELIX, Ed. *A Book of Puppets.* Columbus, Ohio: Design Publishing Co., 1936.
A collection of miscellaneous articles about puppets, with a number of good illustrations.

Technique (Hand-Puppets)

FICKLEN, BESSIE A. *A Handbook of Fist Puppets.* New York: Frederick A. Stokes Co., 1935.
A good all-round treatment of hand-puppets.

FLEXNER, MARION; CANE, ALICE and CLARK DOROTHY *Hand-Puppets,*

Bibliographies

A Practical Manual for Teachers and Children. New York: Samuel French, 25 W. 45 St. 1935.

A useful book for beginners.

MILLIGAN, DAVID F. *Fist Puppetry.* New York: A. S. Barnes and Co., 1938.

Various methods of constructing hand-puppets and presenting plays are described.

MUNGER, M. P. and ELDER, A. L. *The Book of Puppets.* Boston: Lothrop, Lee and Shepard Co., 1934.

A well-illustrated practical guide to simple hand-puppet making.

Technique (Shadow-Puppets)

MARCH, BENJAMIN. *Chinese Shadow-Figure Plays and Their Making.* Puppetry Imprints, 155 Wimbleton Drive, Birmingham, Mich., 1939.

A brief description of mechanics, a series of photographs showing puppeteers and stage, and three characteristic plays.

MILLS, W. H. and DUNN, LOUISE M. *Shadow Plays and How to Produce Them.* New York: Doubleday, Doran and Co., 1939.

The Chinese method of shadow-figure making adapted for children. Construction details and plays are included.

WIMSATT, GENEVIEVE. *Chinese Shadow Shows.* Cambridge, Mass.: Harvard University Press, 1936.

More general information and fewer illustrations than in the March volume listed above.

Technique (String-Puppets)

ACKLEY, EDITH FLACK. *Marionettes, Easy to Make! Fun to Use!* New York: Frederick A. Stokes Co., 1929.

Complete directions for making stuffed cloth marionettes.

DWIGGINS, W. A. *Marionette in Motion.* Puppetry Imprints, 155 Wimbleton Drive, Birmingham, Mich., 1939.

A full description of the counterbalanced marionette now used by many professional showmen. Although more difficult to construct, this type of figure has better movement than marionettes made by other methods.

McPHARLIN, PAUL. *Animal Marionettes.* Puppetry Imprints, 155 Wimbleton Drive, Birmingham, Mich., 1936.

Sketches and suggestions for making a wide variety of string-puppet animals.

NELSON, NICHOLAS and HAYES, JAMES J. *Trick Marionettes*. Puppetry Imprints, 155 Wimbleton Drive, Birmingham, Mich., 1935.

For the skilled puppet maker, this book offers descriptions and stringing for most of the stock marionette tricks.

BOOKS ABOUT THE THEATRE

A few books which may be useful to the puppet maker are here listed. Most of them can be purchased from the Drama Bookshop, 48 W. 52nd St., New York City 19. For general articles about the theatre, past and present, *Theatre Arts*, 130 W. 56th St., New York City 19, is one of the best sources.

Bibliography

BAKER, BLANCH M. *Dramatic Bibliography*. New York: H. W. Wilson Co., 1933.

Interior Design

EBERLEIN, H. D., McCLURE, ABBOTT and HOLLOWAY, EDWARD S. *The Practical Book of Interior Decoration*. Philadelphia: J. B. Lippincott, 1919.

Useful for the designing of period settings and furniture.

For suggestions about contemporary interior design and furniture see the periodicals *Interiors* and *Architectural Forum*.

Masks

In addition to the books listed below, illustrations of masks may be found in many books dealing with the Chinese theatre, the Japanese no drama, and the theatrical art of Java and Bali. In primitive civilizations throughout the world the mask has been used in religious ceremonial; the puppet maker can find some of his best inspiration in the masks of the American Indian, and the people of the South Seas. Masks used in the dramas of the Greeks and Romans can be found in books on the subject, while the Italian *commedia dell'arte* of the sixteenth and seventeenth centuries provides still other masks for the puppet designer to study.

Bibliographies

BENDA, W. T. *Masks*. New York: Watson-Guptill Publications, Inc., 1944.
Benda's preliminary sketches as well as his finished masks are valuable for the puppet designer.

INVERARITY, R. BRUCE. *Movable Masks and Figures of the North Pacific Coast Indians*. Bloomfield Hills, Mich., Cranbrook Institute of Science, 1941.
Although not obtainable except in libraries, this book has a group of unusually fine illustrations of Indian masks.

KNIFFIN, HERBERT R. *Masks*. Peoria, Ill., The Manual Arts Press, 1931.
A good general book on mask making.

LINTON, RALPH and WINGERT, PAUL. *Arts of the South Seas*. New York: The Museum of Modern Art, 1946.
Many fine examples of primitive masks are included in this book, which is especially recommended to puppeteers.

MACGOWAN, KENNETH and ROSSE, HERMAN. *Masks and Demons*. New York: Harcourt Brace and Co., 1923.
A general survey of masks of all periods, with historical notes and illustrations.

McPHARLIN, PAUL. *Masks, Occult and Utilitarian*. Bloomfield Hills, Mich., Cranbrook Institute of Science, 1939.
Photographs and sketches of all types of masks, with a brief history are included in this catalogue.

SWEENEY, J., Ed. *African Negro Art*. New York: The Museum of Modern Art, 1935.
The stylistic quality of this art is helpful to the puppet designer.

Stage Costuming

BARTON, LUCY. *Historic Costume for the Stage*. Boston: Walter H. Baker Co., 1935.
Contains descriptions and cutting patterns.

BEAUMONT, C. W. *Five Centuries of Ballet Design*. New York: Studio Publications, 1939.
A stimulating source of inspiration for the puppet costume designer.

BOEHN, MAX VON and FISCHEL, OSKAR. *Manners and Modes in the Nineteenth Century*. London: J. M. Dent and Sons, Ltd.
A good reference work for this period.

BROOKE, IRIS. *Western European Costume and Its Relation to the Theatre*. London: G. G. Harrap and Co., Ltd., 1939.

Vol. 1 covers the thirteenth to sixteenth centuries; vol. 2, the seventeenth to the mid-nineteenth. This is an excellent source for period costumes.

Harrap has also published a series of books on English costume by the same author: Early Middle Ages (tenth to thirteenth centuries); Later Middle Ages (fourteenth to fifteenth centuries); Age of Elizabeth (sixteenth century); Seventeenth Century; Eighteenth Century; Nineteenth Century; English Children's Costume.

DABNEY, EDITH and WISE, C. M. *A Book of Dramatic Costume*. New York: F. S. Crofts and Co., 1930.

Contains good practical hints for stage costuming.

EXMOUTH, CHAS., and PELLEW, ERNEST. *Dyes and Dyeing*. New York: Robert M. McBride and Co., 1928.

Useful information for the stage and costume designer.

FERNALD, MARY and SHENTON, EILEEN. *Costume Design and Making*. London: Adam and Charles Black, 1937.

Covers the period from the Saxons to the 1880's. Illustrations from contemporary paintings, manuscripts, etc. Particularly valuable for the excellent cutting patterns it contains.

KOEHLER, CARL. *A History of Costume*. London: G. G. Harrap and Co., Ltd., 1928.

A good general reference book.

RACINET, A. C. A. *Le costume historique*. Paris: Firmin-Didot et Cie., 1888. 6 vols.

Large libraries have this work, which is one of the most complete histories of costume. Accessories and sketches of rooms of the various periods are included.

WALKUP, MRS. FAIRFAX. *Dressing the Part. A History of Costume for the Theatre*. New York: F. S. Crofts and Co., 1938.

Excellent suggestions for adapting period costume to the stage. Lists of best materials to use also included.

Stage Scenery and Lighting

CORNBERG, SOL and GEBAUER, EMANUEL. *A Stage Crew Hand-Book*. New York: Harper & Brothers, 1941.

A good general discussion of scenery making.

Bibliographies

FUCHS, THEODORE. *Home Built Lighting Equipment.* New York: Samuel French, 25 W. 45 St., 1939.
Excellent diagrams, based on professional designs, for constructing various units are included. Some of these are adaptable to the puppet stage.

FUCHS, THEODORE. *Stage Lighting.* Boston: Little, Brown and Co., 1929.
For many years this has been a standard book on the subject.

HEFFNER, HUBERT C., SELDEN, SAMUEL and SELLMAN, HUNTON. *Modern Theatre Practice.* New York: F. S. Crofts and Co., 1939.
A good general book on play production.

KNAPP, JACK STUART. *Lighting the Stage with Homemade Equipment.* Boston: Walter H. Baker Co.
Ways of making lighting units of coffee cans, pails, pans and other easily acquired materials are described.

McCANDLESS, STANLEY R. *A Method of Lighting the Stage.* New York: Theatre Arts, Inc., 1932.
One of the best handbooks on lighting. It is brief but thorough, and a valuable aid to the puppet stage electrician.

SELDEN, SAMUEL and SELDEN, HUNTON D. *Stage Scenery and Lighting: A Handbook for Non-Professionals.* New York: F. S. Crofts and Co., 1930.
Covers the elements of the subject; a particularly useful book for the puppet scenery designer.

SIMONSON, LEE. *The Stage Is Set.* New York: Harcourt Brace and Co., 1932.
A stimulating book about general aspects of the theatre.

PUPPET PLAYS AND SOURCE MATERIAL

Because of the dearth of published puppet plays, there is here included a wide variety of sources from which the puppeteer can make his own plays. As far as possible, fresh material has been suggested.

Published Puppet Plays

BARING, MAURICE. *Palæmon and Arcite.* Oxford: B. H. Blackwell, 1913.

BUFANO, REMO. *Magic Strings*. New York: The Macmillan Co., 1939.
A group of delightful puppet plays for a young audience.
The Show Book of Remo Bufano. Seven Plays for Marionettes and People. New York: The Macmillan Co., 1930.
Dramatizations of the most familiar fairy stories such as "Jack and the Beanstalk."
BROWN, FORMAN. *The Pie-Eyed Piper and Other Impertinent Puppet Plays*. New York: Greenberg, Inc., 1933.
A number of sophisticated puppet plays designed for adults.
FLEXNER, MARION W. and CLARK, DOROTHY PARK. *Poor Giraffe and Other Puppet Plays*. New York: Samuel French, 1935.
Simple plays for children.
JAGENDORF, MONTY ADOLF. *Penny Puppets, Penny Theatre and Penny Plays*. Indianapolis, New York: The Bobbs Merrill Co., 1941.
A book about the toy paper theatre.
Junior League Puppet Plays. New York: Samuel French, 25 W. 45 St.
A group of children's plays written by various authors. Write for titles.
KREYMBORG, ALFRED. *Puppet Plays*. London: M. Secher, 1923.
Seven plays for adults.
McPHARLIN, PAUL. *A Repertory of Marionette Plays*. New York: The Viking Press, 1929.
An excellent selection of plays by well-known authors from vari-, ous countries, including Goethe and Maeterlinck.
MAETERLINCK, MAURICE. *Alladine and Palomides, Interior and The Death of Tintagiles*. London: Duckworth and Co., 1899.
PRESTON, EFFA E. *Punchinello Puppet Plays*. Chicago: T. S. Denison and Co., 1936.
Plays for grade school children.
Puppetry Imprints: Plays. Published by Paul McPharlin, 155 Wimbleton Drive, Birmingham, Mich.
Nine plays by various authors: *The Wolf at the Door, Lincoln and the Pig, Weather, De Courtin' Couple, Punch and Judy, St. George and the Dragon, Pensive Puppets, The Sorcerer's Apprentice*.
REIGHARD, CATHERINE. *Plays for People and Puppets*. New York: E. P. Dutton and Co., 1929.
Contains *Pierre Pathelin, Jack and the Beanstalk, The King of the Golden River, Rumpelstiltskin, Aladdin*.

Bibliographies

SAND, MAURICE. *Maurice Sand's Plays for Marionettes*. Trans. by Babette and Glenn Hughes. New York: Samuel French, 1931. Clever, sophisticated plays, but with a limited appeal.

SHELDON, MARY (STEWART). *The Land of Punch and Judy*. New York: Fleming H. Revell Co., 1922.

STODDARD, ANNE and SARG, TONY. *A Book of Marionette Plays*. New York: Greenberg, 1927.
Plays for children.

WALTERS, MAUDE OWEN. *Puppet Shows for Home and School*. New York: Dodd Mead and Co., 1929.
Plays for young children.

WHANSLAW, H. *Book of Marionette Plays*. London: W. Gardner, Darton and Co., Ltd., 1936.

Epic Poems

The epic poetry of various nations has many episodes which lend themselves well to puppet production—if they are interpreted in puppet terms. Be careful about using too much of the exalted language in which these works abound.

Aeneid (Latin); *Beowulf* (English); *Cid* (Spanish); *Iliad and Odyssey* (Greek); *Mahabharata* and *Ramayana* (Hindu); *Niebenlungenlied* (German); *Orlando Furioso* (Italian); *Song of Roland* (French). See various editions and translations.

Fables

AESOP's *Fables*

FONTAINE, JEAN DE LA. *Fables*.

KOMROFF, MANUEL. *The Great Fables of all Nations*. New York: Tudor Publishing Co., 1936.
An excellent collection.

THURBER, JAMES. *Fables for Our Time*. New York: Harper & Brothers,1940.
These fables are satirical, and would make excellent puppet plays for adults.

Fairy Tales

There are hundreds of fairy tales besides the well-known collections of the Brothers Grimm and Hans Andersen. The extent of this literature should make it easy to find unhackneyed material, and avoid such overworked stories as "Hansel and Gretel," "Jack and the Beanstalk" and "Little Red Riding Hood."

BARING, MAURICE. *The Glass Mender and Other Stories.* London: James Nisbet and Co., Ltd., 1910.

Unusually good stories for interpretation by puppets. The material is fresh and offers opportunities for transformations and tricks.

CURTIN, JEREMIAH. *Fairy Tales of Eastern Europe.* New York: McBride, Nast and Co., 1914.

A good collection of Russian, Hungarian, Bohemian, and Serbian tales.

DEMORGAN, MARY. *On a Pincushion.* New York: Duffield and Co., 1922.

A pebble brooch, a jet shawl and a common pin on a pincushion tell a series of fantastic stories to drown out the talking of the bracelet hanging over the looking glass. An excellent collection of unusual stories.

———. *The Windfairies and Other Tales.* London: Seeley and Co., Ltd., 1900.

EASTMAN, MARY H. *Index to Fairy Tales, Myths and Legends.* Boston: The Boston Book Co., 1915.

Lists titles of tales, names of heroes, and collections of stories.

FAULKNER, GEORGENE. *The White Elephant and Other Tales.* New York: The Wise-Parslow Co., 1929.

Indian (Hindu) stories about animals, some of which are adaptable to puppet plays.

GATE, ETHEL MAY. *Tales from the Secret Kingdom.* New Haven: Yale University Press, 1919.

A good group of stories.

JACOBS, JOSEPH. *Celtic Fairy Tales.* New York: G. P. Putnam's Sons, 1923.

JAMES, HARTWELL. *The Magic Jaw Bone.* Philadelphia: Henry Altemus Co., 1906.

Three Maori stories, full of adventures, which would be adaptable to puppet plays.

KAVANAUGH, BRIDGET and JULIA. *The Pearl Fountain and Other Fairy Tales.* New York: Henry Holt and Co., 1876.

An old collection, but many of the stories would make good puppet plays.

Bibliographies

MARTENS, FREDERICK H. *Fairy Tales from the Orient*. New York: Robert M. McBride and Co., 1923.

A selection of exotic tales on the order of the Arabian Nights.

NEWMAN, ISIDORA. *Fairy Flowers, Nature Legends of Fact and Fancy*. New York: Henry Holt and Co., 1926.

Whimsical stories about flowers which are usable for puppet plays.

O'FAOLAIN, EILEEN. *King of the Cats*. New York: William Morrow and Co., 1942.

A story of cats, an old woman, two boys and their strange adventures at a fair, a castle, etc.

PYLE, HOWARD. *The Garden Behind the Moon*. New York: Charles Scribner's Sons, 1895.

An adventure story about a little girl who went to the garden behind the moon.

SINCLAIR, UPTON. *The Gnomobile*. New York: Farrar and Rinehart, 1936.

A modern fairy tale in which a little girl and her uncle discover two gnomes in the California redwood forest. Their adventures are recounted with an ironical touch which would interest adults.

STEEL, F. A. *English Fairy Tales*. New York: The Macmillan Co., 1922.

Contains many of the usual stories but there are some less familiar ones.

STEPHENS, JAMES. *Irish Fairy Tales*. New York: The Macmillan Co., 1920.

An excellent collection of stories of special interest to adults.

WILDE, OSCAR. *Happy Prince and Other Tales*. Garden City Publishing Co.

These stories for adults might be dramatized for puppets.

WIMBERLY, LOWRY C. *The Famous Cats of Fairyland*. New York: E. P. Dutton and Co., 1938.

An excellent selection of cat stories including well known ones like "Dick Whittington" as well as less familiar ones.

Folk Dances

The following books are listed as aids in working out dance routines and selecting appropriate music for various national dances. Most of these books give directions for performing the dances, as well as costume sketches.

BURCHENAL, ELIZABETH. *Five Folk Dances from Austria, Germany,
Holland.* Boston: The Boston Music Co., 1929.

————. *Folk Dances of Denmark; Folk Dances of Finland; Folk
Dances of Germany* (29 dances and singing games); *American
Country Dances.* New York: G. Schirmir.
Each of these volumes contains music, descriptions of the dances
and a few illustrations.

BREWSTER, MELA SEDILLO. *Mexican and New Mexican Folk Dances.*
Albuquerque: University of New Mexico Press, 1937.
Brief descriptions of dances, notes on costumes, and simple ar-
rangements of music.

CHAPLIN, NELLIE. *Ancient Dances and Music.* London: J. Curwen
and Sons, Ltd., 1909.
The same author has also edited: *Court Dances and Others; Dances
of the Suite; Elizabethan Dances; Minuet and Gavotte.* All these
volumes contain photographs of dancers in costume, music and
directions.

FROST, HELEN. *Oriental and Character Dances.* New York: A. S.
Barnes and Co., 1930. Music by Lily Strickland.
Part I contains 10 Indian, Moslem, Burnese and Tibetan dances;
Part II, clog and character dances. Illustrations of the latter are
out of date.

GATES, EDITH M. *Old Folk Dances from New Nations.* Chicago: C.
F. Summy Co., 1932.
Dances from Estonia, Latvia, Poland and Russia, with music and
illustrations of dancers in costume.

KIMMINS, C. W. *Peasant Dances of Many Lands.* London: Evans
Bros., Ltd., 1919.
Music and description of a large number of dances; illustrations
poor, but the book as a whole is useful.

Folklore

Folk stories are often highly imaginative, even fantastic, and usually
make good puppet plays if they have sufficient action.

BARHAM, RICHARD HARRIS. *Ingoldsby Legends.* Blackie and Son. Ltd.

BOTKIN, B. A. *A Treasury of American Folklore.* New York: Crown
Publishers, 1944.

A rich collection of stories and ballads; one of the best sources for this type of material.

California Folklore Quarterly. Berkeley and Los Angeles: University of California Press.

CHAUCER, GEOFFREY. *Canterbury Tales.* George G. Harrap and Company, Ltd.

FENNER, PHYLLIS R. *There Was a Horse: Folktales from Many Lands*. New York: A. A. Knopf, 1941.

A good collection of sixteen stories about horses.

Journal of American Folklore. Boston and New York: Houghton Mifflin Co.

LEE, FRANK H. *Folk Tales of all Nations*. New York: Coward McCann, 1930.

A fat volume of 942 pages containing stories from all over the world.

PHILLIPS, GRACE DARLING. *Far Peoples*. Chicago: University of Chicago Press, 1929.

An interesting collection of fables, stories, poems, games, music, recipes for national dishes—everything necessary for programs about India, China, Korea, Russia, Africa and other countries.

STEVENS, JAMES. *Paul Bunyan*. Garden City, New York: Garden City Publishing Co., 1925.

Folk Songs and Ballads

There are many collections of ballads from all parts of the United States. Many of these are related to various occupations such as coal mining, lumber milling and other regional activities. Every country and every period of history are represented in folk songs. Many of these are dramatic in quality, and if they have sufficient action, can be made into good puppet plays.

BORROW, GEORGE. *Ballads of all Nations*. London: A. Rivers, Ltd., 1927.

BROWN, JAMES DUFF. *Characteristic Songs and Dances of all Nations*. London: Bailey and Ferguson, 1901.

Most of the songs are too brief for puppet action, but there are many good bits of national music included, such as the hornpipe, reel, French branle.

DEUTSCH, LEONHARD. *A Treasury of the World's Finest Folksong*. New York: Howell, Soskin, 1942.
An excellent collection of songs with piano accompaniment.

DOWNES, OLIN. *A Treasury of American Song*. Music arranged by Elie Seigmeister. New York: A. A. Knopf, 1943.
A fine selection of American songs.

GILBERT, HENRY F. BELKNAP. *One Hundred Folk Songs from Many Countries*. Boston: C. C. Birchard and Co., 1910.
An excellent collection with many songs having enough action to be done with puppets.

GILBERT, W. S. *The Bab Ballads*. Hutchinson and Company.

KIPLING, RUDYARD. *Ballads* and *Barrack Room Ballads*. Grosset.

LAWTON, V. B. *Ballads for Acting*. London: Sheldon Press, 1927.
Although these dramatizations are not too good for puppets, they indicate how ballads may be adapted.

LOMAX, JOHN and ALLEN, Ed. *American Ballads and Folk Songs*. New York: The Macmillan Co., 1934.
Macmillan has also published by the same authors: *Cowboy Songs and Other Frontier Ballads*, 1938; *Our Singing Country*, 1941. These three collections contain both words and music.

Myths and Legends

There is a wealth of material for puppet plays in the myths and legends of all countries. Every region has its local heroes and legendary stories. In America these have not received the attention which is their due, hence a few books have been listed which contain stories from various parts of the country. In addition to these, the lives of many of our pioneer explorers, such as Daniel Boone, offer exciting material for dramatization.

BOYER, WARREN E. *Vanishing Trails of Romance*. Denver, Colo.: Great West Publishers, 1923.
Legends about happenings in Colorado.

BULFINCH, THOMAS. *Bulfinch's Mythology*. New York: Modern Library, 1934.
Contains "The Age of Fable"; "The Age of Chivalry," and "The Legends of Charlemagne."

CHAPMAN, IVA. *Twelve Legendary Stories of Texas*. San Antonio, Texas: The Naylor Co., 1940.

Bibliographies

DOBIE, JAMES FRANK. *Apache Gold and Yaqui Silver*. Boston: Little, Brown and Co., 1939.

EDMUNDS, POCAHONTAS WIGHT. *Land of Sand; Legends of the North Carolina Coast*. Richmond, Va.: Garrett and Massie, Inc., 1941.

FORBUSH, W. B. *The Wonder Book of Myths and Legends*. Philadelphia: J. C. Winston, 1928.

GRAY, LOUIS HERBERT. *The Myths of all Races*. Boston: Marshall Jones Co., 1916-1937.
This 13-volume work is one of the most complete reference sources on the subject.

HALLENBECK, CLEVE and WILLIAMS, J. H. *Legends of the Spanish Southwest*. Glendale, Calif.: The Arthur H. Clark Co., 1938.

Heroes of Myth and Legend. Introduction by Benjamin Ide Wheeler. New York: P. F. Collier and Son, 1903.
A collection of stories by various authors about famous legendary heroes.

MACKENZIE, DONALD ALEX. *Egyptian Myth and Legend*. London: Gresham Publishing Co., 1913.
By the same author are: *Indian Myth and Legend*, 1913; *Myths of Babylonia and Assyria*, 1915; *Myths of China and Japan*, 1923; *Myths from Melanesia and Indonesia*, 1930; *Myths of Pre-Columbian America*, 1924.

———. *Tales from the Moors and the Mountains*. London: Blackie and Son, Ltd., 1931.
A group of Scottish legends.

MONCRIEFF, ASCOTT ROBERT H. *Romance and Legend of Chivalry*. New York: W. H. Wise and Co., 1934.

PRICE, SAMUEL G. *Black Hills, the Land of Legend*. Los Angeles: De Vorss and Co., 1935.

SHOEMAKER, HENRY W. *In the Seven Mountains*. Reading, Pa.: The Bright Printing Co., 1913.
A group of legends collected in central Pennsylvania.

SPENCE, LEWIS. *Myths and Legends of Ancient Egypt*. London: G. G. Harrap and Co., Ltd., 1915.

———. *Myths of Babylonia and Assyria*. New York: F. A. Stokes Co., 1916.

———. *The Myths of Mexico and Peru*. New York: F. Y. Crowell Co., 1913.

[275]

————. *The Myths of the North American Indian.* London: G. G. Harrap and Co., Ltd., 1914.

Poems and Nonsense Verses

The following titles are only a few of many similar ones which could be used for puppet turns and plays.

CARROLL, LEWIS. *Hunting of the Snark.* Antioch Press.

HOOD, THOMAS. *Comic Ballads.* Peter Pauper.

LEAR, EDWARD. *The Complete Nonsense Book.* Edited by Lady Strachey. New York: Duffield and Co., 1912.

MILNE, A. A. *When We Were Very Young.* E. P. Dutton and Company, Inc.

————. *Now We Are Six.* E. P. Dutton and Company, Inc.

————. *Songs from Now We Are Six.* Music by H. Fraser-Simson. London: Methuen and Co., Ltd., 1927.

Arranged for voice with piano accompaniment.

Mother Goose. In Stevenson, B. E., *Famous Single Poems,* New York: Harcourt Brace, 1923.

THAYER, ERNEST LAWRENCE. *Casey at the Bat.* Various editions.

A Treasury of Gilbert and Sullivan. Words and music of 102 songs from 11 operettas, ed. by Deems Taylor. Illustrated by Lucille Corcos. New York: Simon and Schuster, 1941.

The illustrations are imaginative and offer inspiration for puppet costumes. These songs are excellent puppet material.

Stories

Good puppet play material can be found in short stories or adventure stories which have sufficient action. There are many collections, a few of which are here listed.

King Arthur and the Knights of the Round Table.

The Arabian Nights Entertainment.

Stories from the *Bible*, such as David and Goliath, Esther, The Prodigal Son, The Judgment of Solomon, Noah's Ark, Jonah and the Whale.

CERVANTES, MIGUEL DE. *Don Quixote.* Various editions.

COPPARD, A. E. *Pink Furniture.* The Fabulous Adventures of Toby Tottel. Jonathon Cape, Ltd.

A child's story, with many adventures.

Bibliographies

DEFOE, DANIEL. *Robinson Crusoe*. Blackie and Son, Ltd.

DUNSANY, LORD. *The Book of Wonder*. Boston: J. W. Luce & Co.

———. *The Charwoman's Shadow*. Boston: Little Brown & Co., 1926.

———. *Fifty One Tales*. Boston: Little Brown & Co., 1920.

———. *Five Plays*. Boston: Little Brown & Co., 1925.

———. *Plays of Near and Far*. New York and London: G. P. Putnam's Sons, 1923.

GOODMAN, JACK. *The Fireside Book of Dog Stories*. New York: Simon and Schuster, 1943.

HARRIS, JOEL CHANDLER. *Uncle Remus*. Various editions.

KIPLING, RUDYARD. *Children's Stories; Kipling's Boys Stories; Collected Dog Stories; Jungle Books; Just So Stories*. Various editions.

Just So Song Book. Songs set to music by Edward German. Garden City, New York: Doubleday, Doran and Co., 1928.

LIEBER, MAXIM and WILLIAMS, B. C. *Great Stories of All Nations*. New York: Brentano's, 1927.

MAUGHAM, SOMERSET, Ed. *Tellers of Tales*. New York: Doubleday, Doran and Co., 1939.
One hundred short stories from the United States, England, France, Russia, Germany.

OVERTON, GRANT MARTIN, Ed. *The World's One Hundred Best Short Stories*. New York and London: Funk and Wagnells Co., 1927.
Ten volumes, each containing one type of story: Adventure, romance, mystery, love, drama, courage, women, men, ghosts, humor.

POE, EDGAR ALLAN. *Tales*. Various editions.

RUDWIN, MAXIMILIAN H. *Devil Stories: An Anthology*. New York: A. A. Knopf, 1921.
Stories by Washington Irving, Thackeray, Poe, Baudelaire, Daudet, Garnett, France, Gorky, Masefield, and others.

YARMALINSKY, ABRAHAM, *A Treasury of Great Russian Stories*. New York: The Macmillan Co., 1944.

Puppet History—Addendum

BATCHELDER, MARJORIE. *Rod-Puppets and the Human Theatre*. Columbus, Ohio. Ohio State University Press, 1947.
A historical, technical and theoretical monograph.

Supplementary Materials

~~~~~~

Variety Acts

There are dozens of good variety numbers which can be done without resorting to overworked ones such as the piano player, the singer with heaving bosom and the strip tease. Originality is better than imitation, and has the further advantage of avoiding direct competition with the work of other puppeteers. Choice of acts should be based upon the capabilities of the type of puppet you are using, rather than upon the exact imitation of variety numbers done by human beings. However, with their natural bent for satire, puppets can comment ironically upon the usual vaudeville acts performed by human actors.

Fights and Combats. Especially with hand- or rod-puppets, combats are effective. Punch's fisticuffs are traditional in the puppet theatre. Mock tournaments (with rod-puppets), boxing bouts, bull fights, conflicts between men and animals are all good puppet material.

Musicians. Comic interpretations, such as two puppets playing an oversize bass viol, are good. An orchestra of animals, each playing an instrument and making his own characteristic noise is amusing. You can also do a satirical interpretation of the sentimental serenader playing a lute, or guitar; or an Italian orchestra of violin, guitar and jug in an exaggerated version of "Santa Lucia."

Tricks, Transformations, Circus Acts, Acrobatic Performances. In McPharlin's *Trick Marionettes* (see p. ooo) are many good string-puppet tricks such as tumblers, knife throwers, popouts, unicycle rider on a rope, etc. You can also do come-apart flip-flops, contortionists, acrobats performing on a taut canvas, auto races, trained animals, bareback riders (with the horse moving from under the rider who walks through the air and finally catches up), and many other similar acts.

Dances. Many kinds of dance movements are suitable for puppets (see pp. 222-25). Peasant dances often make charming numbers if done in costume and based upon characteristic movement (see references on pp. 271-2). National dances, such as the Russian hopak, Spanish and Mexican routines, and American Indian ritual dances are good material. Puppets do underwater ballets well. For satires on the modern dance, rod-puppets are excellent. Boogiewoogie and adagio dances are fun to do, and there is no limit to what can be done with animal dancers (especially grotesque ones).

Satirical Impersonations. Satires on move stars, trios of animals in the manner of the Andrew Sisters, reversals of the usual order of things such as the dog trainer with a performing man, exaggerated slow motion for an adagio act, a take-off on Harry Lauder offer many possibilities for puppets.

Songs. A song and dance routine from *The Wizard of Oz*, a Gilbert and Sullivan potpourri, blues singers, dramatized ballads—these and similar numbers are excellent.

STAGE EQUIPMENT

Stage Hardware

J. R. Clancy, Inc., Syracuse, N. Y.

Lighting Equipment

Belson Mfg. Co., Chicago, Ill.

Bohling, F. H., St. James Theatre Bldg., 246 W. 44th St., New York City. (Special equipment made to order for the puppet stage.)

Brenkert Light Projection Co., Detroit, Mich.

Broadway Stage Lighting Co., 437 W. 31st St., New York City 1.

Capitol Stage Lighting Apparatus, 527 W. 45th St., N.Y.C. 19.

Century Lighting, Inc., 419 W. 55th St., New York City 19.

Columbia Stage Lighting Co., 341 W. 47th St., New York City 19.

Curtis Lighting, Chicago, Ill.

Display Stage Lighting Co., 102 W. 3rd St., New York City 12.

C. F. Holzmueller, San Francisco, Calif.

Kliegl Bros., Universal Electric Stage Lighting Co., Inc., 321 W. 50th St. New York City 19.

Major Equipment Co., Chicago, Ill.

Pevear Color Specialty Co., Boston, Mass.

Stroblite Co., 35 W. 52nd St., New York City 19.

Supplementary Materials

Dimmers

In choosing the right dimmer for your purpose, figure the total wattage of the unit you plan to use, the number and wattage of the individual units, the number and wattage of the separate circuits, the degree of dimming you require, and the line voltage. Then consider the various types of dimmers—plate, ring, slide, and auto-transformer—and write for catalogues. The stage lighting companies listed above handle plate dimmers commonly used in theatres. Below are suggested other firms which make various types of dimmers. Any of them will be glad to help you select the dimmer, if you give them full information about your light setup. Be careful to check the size and weight of the dimmer you are considering, especially if you plan to tour, because some of them are too heavy for easy transportation.

Cutler-Hammer, Inc., 315 N. 12th St., Milwaukee 1, Wis. New York office, 8 W. 40th St., New York City 18.

Besides plate dimmers and slide-type spotlight dimmers, this company has auto-transformer dimmers of 1000- and 4000-watt capacity. These work by a reduction in voltage instead of by resistance. They will dim one lamp, no matter how small, as well as lamps which total the wattage capacity. They generate less heat than resistance dimmers, and are smooth in operation. They can be used *only* on A-C current. The type made by this company is too heavy (90 lbs.) for a touring company, but would be satisfactory for a permanent theatre.

General Radio Co., Cambridge, Mass. New York office, 90 West St., New York City 6.

This company makes excellent auto-transformers called Variacs. They range from 170 to 2000 volt-amperes (for purposes of lighting control, volt-ampere and wattage rating are the same). The 860 volt-ampere, weighing only 8¼ lbs. unmounted, is especially suitable for the puppet stage. The 2000 volt-ampere model weighs 30 lbs. but is very compact. These dimmers are smooth in operation, they generate little heat, they will dim a 5-watt lamp as completely as a full complement of lamps, but they can be used *only* on A-C current. They are moderately priced.

International Resistance Co., Philadelphia, Pa. New York office, 165 Broadway, New York City 6.

Small ring-type rheostats up to 50-watt capacity, and slide resistors from 10 to 200 watts can be purchased here. More powerful resistors can be made to order, if you write full particulars of your requirements. These dimmers are useful for small stages, because they are compact and relatively inexpensive.

Ohmite Mfg. Co., 4835 Flournoy St., Chicago 44, Ill.

Lamp dimming rheostats from 24 watts to several kilowatts are handled by this company. Write for catalogue and prices.

Ward-Leonard Electric Co., 31 South St., Mt. Vernon, N. Y.

Vitrohm ring-type rheostats, 4″ in diameter, 150-watt capacity can be purchased for a moderate price. The advantage of these is their compactness, but they are relatively expensive if the total wattage is great. With them, of course, individual circuits can be dimmed. Plate dimmers can be used for master dimming, with the rheostats for individual lights or circuits. Ask for catalogue and prices.

Scenery, Drapery, and Properties

Arthur B. Albertis Co., Inc., 440 W. 42nd St., New York City 18.
For properties.
Century Drapery Studios, 118 W. 47th St., New York City 19.
Praetorius Papier Mache Properties Studio, 607 W. 46th St., New York City 19.
Frank W. Stevens, 641 W. 43rd St., New York City 18.
For scenery.
Theatre Production Service, 1430 Broadway at 40th St., New York City 18.
Theatrical Properties Studios, 320 W. 48th St., New York City 19.
Universal Scenic and Drapery Studios, Inc., 315 W. 47th St., New York City 19.

Costume Fabrics

Mill-end shops, especially those which handle knitted goods, are excellent sources for costume fabrics. The local department store is also a possibility. For theatrical fabrics see:

Associated Fabrics Co., 1600 Broadway, New York City 19.
Dazian's, Inc., 142 W. 44th St., New York City 18.
Gladstone Fabrics, 117 W. 47th St., New York City 19.
Kalmo Theatrical Textiles, Inc., 110 W. 45th St., New York City 19.
Waas and Son, 123 S. 11th St., Philadelphia, Pa.
Wolff, Fording and Co., 46 Stuart St., Boston, Mass.

Supplementary Materials

Flameproofed Materials

The Antipyros Co., 338 Berry St., Brooklyn, N. Y.
This company also has chemicals for flameproofing.

Scene Paint

Ready-sized concentrated dry colors can be purchased from paint stores which handle water paint such as Muralo, Kalsomine, etc. Casein paint in paste form may also be used. Kindergarten paints, dry tempera, or ordinary tempera (which can be purchased at any of the school supply companies) are usable for small settings. Standard scene paint may be bought at:

A. Leiser and Co., 48 Horatio St., New York City 14.
Abraham Bros., 38 W. 28th St., New York City 1.
Aljo Mfg. Co., 130 W. 21st St., New York City 11.

PUPPET WORKSHOP EQUIPMENT

It is not necessary to have all the materials listed here in order to make puppets. Each person must plan for himself the amount of equipment he will need; for simple shadow-puppets, a bit of cardboard, some scissors, thread and a few stiff wires would be adequate. For carved marionettes of the professional type, you would need more tools. The following list suggests the kind of equipment commonly used by puppeteers. An excellent plan for a complete puppet workshop designed by Lemuel Williams, can be found in *Puppetry 1942-43*, pp. 56-57.

Drawing Materials

Paper: Drawing, assorted colored, tracing, black cover; pencils; rulers (12" and architect's scale rule); stencil knife; ruling pen; compass; paint brushes; India ink; drawing board; eraser.

Hand Tools

Most of the tools listed below can be purchased at the average hardware store: Hammers; saws (coping and hand); screw drivers (plain and ratchet); pliers (flat nose and electrician's); plane; brace with ¼" to 1" bits and extension bit; hand drill and assorted drills; riffler rasps (Nos. 139-152); cabinet rasps; tin shears; squares (steel and try); small nail set; yardstick and 6′ steel measuring tape; small ticket punch; soldering iron and acid core solder; carving tools (skew, straight gouges, back bent gouges, parting tool, fishtails, gouge sweeps); wood carver's mallet.

Linoleum and wood carving tools can be found listed in most of the school supply and art materials catalogues, but better ones can be purchased at: William Dixon, Inc., Newark, N. J.; Broadhead Garrett Co., Cleveland, Ohio; Hammacher Schlemmer, 145 E. 57th St., New York City 22.

Power Tools

For the small workshop, the Delta line of power tools is excellent. The Craftsman tools, handled by Sears Roebuck and Co., are inexpensive and of good quality.

The most useful tools are: Band saw, lathe with assorted turning chisels, small bench saw, jig saw, sander, drill press with assorted drills.

Electrical Supplies for Shop

Electric cord, friction tape, miscellaneous switches, plugs and sockets.

Paint and Dye

Tube oil colors, or half-pint cans of concentrated color ground in oil.
Turpentine, boiled linseed oil, japan dryer.
Tempera, scene paint (see p. 283), whiting.
Satin finish varnish, paste floor wax.
Metallic powders and bronzing liquid.
Textile paint. Prang Textile Paints, made by the American Crayon Co., Sandusky, Ohio, are satisfactory for block printing, stenciling, and painting freehand on textiles. Printer's ink can be used for block printing, but it stiffens the textile, which is a disadvantage for costumes, although it is all right for stage fabrics. Water soluble block printing ink can be used for material which does not have to be washed, or for printing on paper.
Dye. Ordinary Diamond or Putnam dye purchasable at drugstores can be used for many purposes; cold batik dye is more concentrated and can be mixed for any color by using red, blue and yellow. The Aljo Mg. Co., 130 W. 21st St., New York City 11, makes a good dye, and so does Fezandie and Sperrle, Inc., 205 Fulton St., New York City 7.

Supplementary Materials

Sewing Materials

Pins, scissors, needles, thimbles, hooks, eyes, snap fasteners, elastic, and all the colored threads obtainable at the ten-cent store.

Scrap Boxes and Files

The puppet maker will find continual use for a collection of illustrations of costumes, accessories, dance groups, furniture, architecture, animals, character studies of interesting faces, reproductions of contemporary paintings and sculpture (especially of the abstract type).

There should also be a scrap box of odds and ends such as beads; buttons; pieces of fur, leather, and materials with good texture; wooden balls and beads; sacks of wood turnings from the ten-cent store; glass marbles; scraps of sheet metal; ribbons; braid; trimmings of all kinds; costume jewelry, etc. In fact, anything which might be used to bedeck a puppet's costume or suggest features for stylized heads (see p. 80) should be saved.

A good supply of costume materials is important, not only for the actual making of puppet clothes, but for experiments with colored lights and selection of textures. Wise puppeteers buy pieces of material when they see them, whether there is a specific use for them or not. Discarded clothes often provide good material for puppet costumes.

Supplies for Puppet Construction

Assorted nails, bolts, screws, screw eyes (especially No. 215), tacks, and blind staples. ½" wire headed nails are particularly useful.

Pots, pans, tin cans, kitchen spoons and knives, empty glass jars. Plenty of containers in which to mix paint and to store things make all shop work easier.

Wood. Assorted dowels, soft wood scraps, sugar pine, balsa, thin sticks for handles of shadow-puppet control wires, old curtain blinds, stocking darners and other wooden forms.

Plastic. Scraps of Plexiglas or other available plastic in both sheets and chunks have many uses. Successful shadow-puppets have been cut from Vinylite, Plastecele and other plastics. Sheet plastic is good for joints and is easier to cut than trunk fiber. Cellophane and gelatin are useful. Each plastic has its own solvent which should be used to cement pieces together. Chloroform works well with Plexiglas. The companies listed below are useful sources of supply; for others consult the periodical *Plastics*.

> Carbide and Carbon Chemicals Corporation, 30 E. 42nd St., New York City 17.
> For Vinylite.
> Catalin Corporation, 1 Park Ave., New York City 16.
> Du Pont de Nemours E I and Co., 350 5th Ave., New York City 1
> Monsanto Chemical Co., Plastics Division, Springfield, Mass. New York office, 30 Rockefeller Plaza, New York City 20.
> Virginia Plastic Co., 270 Madison Ave., New York City 16.

Modeling clay. Water clay can be used if it is kept damp. For casting or building papier-mâché heads, it has to be greased or given a thin coat of hot paraffin to keep it from sticking to the plaster or paper. A clay with an oil base is better because it needs no greasing, does not dry out nor crack. The Ettl Studios, Inc., 213 W. 58th St., New York City 19, handle a fine quality of oil clay; other brands may be obtained from school supply companies (see p. 288).

Fishline. Eighteen pound test is average for most marionettes. For rod-puppets and heavy marionettes, twenty-five pound test is necessary. Black is the usual color, but gray is less conspicuous against some backgrounds. Fishline should be of woven silk or rayon.

Glue. Prepared glue such as Le Page's can be used for many purposes. For scene paint size, white flake or gelatin glue is best. Ground or flake glue (brown) can be purchased at any hardware shop, and is a good general utility glue. Casein glue and Weldwood are waterproof. Airplane cement is invaluable for puppet work. It is colorless and especially good for fastening hair to heads, securing details of costume, etc. For mixing glue, a glue pot or double boiler is essential to prevent burning.

Plastic Wood. Made by Boyle-Midway, Inc., 22 East 40th St., New York City 16. The product is sold in one-pound tins, but it is more economical to order it direct from the company in five-, ten- or twenty five-pound cans. A good supply of solvent makes working with this material much easier.

Water putty. The Old English brand is recommended. For patching wood or Plastic Wood, water putty is excellent because it can be mixed in any quantity needed and is easy to apply.

Supplementary Materials

Trunk fiber. Any company which makes trunks can supply scraps which are useful for puppet joints. The material is practically unbreakable.

Wire shanks. For shadow-figure joints, No. oo wire shanks can be used, and they are also useful for jointing puppets made of sheet metal.

Umbrella ribs. Men's umbrellas, which have long rods, are particularly good for rod-puppets. Hand-and-rod figures can be fitted with the shorter rods from women's umbrellas. To lengthen the ribs, splice the long section with the short piece, or splice together two long sections. The overlapping joint should be wound first with fine wire, then with friction tape. Keep in touch with Lost and Found bureaus, because they are your best source for old umbrellas.

Unbleached Muslin. Essential for scenery, bodies, backdrops, and protecting bags for the puppets.

Elastic cloth. For puppet body covering, the material used in women's girdles is good.

Lead. Various kinds of weights are often needed for balancing puppet bodies, weighting draperies, etc. Shot, sinkers of assorted sizes, round dress weights, sheet lead (which can be cut any size or shape), and solder (without an acid core) are often used.

Grease and oil. Any equipment which rolls (including movable stools for puppeteers) should be well greased. Oil is of course essential for machinery and sharpening stones.

Jack chain. For fastening rods to screw eyes, a link of small jack chain helps to keep the rod from locking and permits free movement.

Springs. Those used for screen doors are good for rod-puppet waist joints. Smaller springs are useful for flexible necks, tails, feet, etc.

Sponge Rubber. Before the war, scrap sponge rubber could be obtained from the school supply companies. When it becomes available, the foam rubber used for mattresses and upholstering will be an ideal material for puppets, especially rod-puppet animals, because it is several inches thick and very soft.

Sources for Various Supplies

Art materials such as paper, drawing instruments, tools for linoleum carving, brushes, block printing outfits, etc. can be purchased at:

Abbott Educational Company, S. Wabash Ave., Chicago, Ill.

Arthur Brown and Bro., 67 W. 44th St., New York City 18.

E. H. and A. C. Friedrichs Co., 140 Sullivan St., New York City 12.
Eugene Dietzgen Co., 218 E. 23rd St., New York City 10.
A still wider variety of materials can be bought from the school supply companies such as:
The American Crayon Co., Sandusky, Ohio.
American Handicrafts Co., Inc., 45-49 South Harrison St., East Orange, N. J., or 915 South Grand Ave., Los Angeles 15, Calif. Retail store at 12 E. 41st St., New York City 17.
Binney and Smith, 31 E. 42nd St., New York City 17.
Dennison Mfg. Co., 220 5th Ave., New York City 1. Many kinds of paper products and novelties can be found at Dennison's, which has stores in various cities.
Milton Bradley Co., 200 5th Ave., New York City 10.
Talens School Products, Inc., 41 E. 42nd St., New York City 17.
Universal Handicraft Service, 1267 6th Ave., New York City 19.
School Arts Magazine carries ads of all the leading craft supply companies. *Theatre Arts* is a good source for ads of theatrical supplies.

RECORDED SOUND EFFECTS AND MOVIES

Sound Effects

Gennett Records, Indiana.
Major Records, obtainable from Thomas J. Valentino, Inc., 1600 Broadway, New York City 19.

Movies

George Pal's Puppetoons are puppetlike, although they are done with stop motion, which is not strictly a puppet technique. The Russian film *The New Gulliver* is of the same type.
A number of years ago *I Am Suzanne* was produced, with the Italian puppets from the Teatro dei Piccoli and those of the Yale Puppeteers.
Rufus Rose produced a commercial film for the American Can Company entitled *Jerry Pulls the Strings* which tells the story of the discovery and use of coffee.
The above films can be rented through the visual aids department of schools and colleges.
Several process films were made in the School of Fine and Applied

Arts at Ohio State University, Columbus. One shows the making of shadow-figures. In *The Making of a Marionette*, Marjorie Batchelder constructs a wooden string-puppet. Her rod-puppets are seen in *St. George and the Dragon*, and construction details are given in *How to Make a Rod Puppet*. These films are obtainable from the university.

Notes

CHAPTER I. THE PUPPET THEATRE AND ITS USES

1. "Actor with Puppet: Obrazsov," *Puppetry 1941*, p. 7.
2. PETTY, EMMA, "School Aspects of Puppetry," *Puppetry 1930*, p. 42.
3. WOLTMAN, ADOLF, "Therapeutic Aspects of Puppetry," *Puppetry 1942-1943*, p. 20.
4. WARFIELD, EMMA, "Health Via Puppetry," *Puppetry 1940*, p. 24.
5. COHEN, LT. COL. R. ROBERT, "Visual Aids in Group Psycho-Therapy," *Occupational Therapy and Rehabilitation*, Vol. 23, No. 6, Dec., 1944. This material is used by permission of the publishers, the Williams and Wilkins Co.
6. Other articles about puppets in occupational therapy are:
BROWN, SARAH GOODWIN. "Puppetry in Occupational Therapy," *Occupational Therapy and Rehabilitation*, Vol. 16, 1937.
———. "Puppets in Occupational Therapy." *Puppetry 1936*, p. 46.
BENDER, L. and WOLTMAN, A. G., "The Use of Puppets as a Psychotherapeutic Method for Behavior Problems in Children," *American Journal of Orthopsychiatry*, Vol. 6, No. 3, July 1936. A shorter article with the same title appeared in *Puppetry 1939*, pp. 6-7.
FABER, A. D., "Puppetry as a Rehabilitation Measure," *Occupational Therapy and Rehabilitation*, Vol. 23, No. 4, August, 1944.
WOLTMAN, A. G., "The Use of Puppets in Understanding Children," *Mental Hygiene*, Vol. 24, No. 3, July, 1940.
———. "Puppetry as a Means of Psychotherapy," *Encyclopedia of Child Guidance* (New York: The Philosophical Library, 1943).

7. AYALA, SISKA, BAKER, BOB, McGUIRE, VERA, "Commercial Film Possibilities," *Puppetry 1943-1944*, p. 19.
8. JOHNSON, EDWARD, "Electronics Futures," *Puppetry 1942-1943*, p. 17.
9. LONGFIELD, ANDRE VERN, "Puppets in Radio and Television," *Puppetry 1937*, p. 20.
10. JOHNSON, EDWARD, *Op. cit.*

CHAPTER II. PLANNING THE PUPPET SHOW

1. ROSE, RUFUS, "Marionette Technique," *Puppetry 1936*, p. 33.
2. BUFANO, REMO, "What Not To Do," *Puppetry 1935*, p. 36.
3. HASTINGS, SUE and RUTHENBURG, DORCAS, *How to Produce Puppet Plays*, p. 12. This and other passages quoted from the same book are used by permission of the publisher, Harper and Brothers.

CHAPTER III. PUPPET CONSTRUCTION

1. ROSE, RUFUS, "Marionette Technique," *Puppetry 1936*, p. 33.
2. FICKLEN, BESSIE A., *A Handbook of Fist Puppets*, p. 77.
3. TOZER, H. V., "The Puppet Theatre in Barcelona," *Puppetry 1932*, p. 25.
4. EFIMOVA, NINA, *The Adventures of a Russian Puppet Theatre*, p. 91.
5. FICKLEN, *Op. cit.*, p. 77.
6. Patterns and full directions for making cloth marionettes may be found in Ackley, *Marionettes, Easy to Make, Fun to Use* (see bibliography).
7. WILLIAMS, LEMUEL, *Puppet Head Construction*, p. 11.
8. DWIGGINS, W. A., *Marionette in Motion*, p. V. This book treats the counterbalanced marionette in detail.
9. DWIGGINS, *Ibid.*, p. XIX.
10. ROSE, RUFUS, "A Method of Casting Puppet Heads and Body Parts of Composition Material," *Puppetry 1934*, pp. 63-4.
11. ROSE, *Ibid.*
12. WILLIAMS, *Op. cit.*
13. EFIMOVA, *Op. cit.*, p. 86.

CHAPTER IV. COSTUME DESIGN AND CONSTRUCTION

1. EFIMOVA, NINA, *The Adventures of a Russian Puppet Theatre*, p. 95.
2. Most of the material on puppet costuming in this chapter was drawn from an unpublished manuscript "Costuming the Production" by David Gibson.

CHAPTER VI. SCENERY, LIGHTING, PROPERTIES AND SPECIAL EFFECTS

1, 2, 3. STEVENS, MARTIN. Notes written for this book.
4. Most of the material on special effects was written and illustrated by Lemuel Williams for this book.
5. BRANT, F. L., "Formula for Smoke Cartridge," *Puppetry 1932*.
6. The best example which the author has seen of this kind of writing was in a Czech puppet show given in honor of visiting Americans.

CHAPTER VII. PLAYWRITING AND PUPPET PLAYS

1. EASLY, CLEM, "Playwriting for Puppets," *Puppetry 1937*, p. 17.
2. HARGRAVE, MARTHA. Notes written for this book.
3. HASTINGS, SUE and RUTHENBURG, DORCAS, *How to Produce Puppet Plays*, p. 28.
4. BUFANO, REMO, *Be A Puppet Showman*, p. 131. This passage is quoted by permission of the publishers, D. Appleton-Century Co., Inc.
5. FOWLER, HARRY. Notes written for this book.
6. MERLE SWINEFORD (Dilley) in her Master's thesis, "The Use of the Puppet Theatre in the College Speech Curriculum" (Ohio State University, 1942) proves the validity of the improvisation method for stimulating playwriting for puppets.
7. WILKINSON, WALTER. Notes written for this book.

CHAPTER VIII. PRODUCING THE PUPPET SHOW

1. "Floor Showmanship," *Puppetry 1942-1943*, p. 24.
2. MARTIN, LOUISE. Notes written for this book.
3. MARTIN, *Ibid*.
4. GIBSON, DAVID, "Music for Puppet Drama," *Puppetry 1944*.

Notes

5. HASTINGS, SUE and RUTHENBERG, DORCAS, *How to Produce Puppet Plays*, pp. 84-85.
6. VAN VOLKENBURG, ELLEN. Notes written for this book.
7. INVERARITY, R. BRUCE, *A Manual of Puppetry*.
8. DILLEY, PERRY, "Notes on the Manipulation of Hand-Puppets," *Puppetry 1930*, pp. 61-62.
9. HASTINGS and RUTHENBERG, *Op. cit.*, pp. 92-3.
10. HOUGHMASTER, JOHN, "Voice in the Theatre," *Puppetry 1939*, p. 7.
11. GIBSON, DAVID, "The Art of Puppet Manipulation." Unpublished MS.
12. WILKINSON, WALTER. Notes written for this book.
13. FICKLEN, BESSIE A., *A Handbook of Fist Puppets*, p. 104.
14. DILLEY, *Op. cit.*, pp. 59-61.
15. FICKLEN, *Op. Cit.*, p. 103.
16. FICKLEN, *Ibid.*, p. 105.
17. EFIMOVA, NINA, *Adventures of a Russian Puppet Theatre*, pp. 147-8.
18. HASTINGS and RUTHENBURG, *Op. cit.*, p. 89.
19. HASTINGS and RUTHENBURG, *Ibid.*, p. 90.
20. MABLEY, EDWARD, "The Business End," *Puppetry 1932*, p. 56.